The
HUNT
FOR
ANNA
PAVLOVNA'S
STOLEN
JEWELS

THE HUNT FOR ANNA PAVLOVNA'S STOLEN JEWELS

DECEPTION, DIPLOMACY & AN IMPERIAL HEIST

JENNI WILTZ

PEN & SWORD HISTORY

AN IMPRINT OF PEN & SWORD BOOKS LTD.
YORKSHIRE – PHILADELPHIA

First published in Great Britain in 2026 by
Pen & Sword History
An imprint of
Pen & Sword Books Ltd
Yorkshire - Philadelphia

ISBN 978 1 03614 986 4

Typeset in INDIA by IMPEC eSolutions
Printed and bound in England by CPI Group (UK) Ltd, Croydon, CR0 4YY

The Publisher's authorised representative in the EU for product safety is Authorised Rep
Compliance Ltd., Ground Floor, 71 Lower Baggot Street, Dublin D02 P593, Ireland.
www.arccompliance.com

For a complete list of Pen & Sword titles please contact:

PEN & SWORD BOOKS LIMITED
George House, Units 12 & 13, Beevor Street, Off Pontefract Road,
Barnsley, S71 1HN, UK
E-mail: enquiries@pen-and-sword.co.uk
Website: www.pen-and-sword.co.uk

or

PEN AND SWORD BOOKS
1950 Lawrence Rd, Havertown, PA 19083, USA
E-mail: uspen-and-sword@casematepublishers.com
Website: www.penandswordbooks.com

Contents

A Note on Dates and Names   vii

Chapter 1   The Robbery   1

Chapter 2   Happily Never After   11

Chapter 3   Meanwhile in America   21

Chapter 4   The Husband Did It   25

Chapter 5   The Belgian Revolution   30

Chapter 6   An American Scandal   37

Chapter 7   A Suspect Emerges   46

Chapter 8   The Best Laid Plans   55

Chapter 9   Welcome to New York   66

Chapter 10   The First Betrayal   74

Chapter 11   Buried Treasure   82

Chapter 12   The Second Betrayal   88

Chapter 13   A Reputation Rehabilitated   96

Chapter 14   The Third Betrayal   100

Chapter 15   Law and Disorder   112

Chapter 16   A Hero, a Spy, and a Scoundrel   120

Chapter 17   Cholera   128

Chapter 18   Extradition   134

Chapter 19   The Brink of War   142

Chapter 20   A Dubious Confession   150

Chapter 21   The Trial   155

Chapter 22   A Walking Stick in America   166

Acknowledgements   175

Notes   176

Bibliography   206

Index   210

A Note on Dates and Names

Anyone writing about history that takes place in multiple countries must decide how to present foreign names to the reader. This is no small task when a Russian grand duchess and a Dutch prince address each other in French, or when Dutch bureaucrats enforce the use of their language in a kingdom that also includes Walloons, Flemings, and Belgians. Would Anna Pavlovna prefer I use the French version of her name, Anne, as her husband and mother did? Would a Flemish painter prefer his name appear in French or Dutch? The humble writer must confront a minefield of such choices, many of which carry political overtones. In the end, I chose to use a mix of foreign and familiar spellings. Anna Pavlovna's father-in-law and husband are Willem rather than William, for example. For Russian names, I have used the versions most familiar to English-language readers. Similarly, for the sake of readability and consistency, I used the most familiar present-day spelling of place names, hence Namur rather than Namour and Leuven rather than Louvain.

As for dates, Russia used the Julian (Old Style) calendar until February 1, 1918. In the nineteenth century, this calendar was twelve days behind the Gregorian (New Style) calendar, used by the French, Dutch, and Americans. I have presented all dates in the Gregorian (New Style) calendar.

Chapter 1

The Robbery

Brussels
The United Kingdom of the Netherlands
September 25, 1829

The Princess of Orange's carriage sped through the Namur gate, leaving Brussels and its obligations behind. Rather than put in an appearance at her brother-in-law's party, she preferred to spend the night under the same roof as her children, in her white-columned country villa.

Socializing didn't come easily to Anna Pavlovna, although she loved the glamorous gowns and dazzling jewels formal occasions required. Once, she had entered the royal box at the theater wearing a tiara that, according to one overwhelmed observer, 'displayed a greater profusion of diamonds than perhaps any individual ever beheld upon one person at one time.'[1] Her grandmother, Catherine the Great, had also used jewels to convey power and majesty. From the 189.62-carat Orlov diamond in the Imperial Scepter to the 400-carat red spinel topping the Imperial Crown, Catherine had dazzled her Russian subjects with one clear purpose in mind.[2] Splendor created awe, and awe inspired respect. If a Russian monarch lost that respect, he could lose his life – as had Anna's father and grandfather, both murdered in palace revolutions. It was a lesson she had absorbed to the very marrow of her bones.

When Anna arrived at Tervuren, two-and-a-half leagues from Brussels, her chambermaid, Natalia Petrovna Chernysheva, helped her get ready for bed. For thirteen years, Natalia had been a trusted companion who reminded her of home. It was Natalia who cleaned and cared for all her jewels, preserving the links they represented to the people she loved. Many had been wedding presents from her husband, Prince Willem of Orange, and her brother, Emperor Alexander I. Every year on her birthday and name day, her mother sent more. One year, it was a pair of bracelets set with gleaming topaz, her favorite stone. Another year, it was a tiara set with turquoise, a stone that symbolized a happy marriage.

Wearing these gifts made Anna feel closer to her family, despite being over 1,500 miles from St. Petersburg. As a young bride, she had once thought she was being criticized for wearing too many jewels. When she asked her mother for advice, Dowager Empress Maria Feodorovna reassured Anna that her position required her to dress the part. With her mother's blessing, Anna continued to wear her diamond butterfly, her chain of Siberian amethysts, and the pearls said to have belonged to Marie Antoinette.[3]

Recently, Anna had worn her perfectly matched drop pearl earrings with an off-the-shoulder blue velvet gown to sit for a portrait by Jean Baptiste van der Hulst.[4] Hairstyles of the time were not small, featuring sections of hair curled and looped across the head. As fashionable as it was, Anna's coiffure couldn't compete with her tiara: a large diamond kokoshnik in a foliate scroll design, topped with a row of circular brilliants and large diamond drops. Part of her Russian trousseau, it symbolized her wealth, origin, and position. But by the time Van der Hulst delivered the completed painting, her tiara had vanished. Its real-life luster had been reduced to a memory, just a few dots of white paint pressed into canvas. She would never see it again.

A few hours after Anna went to bed, a workman walked the well-worn path outside the Brussels city wall. Despite the pre-dawn darkness, he saw a ladder propped against the wall near the Leuven gate. He walked over to inspect it and saw something else on the ground nearby: a woman's shawl, soft and luxurious. Before anyone could see what he'd done, the workman hurried away with the shawl. Later that night, over a beer, he would tell his friends at the *estaminet* about his good luck.[5]

An hour or so later, inside the city, another workman left home before sunrise. Étienne Parfait made his way down Rue de la Madeleine, across the Place Royale, and past the king's palace to that of his son and heir, Prince Willem of

Orange. Even in the dim morning light, the palace was imposing. Its austere neoclassical design featured a long row of columns and pilasters facing the public park. Built with three shades of Arquennes blue stone, it was one of the few buildings in the city not plastered or painted. The opulent interior featured a grand marble staircase, Corinthian columns, golden candelabra, and furniture from the Princess of Orange's dowry, crafted with lapis lazuli, malachite, and other precious materials. The glittering treasures of the princess's trousseau complemented the prince's art collection, including paintings by Van Eyck, Memling, and Rembrandt. When no one was home, palace caretakers admitted visitors to gawk at the royal couple's art and objects. They handed out shoe covers to protect the floor and told visitors to slide, as if on skates, to avoid a fall.[6]

No tourists were present that Saturday morning when Parfait climbed the palace stairs to clean the princess's bedroom. But someone had been there before him – someone who should never have been there at all. The princess's jewelry chest stood against a wall near the fireplace, like it always had, but the upper cabinet was no longer surrounded by thick plate glass. Someone had shattered it, then flung open the doors of the lower cabinet.

Parfait ran to tell the concierge, Nicolas Cavanillas. An elderly Spanish man, Cavanillas had worked for Prince Willem of Orange for years and was responsible for the second floor of the palace. One glance at Anna's bedroom convinced Cavanillas the situation was grave, too much for him to handle on his own. He left the palace and hurried to the home of Anna's secretary, arriving at 524 Rue de l'Abricot between 8 and 9 a.m.[7]

Born in St. Petersburg in 1793, Karl Ivanovich Schultz had come with Anna to the Netherlands upon her marriage. He worked as her private secretary and held a commission in the Russian Ministry of Foreign Affairs. But he and his English wife weren't expecting company that morning. Confused, Schultz asked Cavanillas if he'd come to announce Anna's arrival. Perhaps she had come back early from Tervuren and needed him? The look on the older man's face told Schultz it was something else. With a glance up the street, aware of prying eyes, he took Cavanillas upstairs.[8] There, the Spaniard told Schultz what had happened: someone had stolen the Princess of Orange's jewels.

The Brussels Director of Police, Chevalier Pierre Michel-Charles de Knyff de Gontrœul, had been on the job for almost fifteen years. Born in Antwerp in 1784, he came from a long line of public servants, including a great-grandfather knighted by Holy Roman Emperor Charles VI. In 1819, he had uncovered a plot to kidnap Anna's brother, Emperor Alexander I. He rose to fame when he arrested the conspirators near the French border.[9] Nine years later, however, that fame had waned. But when Nicolas Cavanillas reported the jewel theft, he saw another opportunity to shine in the eyes of the royal family. De Knyff de Gontrœul hurried to the scene of the crime with the Commissioner of Police, Théodore-Emmanuel Barbier, in tow.

Meanwhile, Schultz and Cavanillas had already returned to the palace. A dark suspicion had entered Schultz's mind and he asked Cavanillas to take him to Anna's library, two doors down from her bedroom. There, he threw open the lids of two trunks and peered anxiously inside. The jewel casket in each lay undisturbed. To him, this meant the thief couldn't have had an informant inside the palace or these jewels would have been gone, too.[10] When De Knyff de Gontrœul and Barbier arrived, Schultz told them about his discovery, believing it exonerated palace staff.

The two men asked to be taken to Anna's jewelry chest. Called a *diamantaire*, its upper section had a thick glass lid, now broken, with mirrored doors that had opened outward like a writing desk. Anna's chambermaid, Natalia, held the only key. There, Anna had stored loose diamonds, covered with silk, along with the key to the lower section. In the bottom, she kept three boxes full of jewels, a white cashmere shawl given to her by her mother, and leather portfolios with important papers. The thief had left the key to the lower section in the lock, which also bore the marks of a sharp instrument. De Knyff de Gontrœul and Barbier concluded the thief had tried to break the lower lock, failed, and smashed the top of the diamantaire, where he discovered the key. He had taken everything except the portfolios, likely discarded when they revealed no cash or valuables.[11]

But how had the thief entered the palace in the first place? The two men asked about the staff, only to be told most went home each day. A few had rooms on the ground floor, but with Anna and her husband away, there would have been no one on the second floor that night. Cavanillas had offered to have someone stay in Anna's apartment while she was gone, but no one in the royal family had thought there was any need.[12]

The thief, then, had likely come from outside.

De Knyff de Gontrœul and Barbier found proof in the nearby Red Marble Room, where a spray of broken glass littered the parquet floor, along with several drops of blood. The glass had come from the adjacent French door, which only opened from the inside. The Red Marble Room was an ideal entry point, situated on a short side of the rectangular palace, overlooking an unpaved side street. A stone wall at the edge of the property kept passersby out and protected the garden and its main feature: a tall earthen terrace.[13] That terrace – a ramp of packed earth – led from the garden straight to the French door in the Red Marble Room. Built for use during the palace's construction, it was never supposed to be a permanent feature.

As he studied the broken glass, De Knyff de Gontrœul realized the thief had come prepared. Approaching from the outside, the thief had coated one pane of glass with clay to deaden any sound, then smashed it to access the door latch. Reaching in, he must have dragged his arm across a jagged shard, drawing blood. A few steps away, the two investigators found multiple used match heads and dirty handprints on the furniture.[14]

Tracking the thief's path in reverse, the two men stepped onto the terrace. They found two sets of footprints, described as 'the steps of a man, whose foot would be very well made, and who would have a light and elegant shoe, and other steps of a naked foot, whose strides were very big…'[15] They traced a copy of both prints for reference. De Knyff de Gontrœul thought the bare footprints had more depth, perhaps because the person was weighed down by the boxes from the diamantaire. Oddly enough, the bare footsteps didn't continue all the way down the terrace. Instead, they veered toward the steep side of the earthen ramp and disappeared. Had the thief scrambled down the side of the terrace to avoid being seen?

In the garden, the two men found the same shoe print heading from the palace to the garden wall and a pearl-encrusted watch, presumably dropped in haste. Near the wall, they saw two faint indentations on the ground, as if a ladder had been pressed into the earth. On the other side of the wall, in the side street, they found two more indentations. They also found a slight scrape and a bit of dirt on top of the garden wall, evidence of the thief's passing.[16]

After his walk-through, De Knyff de Gontrœul spread the news to jewelers, police chiefs in major cities, and customs inspectors on the French and Prussian borders. He requested a list of people who had left Brussels by stagecoach or checked out of their hotel that morning. He even began arresting sex workers, hoping one of them might have seen someone near the palace.[17]

Although De Knyff de Gontrœul was the Director of Police, he wasn't senior enough to act as liaison with the royal family. That job fell to the Minister of Justice, Cornelis Felix van Maanen, the king's close collaborator. When Van Maanen arrived to deliver the bad news, King Willem I was still groggy. Prince Frederik's party had carried on long into the night, and the king had gone to bed later than usual.[18] News of the theft woke him like a splash of cold water. Horrified, he ordered Van Maanen to find the jewels and the person responsible.

After the two investigators left the palace, Schultz ordered a carriage and driver. It fell to him to bring the news to Anna in person in Tervuren. Investigators, he said, needed a full inventory of what had been stolen. Immediately, Anna and Natalia returned to Brussels to provide it. Never a strong woman physically or emotionally, it must have been a struggle for Anna to keep the surging feelings of loss and violation at bay as she walked through her rooms and saw the shattered glass and bloodstains on her parquet floor. But she had learned from her mother and grandmother – two extraordinarily composed royal women – that duty came first.

Together, Anna and Natalia identified 77 missing items. Among them was her bouquet of gemstone flowers, which included a rose, daffodil, two lilies, and other diamond-encrusted blossoms, all tied with a knot of rubies. A string of 58 large pearls. A cross in turquoise and gold, with an engraved motto – *Ne m'oubliez pas* (don't forget me) – on the back. A tiara of diamonds and cameos. A golden snake bracelet. Large oval sapphires, pear-shaped emeralds, topaz, turquoise, opal, carnelian, brooches, buckles, and loose diamonds – all gone. Later, it would be estimated the stolen pieces contained 2,091 carats of diamonds and 13,462 additional gemstones.[19] Many had sentimental value. The smallest box stolen, labeled 'Inheritance from my dear mother the Empress of Russia,' held portraits of Anna's brothers, a bracelet with portraits of her parents, and a turquoise and gold talisman bracelet that Anna was attached to 'far beyond its intrinsic value.'[20]

Working from memory, Natalia began to sketch many of the missing jewels. A grateful Anna told her brother that Natalia 'did in two days what might enable me at some time to retrieve the jewels that were taken from me.'[21] While he waited for the sketches, De Knyff de Gontrœul sent the list to police and local jewelers. Anyone who spotted a match was to notify Joseph-Germain Dutalis, the Brussels court jeweler, who prepared detailed drawings based on Natalia's sketches, ready for the moment someone recognized one of the stolen jewels.

Late that night, Anna's husband, Prince Willem of Orange, arrived home from the spa town of Ems. It would be a short, frustrating stay, with little time to soothe a distressed wife. He had appointments to inspect the *Schuttery*, the country's militia, in Brussels early the next morning and in Ghent early Monday morning. As a former soldier, he took his military duties seriously and refused to reschedule them. On Sunday morning, Willem rose early for the Brussels inspection. Afterward, he vented his frustration to Van Maanen and De Knyff de Gontrœul. Why had palace staff been allowed to clean up the crime scene? What if valuable evidence had already been lost? With nothing else to be done, Willem left Brussels in the early morning hours. He complained to his brother-in-law, Emperor Nicholas I, 'I had to leave my house to be searched by the police and the justice system during my absence.'[22]

Meanwhile, the police worked their only lead: the shoe print. They compared it to the shoes of everyone in the palace, but found no match. They checked the cleaning man, Étienne Parfait, against the bare footprint as well, but there weren't enough similarities to cast him as a suspect. Both Cavanillas and Parfait's previous employer confirmed his excellent references, placing him above suspicion. But if not Parfait, then who? De Knyff de Gontrœul believed their culprit had 'extensive knowledge of the localities,' which meant he *had* to be connected to the palace.[23]

Police spread out to canvass nearby residences. An Englishman reported a ladder stolen from his courtyard, but none of the four guards at the palace gates had seen a person carrying a ladder. Even worse, no guards had ever been posted along the side street facing Anna's rooms. Cavanillas told De Knyff de Gontrœul he had warned the prince and princess about this two months ago, but no action had been taken. When night fell that Sunday, the police still had no witnesses and no leads.

On Monday, three public prosecutors and an examining magistrate arrived to review the scene. Despite heavy rain over the weekend, they confirmed the presence of two sets of footprints. Next, the group re-interviewed the concierge, Nicolas Cavanillas. He told them that Anna's golden breakfast service, set out for her each morning, was visible through the palace window.[24] That gleaming golden beacon could have inspired the thief to break in. No one on the outside knew it was locked away each night, which could have resulted in a confused thief fumbling with matches to find it once inside.

While De Knyff de Gontrœul was at the palace, a messenger brought word of an important discovery. Police had recovered a cashmere shawl from a worker who'd found it early Saturday morning in Saint-Josse-ten-Noode, outside the city's Leuven gate. While inspecting the discovery site, they also recovered a ladder and found traces of the shoe print from the palace garden. When the shawl was brought to the palace, Schultz confirmed it as Anna's. When he saw the visible smudges, De Knyff de Gontrœul concluded the thief had used it to bundle and transport the boxes of jewels.[25]

At 3 p.m., Anna left Brussels for Tervuren. The theft had shaken her, and its aftereffects would soon be visible in her physical and mental health. Without having to worry about disturbing her, the public prosecutors descended on her rooms, but there was nothing new to find. With no further clues, investigators turned to Minister of Justice van Maanen to widen the search.

With snow-white hair, deep-set blue eyes, and a stern expression, Cornelis Felix van Maanen looked like the strict headmaster of a boys' school. Instead, he was the Dutch king's most powerful minister and keeper of the royal family's darkest secrets. A political chameleon, he had survived multiple regime changes by following orders rather than principles, serving a stadtholder, a republic, a Bonaparte king, and now the restored House of Orange. A famous pamphlet of 1813 lambasted his 'deceitful display' of friendship, designed only to keep his job.[26] But the display, deceitful or not, suited the new king.

In return, Van Maanen wielded the law as a weapon, punishing and silencing the king's enemies.

By Sunday evening, Van Maanen had drafted letters for Dutch diplomats across Europe, asking them to look for the items on Anna's list. Closer to home, he ordered searches at all Dutch entry and exit points. When the packet ship *Fury* arrived in England from Ostend on September 30, passengers said their luggage had been searched before departure, as did passengers on the *Earl of Liverpool* on October 5.[27]

It didn't take long to figure out why.

Newspapers in Brussels and The Hague reported the theft within 24 hours. On October 2, the *Dagblad van 's Gravenhage* published a full inventory of the missing items, estimating their value at two million guilders. The story included details on the broken window, footprints outside the palace, and the recovered cashmere shawl. 'What is strange,' the author noted, 'is that they [i.e., the thief or thieves] were able to locate the place where all these valuables were located without any internal contacts.'[28] While the citizens of Brussels puzzled over these clues, investigators continued the search but found no sign of the jewels or the thief.

Their lack of progress wore on Anna's nerves. On October 18, less than a month after the theft, a chimney sweep came into her room by mistake. He frightened Anna so badly her ladies-in-waiting called the doctors to her side.[29] Unsurprisingly, they prescribed rest and calm. When the royal family moved to The Hague in late October, Anna must have been relieved. She had no way of knowing she would never see Brussels or her palace again.

With no leads or suspects in sight, Attorney General Anthoni Willem Philipse announced a reward: 25,000 guilders for the jewels' safe return, 50,000 if the tipster also identified the thief. Across the globe, Dutch envoys relayed the offer to their host countries. On November 19, the Dutch minister to the United States of America, Chevalier Christiaan Bangeman Huygens, requested full cooperation if the jewels surfaced at a US Customs house. Secretary of State Martin Van Buren promised his support.[30] But as the days of autumn shortened and grew colder, no word arrived from foreign ports.

Despite continued searches, not a single stolen topaz surfaced from a tourist's trunk or merchant's crate. It seemed impossible: how could a 162-carat sapphire, one of the largest in the world, simply vanish? There was no sign of it anywhere, and gossip in Brussels hinted there never would be – because there hadn't been a theft at all.

Chapter 2

Happily Never After

On the night of January 16, 1795, Grand Duchess Maria Feodorovna of Russia went into labor. At five the next morning, her mother-in-law, Catherine the Great, reported that their 'number is increased by a lady Anne, of enormous size in length and weight; this one neither sings nor shouts so far.'[1] Anna was the eighth child and sixth daughter born to Catherine's heir, Grand Duke Paul Petrovich.

Anna's oldest brothers were already married when she was born, so she bonded with the two who came after her: Nicholas and Michael. They formed a club called Triopathy, solemnized by gold rings inscribed with 'steadfastness and hope.'[2] The members of Triopathy pledged their undying devotion, confiding in each other through numerous schoolroom tribulations. The first of those tribulations would come in 1801, when their father was murdered in a palace coup.

Since childhood, Anna's father had displayed a violent temper and mood swings. His tutor, Semyon Andreevich Poroshin, had warned him, 'With the best intentions in the world, you will be hated, my lord.'[3] Poroshin was right. In his manic efforts to promote discipline, morality, and punishment, Paul alienated the army, the aristocracy, the general populace, and his European allies. Finally, to protect their country and themselves, a handful of conspirators strangled him in his fortress of a palace. Alexander, Anna's oldest brother, had given the conspirators his tacit agreement on the condition they spare his father's life. The guilt-stricken son faced his mother the morning after the murder. Brought to the Winter Palace after a sleepless night spent begging for permission to see her husband's body, Maria Feodorovna screamed at her son, 'Alexander, are you guilty?'[4] The new emperor took his mother behind closed doors, where no witness could see his tears or hear his excuses. When they emerged, all had been settled between them. In a pact born of blood and shame, Alexander gave Maria Feodorovna the freedom to run their family and the court as she saw fit. Instantly, she became more powerful than she had ever been as Paul's empress.

Unsurprisingly, it was Maria Feodorovna who influenced young Anna the most. At the age of three, her mother assigned her a Swiss governess, Elisabeth-Louise de Sybourg ('Bourcis'), who taught Anna French and German in addition to her native Russian. Like her sisters, she had lessons in math, history, geography, religion, botany, geometry, painting, and music. Her life was a sheltered one, spent mostly at her mother's side as they visited hospitals, orphanages, and schools. In 1810, Maria Feodorovna wrote that 'my moments belong to my daughter Annette…we live as peacefully as possible… the evenings we spend between us.'[5]

The Napoleonic Wars put a stop to those quiet evenings. After rejecting Napoleon's request for 14-year-old Anna's hand in marriage, Maria Feodorovna and Alexander I faced the French emperor's wrath. The Grande Armée stormed across their heartland in 1812 but could not supply their soldiers with enough food, clothing, or matériel to defeat the Russian winter. After Napoleon's abdication in 1814, an exhausted Europe fêted Alexander as its savior. He became an international celebrity and the entire family's prestige grew considerably. And now that Anna was old enough to marry, the question became: who was good enough for a savior's sister?

Prince Willem of Orange was born in The Hague on December 6, 1792. His ancestors, the princes of Orange, had risen to power by tossing the Spanish out of the Netherlands and assuming power as hereditary stadtholders of the new Dutch Republic. The apogee of Dutch glory came in the seventeenth century. From Rembrandt's unflinching realism to mathematician Christiaan Huygens's wave theory of light, the Dutch dominated art, science, commerce, and exploration. But a steady two-century decline after these golden years left many ambivalent or even hostile toward the Orange family. During the French Revolution, disaffected Dutch expats asked their host country for help. Ten days after beheading Louis XVI, France's revolutionary government declared war on two-year-old Willem's grandfather, Stadtholder Willem V.

The family fled, taking shelter in Britain and then Prussia. There, young Willem's father enrolled his son in Berlin's military academy and hired a Swiss nobleman, Baron Jean Victor de Constant Rebecque, to guide his son's education. Constant Rebecque and Willem would have a difficult relationship, however, with the older man finding his pupil well-intentioned but moody, restless, and stubborn – typical teenage qualities, but ones that didn't mellow with time. The relationship took its toll on the tutor. At one point, he wrote, '…my hair is turning devilishly gray. Luckily, the wig hides everything.'[6]

The Napoleonic Wars were not kind to the Orange family. Willem's father took the field for his brother-in-law, the king of Prussia, and lost. When he surrendered, Napoleon publicly shamed him as a coward, a disgrace that haunted him for the rest of his life.[7] By this point, the family had lost their hereditary titles, their German principalities, and their prestige. They had nowhere to go but Britain, their first refuge after fleeing the Netherlands. There, Willem's father – Willem Frederik – began to pave his oldest son's way into society. Britain's Prince Regent, the future George IV, had one child, a daughter named Charlotte. If Willem caught her eye, the boy could single-handedly revive their family's flagging fortunes.

To bolster his son's credentials as a future consort, Willem Frederik ordered his heir to join the British army. Charlotte's father made him a Lieutenant Colonel, and he joined the staff of General Arthur Wellesley, then Viscount Wellington, as his aide-de-camp. From 1811 to 1813, Prince Willem of Orange rode at Wellington's side in the Peninsular War. British officers nicknamed him 'Slender Billy,' a nod to his painfully thin frame. Willem was universally liked, according to F. Seymour Larpent, a judge-advocate general on Wellington's staff.[8] But although he could joke with the officers, Willem struggled to find a replacement for the rush of battlefield adrenaline.

When Wellington sent Willem to London with news of a victory in December of 1813, Charlotte's father put him in a room with his daughter, joined their hands, and declared them engaged. The bewildered couple never found their footing, and Charlotte broke the engagement several months later when she realized her father was using the marriage to ship her off to the Netherlands. Publicly embarrassed and lambasted in the British press as a 'Dutch toy,' Willem rejoined the British army in Brussels.[9]

Meanwhile, the regents of the Netherlands – ruling on behalf of Napoleon's crumbling empire – realized the time had come to oust the French. Three Dutch power brokers invited 41-year-old Willem Frederik to become their sovereign prince. He quickly accepted, but saw an even greater title within his reach. He persuaded the victorious allies at the Congress of Vienna to give him the Austrian Netherlands (present-day Belgium) as part of a new, enlarged Kingdom of the Netherlands. As King Willem I, he would rule over the Protestant Dutch-speaking north and the Catholic multi-lingual south.

The first challenge to his rule emerged almost immediately, when Napoleon escaped from exile on Elba and marched straight for the Belgian border. Wellington joined Prince Willem in Brussels, taking charge of 77,000 allied troops. The final confrontation took place on June 18, 1815 at Waterloo, on the edge of the woods nine miles south of Brussels. There, over 180,000 men and 40,000 horses clashed on a three-square-mile battlefield of rain-sodden clay. Near the end of the day, Willem took a musket ball in his left shoulder. In his dispatch to London announcing the allied victory, Wellington praised Willem, who had 'distinguished himself by his gallantry and conduct...' Later, Willem's father ordered a raised mound be built on the spot Willem had been shot, topped with a bronze statue of 'the Lion of Waterloo.'[10]

Willem's injury was a public relations triumph. The House of Orange – newly enthroned over formerly divided territories – had shed its blood in Belgium's defense. What better way to prove the family valued its new acquisition? But the new king knew there was one task left unfinished: his son must marry and produce an heir to solidify the Orange family's hold on their new kingdom.

As the victorious monarchs, diplomats, nobles, and tourists descended on Paris in the wake of Napoleon's abdication, so did Prince Willem of Orange. Traveling against doctor's orders, he arrived on July 16, 1815 and found himself a guest of honor at parties and parades, his wounded arm resting in a black silk sling. At one dinner party, he sat next to Lady Emma Edgcumbe, who cut his meat for him since his injury prevented him from doing it himself.[11]

In Paris, Willem caught the eye of Emperor Alexander I, the man now praised as a savior of Europe. But there was more to the camaraderie than Willem suspected. Alexander had decided the Netherlands would make a good ally, and Willem was its future king. On July 20, Alexander broached the subject of marriage to his youngest sister, Anna. Willem accepted enthusiastically. When news of the engagement broke that August, Princess Charlotte of Wales couldn't help but comment, 'He has none of my good wishes except that of his being *made sufficiently* uneasy by his Grand Dss.'[12] She had likely not expected her rejected suitor to rebound so quickly, or with such a wealthy and glamorous bride.

Willem traveled to St. Petersburg, arriving on December 23. The entire Romanov family welcomed him as if he were their own. When he entered Maria Feodorovna's study in the Winter Palace, he met Anna for the first time: a tall young woman with dark blonde hair, big dark eyes, and a small bow-shaped mouth. Willem thought she looked better than the portrait he'd been sent, noting the beauty of her hands and slope of her shoulders. As for Anna, she saw a very slim man of average height with dark blond hair, who moved quickly and gracefully. His gray eyes were kind, and he had a ready smile. Speaking French – the only language they had in common – they discovered a shared love of art. To his family, Willem described Anna as 'sincere' with a 'tender heart,' calling her his 'Anninka.' Many years later, Anna described theirs as 'love at first sight,' but also added, 'It's a lot to marry someone you don't know.'[13] The emperor provided his sister with the traditional dowry of one million silver rubles, ensuring all her financial needs would be met. Her mother sent her to her new country with everything she needed to set up household, including dinnerware, flatware, vases, gilded mirrors, porcelain, toiletries, fabric, clothes, and the contents and staff for a Russian Orthodox chapel.

The engagement ceremony took place on January 28, 1816 followed by the wedding on February 21. Willem's Aunt Louise confirmed that he was 'very grateful and delighted with his future [wife], of whom he is generally so full of praise…'[14] In the same letter, she reported another royal engagement: Princess Charlotte had rebounded with the handsome but impoverished Prince Leopold of Saxe-Coburg-Saalfeld. Not only was Leopold better looking than Willem – Napoleon called him the 'handsomest young man he had ever seen in the Tuileries' – but he was a third son with few prospects, who would never require her to leave Britain.[15] It was not the last time Leopold and Willem would cross paths, with Leopold emerging victorious.

When Anna became pregnant, the couple left for the Netherlands so the new baby could be born in Willem's homeland. Anna's mother persuaded Mademoiselle de Sybourg, her childhood governess, to go with her. Bourcis accepted, perhaps also eager to be nearer her family in Switzerland. Six months after her arrival in the Netherlands, Anna increased its population by one. Born on February 19, 1817, Willem Alexander Paul Frederik Lodewijk was baptized in the Dutch Protestant church in Brussels. The Belgians were overjoyed with the first prince born in Brussels since the long-ago days of Spanish rule.

Anna wrote to her mother daily, needing reassurance as she adapted to a family whose dynamics she struggled to understand. Willem and his father were openly antagonistic to each other, and although Willem's mother, Wilhelmina ('Mimi'), was a calm and comforting presence, she had none of the influence accorded to Maria Feodorovna. The new Princess of Orange took refuge in the familiar traditions she'd brought with her, including her Orthodox chapel, confessor, and cantors. Every day, she could drink tea from her Russian samovar, pet her Russian dogs, and indulge in steam baths that replicated the feel of a Russian sauna. To the frugal Dutch, Anna's glittering jewels and gilded furnishings looked like exhibitionism. But Anna was her mother's daughter, and Maria Feodorovna believed in the political power of splendor – 'this framework of grandeur,' as she called it, which Catherine the Great had used to give the public 'a motive for respecting herself.'[16] To Anna's credit, she didn't need the Dutch to pay for her luxuries. In addition to the income from her dowry, she received payments from a Romanov family fund and yearly cash gifts from her mother. She put that money to good use, founding a charity to help give it to the poor. She also founded up to 50 orphanages, each supported with her own money.[17]

Anna soon learned that her father-in-law, King Willem I, was not given to displays of wealth. He and Mimi presided over a sedate court and lived a simple life in The Hague, a compact city full of sidewalks, canals, trees, and blooming gardens. The city's palaces, however comfortable, resembled bourgeois mansions more than the Winter Palace. Willem and Anna preferred the sophistication of Brussels, whose citizens appreciated Anna's glamour and Willem's easygoing charm. Together, Anna and Willem threw parties, watched horse races, went to the opera, and attended the theater. There was even a popular saying at the time: live like the Prince of Orange.[18] But while the Princess of Orange could afford such a life, the Prince of Orange could not. His extravagance would cause a host of future problems.

Anna and Willem began married life at the peak of their families' post-Napoleonic popularity. That popularity would soon diminish, at least for the Orange family, as Willem embroiled himself in a number of scandals that eroded his reputation as a war hero of Waterloo. When Willem's former fiancée, Princess Charlotte, died giving birth to a stillborn son in 1817, an unsigned letter from Brussels in London's *The News* accused Willem of breaking mourning protocol by going to the theater and dancing.[19] This was seen as ungallant behavior in a man who should have been grieving the death of a woman he had almost married.

Willem's reputation remained front-page news in late 1817, when he clashed with his father over the reassignment of four officers – his friends – to the Dutch East Indies (present-day Indonesia). Willem fled from a confrontation, leaving a pregnant and exhausted Anna to bear the brunt of the king's verbal assaults. The incident damaged Willem's reputation throughout Europe. The Prussian envoy, Prince von Hatzfeldt, described Willem as 'frivolous and inconsistent…' Lord Clancarty, the British ambassador, suggested 'the Prince should be left altogether unemployed.' Even Wellington, Willem's former mentor, delivered a devastating verdict: Willem 'has already deceived his adherents, and he will deceive them again…I am afraid that there is not in Europe, including Russia, a weaker Prince.'[20] The conflict between father and son did not bode well for the smooth running of their new kingdom. In any other country, these problems might have remained in the personal sphere – but not this one.

The United Kingdom of the Netherlands was an arranged marriage between its constituents, the Netherlands and Belgium, with its citizens divided by language, religion, culture, history, geography, and affinity.

Heavily influenced by French culture and the Catholic religion, Belgium was a melting pot composed of Flemings, Walloons, the descendants of Austrian and Spanish officials, and an influx of French immigrants fleeing war and revolution. The Netherlands, in contrast, was a largely Protestant Dutch-speaking country. As a native of the Netherlands, King Willem I believed Belgians must be forced to adapt to Dutch customs. Taking the side of the Belgians, Willem argued they should not be treated like residents of 'an annexed province.'[21] From the day of the kingdom's creation, the battle lines were clear: the king would always side with the Dutch, and his son and heir would always side with the Belgians.

Because of his affinity for Brussels, Willem befriended a number of its residents, including French political exiles. He found himself swayed by their passionate repudiations of the newly restored Bourbon monarchy. When those repudiations coalesced into a conspiracy, the émigrés looked to Willem as a possible replacement for the hated Louis XVIII. They whispered to him, stroked his ego, and told him he was destined for greatness at their side. Willem began to believe it was true. Like many soldiers, Willem found it hard to adjust to civilian life. He missed the camaraderie, the excitement, and the sense of fighting for the fate of the world. Without a cause to fight for, he was easy prey for anyone who promised him fortune and glory. But Willem and his conspirators weren't careful enough. Foreign spies began to report their movements and conversations. Willem's powerful brother-in-law, Alexander I, warned Willem multiple times to keep the peace and stay away from these conspirators.[22]

Both Alexander I and Willem I understood how easily Willem could be led astray, but they may not have yet known part of the reason why: Willem was bisexual.[23] At the time, it was considered a crime for men to have sexual relations with other men. Homosexual desires were seen as deviant behavior condemned by the church and prevailing social mores. In the minds of his contemporaries, Willem 'committed horrors, which, during the last centuries, were punished by death at the stake.'[24] People with wealth and power could often shield their actions from scrutiny, but Willem was a political figure. To retain public trust, it was crucial he appear strictly heterosexual. This was not easy – especially since, beginning in 1819, Willem would be blackmailed repeatedly to conceal what one blackmailer called his 'disgraceful and unnatural lusts.'[25] Livid with rage at his son's indiscretions, the king relied on Minister of Justice van Maanen to arrest each subsequent blackmailer and quash any hint of scandal.

When Willem and Anna's Brussels palace burned to the ground on the night of December 29, 1820, it shook the entire family. Willem moved his family to The Hague and tried to mend his ways. It was none too soon for Anna, who had been plagued with anxiety, homesickness, poor health, and frequent childbirth for years. When their fourth baby, Casimir, died of encephalitis at five months old in 1822, Anna relied on her strong Orthodox faith to bear the loss. Willem, however, thought Casimir's death made her hard and bitter.[26] Like her father, she was emotional, quick to anger, and fell into periodic bouts of sadness. The couple began to drift apart, physically and emotionally.

Three years later, in October of 1828, Anna and Willem moved into a new palace in Brussels, built to replace the one that had burned. Shortly afterward, Anna received devastating news: her mother had died in St. Petersburg on November 5. She spent the winter wrapped in a shell of misery. By March of 1829, however, she had begun to appreciate her new surroundings. She asked to have a Murillo painting she remembered from her mother's country palace; her fellow Triopathy member, now Emperor Nicholas I, sent it to her. By the terms of her mother's will, Anna inherited a portion of her jewels, including 'brilliants, fine pearls and precious stones.' The Russian Chancellor, Count Karl Vasilyevich Nesselrode, had the jewels appraised and her mother's valet brought them to Anna in person, along with a copy of the will, which she locked in her diamantaire.[27]

That summer, Anna's brother Constantine paid her a visit. He consoled his sister and delivered a loving but stern lecture to Willem. Afterward, he wrote to Anna that he hoped Willem wouldn't hold it against him – everything he'd said had been for Willem's own good.[28] Had Constantine lectured him on his spending, his unsuitable friends, his plummeting popularity, his divided kingdom, or his relationship with his father? Perhaps it was all of these, having done irreparable damage to Willem's reputation. The French envoy captured Willem's position perfectly when he wrote, 'The dangerous errors to which the Prince of Orange indulges would seem incredible if one were not a witness to them. The throne of the Netherlands, barely raised, still totters on foundations that time has only just assured...the House of Nassau cannot have too many friends.'[29] As Willem would find out on the morning of September 26, those friends were in short supply.

Chapter 3

Meanwhile in America

From its earliest days, America's ties to the Netherlands were strong. Many Americans had Dutch ancestry, their grandparents or great-grandparents having been settlers in New Amsterdam. The Dutch West India Company had founded that colony, located at the southern tip of present-day Manhattan, in pursuit of profitable trade in beaver pelts. In 1624, Captain Cornelis May brought thirty families to the area to help create a permanent outpost.[1] Settlers soon spread through the Hudson Valley, founding what would later become Kingston and Albany.

On August 27, 1664, four English ships sailed into New Amsterdam's harbor and demanded the colony's surrender. Governor Peter Stuyvesant acquiesced to avoid violence. The English renamed the colony New York and Dutch influence waned. By 1809, Washington Irving wrote, 'I was surprised to find how few of my fellow-citizens were aware that New-York had ever been called New-Amsterdam…or cared a straw about their ancient Dutch progenitors.'[2] The Dutch legacy lived on in the Hudson Valley, however, where the settlers had less contact with outside influences. Born enslaved in the late 1790s, Isabella Van Wagenen – later Sojourner Truth – grew up speaking Dutch, the language of her enslavers, in Ulster County, New York.[3]

In the post-Napoleonic era, America and the Netherlands both thrived on maritime commerce. A close relationship was desirable, if only to keep an eye on the competition. King Willem I had sent his first diplomatic envoy, François Daniel Changuion, in 1814. Changuion left a year later, unable to do much relationship building during the War of 1812.[4] Ten years later, in 1825, the king decided to send a new permanent representative to the United States. This time, his envoy was a career diplomat who had already served as the Netherlands' representative to the Holy Roman Empire and Denmark. Neither of those posts could have prepared him for one of the biggest social scandals ever to hit the White House.

Born on October 31, 1772, Chevalier Christiaan Bangeman Huygens came from a Dutch family well-known for producing the country's most famous mathematician. He began his career under Prince Willem's grandfather, the last stadtholder, before the French invaded the Netherlands. He quickly moved up the diplomatic ladder, earning promotions from diplomatic secretary at Regensburg (home of the Holy Roman Empire's Imperial Diet) to chargé d'affaires in Denmark to full-fledged minister at the same court.[5] In 1802, he married Elise de Danneskiold Löwendal, the daughter of a Danish count and his wife, an illegitimate great-granddaughter of Louis XIV. The couple had six children, born in three countries between 1803 and 1812. Elise died later that year, leaving Huygens with a large family to raise on his own. He dispersed the six children among relatives while he continued to work for the government.

Huygens survived the turbulent years of the French annexation and found himself working as a Commissioner of Maastricht when the House of Orange returned to claim the throne. In 1814, in conjunction with his co-commissioner, Johannes Bernardus Vrijthoff, he issued a proclamation releasing the city's inhabitants from their oath of allegiance to France. On February 16, 1815, he married a second time, to his co-commissioner's daughter, the widowed Constantia Wilhelmina Vrijthoff van den Santheuvel. Christiaan and Constantia were part of the Dutch court assemblage on hand for Willem and Anna's wedding festivities the following year.[6] Although not part of Anna's inner circle, they saw her at court functions over the years. Constantia took note of her famous jewels, including the towering diadems, the emerald and topaz necklaces, and the sapphires ringed with diamonds.

Then, in March of 1825, the king appointed Huygens as Envoy Extraordinary and Minister Plenipotentiary to the United States of America. Huygens packed up the whole family and brought all six children to America. After landing in New York, they made their way south via Philadelphia and Baltimore until they reached their new home of Washington, DC. On August 26, the American Secretary of State, Henry Clay, introduced him to President John Quincy Adams.[7]

As Huygens settled into his job, he began training his only son, Roger, in the duties of a diplomat. Although Roger held a military rank as an officer of artillery, he worked for his father as secretary to the Dutch legation. In addition to learning English, Roger – who already spoke French – would now learn the paperwork and protocol that underpinned an embassy. When Huygens got word that Prince Bernhard of Saxe-Weimar-Eisenach would be visiting America for an extended tour, he volunteered his son as a traveling companion. Bernhard had joined the Dutch army during the Napoleonic Wars, fighting alongside Willem at Quatre Bras and Waterloo. Now, the prince had the time and money to indulge his curiosity about America. That summer of 1825, Bernhard sailed to Boston and made his way to Washington via New York City, where he picked up Roger. The two of them would travel to New Orleans, then up to Missouri, Indiana, Ohio, and Pennsylvania.[8]

Meanwhile, Huygens made important political and social connections in America. When Congress wasn't in session, diplomats were free to travel to cities like Philadelphia, New York, or Baltimore, where politics took a backseat to networking and entertainment. In 1827, Huygens visited New York and befriended Senator Martin Van Buren, a sociable 45-year-old widower very proud of his Dutch ancestry. 'My family was from Holland,' Van Buren later wrote, 'without a single intermarriage with one of different extraction… embracing a period of over two centuries and including six generations.'[9] A snappy dresser, the five-foot-six-inch Van Buren had engaging deep-set blue eyes, a broad, bald pate, and red mutton-chop whiskers. Dutch was his first language, and he spoke English with a slight accent.[10]

Born in 1782, Van Buren had skipped college and gone straight from his local academy in Kinderhook to a New York City law office. He learned by doing, with a work ethic that made him one of the best lawyers in the city. Later, both he and his son John befriended the Huygens family and enjoyed speaking Dutch together. When the citizens of Albany gave a dinner for Huygens during his visit, they invited residents with Dutch ancestry, including Van Buren. The Dutch New Yorkers toasted Huygens, who replied in praise of Dutch traits and American know-how. He highlighted Albany in particular as 'a living picture of man's industry.'[11] Huygens and Van Buren would remain friends for years, speaking Dutch and traveling together when possible.

Then, in July of 1828, something strange happened. On July 13 at 3 p.m., two Washington police officers were informed of a break-in at the Huygens home. The previous night, at about 11 p.m., someone had forced open a locked room and stolen $300 worth of jewelry and silver. It wasn't hard to figure out who was responsible when three of their servants failed to show up for work the next day. The police sprang into action, and by 6:30 p.m., they had already caught two of them. The perpetrators made it four miles down the road, then stopped at a tavern, where they were caught napping. François Auguste Michand and Jean David Guerraz were apprehended, while Ferdinand Michand managed to escape. Police returned the stolen items to Huygens: three boxes of jewels, a trunk containing 60 silver spoons, and $131.[12]

A dark night. A broken lock. Three stolen boxes of jewels. Huygens must have recalled this incident thirteen and a half months later with an unpleasant sense of déjà vu.

Chapter 4

The Husband Did It

Every day, people in the Netherlands opened their newspapers to read about the latest developments – or lack thereof – in the hunt for the royal jewel thief. While the Brussels police focused on footprints and foreign traffic, the diplomatic corps and those closest to the royal family mulled over their own clues.

It was impossible to ignore the Prince of Orange's constant need for cash. Horses, art, furnishings, travel, parties, his male favorites: Willem had always lived beyond his means. A German soldier in Dutch service, Friedrich von Gagern, wrote, 'His limited income has not sufficed for the irregularities of his life…'[1] As long ago as 1820, the Prussian envoy, Peter Heinrich August von Salviati, had informed his king that Willem's expenses outstripped his income by some 140,000 florins per year.[2] Enquiring minds connected the spendthrift prince with the fortune that had just disappeared from his palace. How could these two facts be unconnected? On October 15, a Brussels civil servant wrote to Minister of Justice van Maanen, '…the most insulting rumors circulate for the Prince of Orange, with regard to the theft committed, which is attributed to H.R.H. himself.'[3] Newspapers even published cartoons depicting Willem stealing from Anna's jewelry box.

Willem seemed oblivious to the rumors. When he wrote to tell Nicholas I about the jewel theft, he called it 'a nasty affair which we do not yet see clearly. God grant that one day we discover the real culprits…'[4] But some felt they saw the matter quite clearly already. In fact, just one day later, the Russian envoy, Count Guryev, informed his foreign minister about a new person of interest. The police, he wrote, 'suspect none other than the dandy Pereira of the theft…'[5] Who, exactly, was this Pereira? And what connected him to the palace and the theft?

❖

Born about 1790, Achilles de Pereira was the son of a Portuguese consul in St. Petersburg. In 1808, he had joined the Portuguese legion of the French army. He became a captain and aide-de-camp to the Marquis d'Alorna, fighting in four Spanish campaigns as well as the invasion of Russia. He survived; d'Alorna did not. Napoleon's chief of staff, Berthier, described Pereira as 'a distinguished officer, very active, and noted for his great zeal and intelligence.'[6] After Waterloo, Pereira left the army and began appearing in fashionable European resorts with wealthy men. He was with a Russian, Count Nikolai Nikitich Demidov, in Spa in 1817, where the pair dined and danced with none other than Willem and Anna.

At some point, Pereira became a secretary to Don Justo José de Machado, a Spanish Consul in Paris. This was the link that worried diplomats like Guryev, because they knew what Machado had been accused of. As part of the settlement after Napoleon's final defeat, France had agreed to pay 1,850,000 francs to Spain for the destruction caused during the Peninsular War. Half the money went directly to Spain, while Machado held the other half in France on Spain's behalf. But when the Spanish king lost power, the new constitutional ministry asked Machado to take the money to England instead. Machado duly cashed out £500,000 and left for England. He refused, however, to give any to the Spanish government. He insisted it belonged only to those with verifiable damage claims from the war. While they sorted things out, the Spanish government asked him to deposit the cash in the Bank of England, where it would earn interest. Machado promised to do so. Instead, he used Achilles de Pereira's name to deposit £200,000 with an English banking firm, Hullett. The pair then moved to the Netherlands, conveniently out of British jurisdiction.[7]

During the struggle over the money, the short-lived Spanish constitutional government had hired a middleman, Juan Álvarez Mendizábal, to request and receive funds from Machado. Mendizábal, now in exile in England, sued Machado for the money, claiming the Spanish government had authorized him to collect it. Machado contested Mendizábal's suit for years, then suddenly had a change of heart. He let it slip to a single witness that he did indeed owe Mendizábal the money, and the Court of Common Pleas awarded Mendizábal a judgment of £146,000. It was widely believed the two former enemies had decided to work together, using the British courts to essentially steal the money. If so, their plan hit a snag when King Ferdinand VII of Spain sued Hullett to get the money back. But by 1826, there was only £100,000 left in the account, according to Hullett's representatives. Machado threatened to sue Hullett for the money he claimed was missing from the account. Mendizábal threatened to sue the king, Machado, *and* Hullett to get the judgment previously awarded him. By the time of the jewel theft, the case had degenerated into an inexplicably tangled web of claims and counter-claims. No one seemed to know what had happened to the money, but they did know Machado had last been in possession of it.[8]

Pereira was never accused of wrongdoing, but he lived and worked with Machado and may have known more than he let on. The relationship troubled the Russian envoy, Count Guryev, who called Pereira an 'adventurer' who was 'well preserved and with a pretty face...'[9] It's unclear when Pereira first met Willem or when their friendship deepened. They were acquainted at least as early as 1817, when a British tourist, Lady de Clifford, saw Pereira with Willem and Anna. They didn't attract attention until 1825, when Guryev saw Willem flaunting Pereira, much to the chagrin of Willem's previous favorite. By 1827, their bond had only strengthened. Pereira bought a house in Brussels, furnished with what may have been Willem's money. Willem also opened an unlimited credit account for Pereira with a tailor and shoemaker.[10] Where, onlookers wondered, did Willem get the money?

The pair made no effort to keep their connection a secret. According to Guryev, they 'were often seen arm in arm and walking together in the countryside...They also often dined alone in the Prince's study and stayed up until three in the morning.' To make it easier to meet, Willem gave Pereira a master key to the palace. Other times, Willem left the palace to meet Pereira away from prying eyes. The French envoy, the Comte d'Agoult, noted Willem's 'absences from the palace during the night' and believed the relationship had to do with Machado. He suspected Willem needed Pereira to connect with Machado, from whom he borrowed money. 'The hereditary prince, as a result of the oddities of his character, of his habitual idleness, has thrown himself into a very unseemly way of life,' wrote d'Agoult.[11]

Whether it was motivated by love or money, Guryev saw the relationship as a potential insult to Anna, and by extension, to Emperor Nicholas I. He told Nicholas, who worried enough to question Willem about Pereira in 1828.

Willem assured Nicholas it was a simple friendship, nothing more. Few in the diplomatic corps believed this explanation. Guryev (and the Austrian envoy, Count Felix von Mier) feared Pereira was an agent of the French secret police, sent to entrap and discredit Willem.

After Anna's jewels disappeared, Willem's friendship with Pereira looked even more suspicious. Gossip had already connected Willem to Machado's money via Pereira. Now, wagging tongues connected one more dot. The Russian envoy heard 'odious rumors' claiming Willem had borrowed from Machado, and 'as a guarantee of payment, Pereira had stolen the diamonds from the Princess.'[12] Anonymous posters appeared in Brussels, indicating that 'all searches would be in vain as the diamonds had been stolen by Pereira, in agreement with the prince, and deposited with the Minister of Spain [Machado].' Although the French envoy, the Marquis de la Moussaye, called this 'absurd slander,' he admitted it was repeated everywhere.[13]

The pieces of the puzzle appeared to be falling into place. Some citizens of Brussels took matters into their own hands. Anna, they decided, must be told who had done this to her. The Marquis de la Moussaye catalogued these hurtful scenes for the French Minister of Foreign Affairs:

> Anonymous letters were addressed to Madame la Princesse d'Orange, containing imputations and details that should never have fallen before her eyes. Deeply hurt, the Princess immediately asked for the sacrifice of a dangerous, if not guilty, intimacy, but could not obtain it. The most vivid scenes have not succeeded in detaching the Prince from his unworthy favorite. Since this episode, Madame la Princesse d'Orange has remained immersed in constant affliction; her health, which had long been shaken, was visibly deteriorating more and more.[14]

Anticipating that Anna would confide in her favorite member of Triopathy, Willem wrote to Nicholas I and broached the subject himself. The public blamed Pereira for the theft, he said, but 'there are no clues in this regard that could authorize police or legal searches, and this gossip is for the moment attributable only to malice.'[15] *For the moment.* Even Willem sounded uncertain of his friend's involvement.

The police offered the prince nothing in the way of damage control, which only fed the gossip. People began to ask: how was it possible they had failed to find a single witness? A single diamond in a pawnbroker's shop? It was easier to believe Willem had taken the jewels to repay Machado. He had sunk from being the hero of Waterloo, with a bronze lion built like a shrine on the site of his spilled blood, to a man who would steal from his wife to keep his lover in style.

From Russia, Nicholas I tried to help Anna untangle the accusations and suspicions. She told him that no guards had ever been present in her rooms because Willem hadn't wanted them. On the night of the theft, '…the valet who should have slept downstairs was not there; and he was just the one recommended by Pereira…he attended an orgy that same night with the people around Machado…I tell you this only to show you the carelessness and negligence that prevail at our home.'[16] She confessed that she knew Willem was deeply in debt, with an unfavorable reputation. Her revelations shook Nicholas, forcing him to ask Willem about Pereira once more. Willem assured him the relationship was 'very innocent and indifferent.'[17] Jealousy, he claimed, made others blame Pereira. As for the theft, there was no evidence Pereira had anything to do with it. But as a concession to Nicholas – and to quiet the gossip – he said he would slowly remove Pereira from his life.

It was just as well. Six months later, the kingdom would be convulsed with revolution and Willem would be more worried about protecting his inheritance than private suppers with Pereira.

Chapter 5

The Belgian Revolution

Prince Willem wasn't the only one whose popularity plummeted in the years leading up to the jewel theft. His father's name had become synonymous with insatiable greed. The British ambassador, Sir Charles Bagot, described King Willem I as a 'huckstering butter and cheese King' whose goals in life were 'to usurp quietly as much power as he possibly can for the Crown, and to fill his pockets as full as they will hold...'[1] He succeeded. He increased censorship, harassed the press, tried to force Belgians to speak Dutch, and attempted to control Catholic clergy and education. Although he stimulated trade and reorganized the country's finances, for many Belgians, the benefits didn't outweigh what he attempted to take away: their identity. Not only was the country less unified than in 1815, but the king's opposition was stronger than ever. Prince Willem described the country as being in a state of 'legally organized anarchy.'[2]

On July 28, 1830, the last Bourbon king of France abdicated. When his attempt to rule as an autocrat had failed, he fled from an outraged populace. Liberal politicians offered his cast-off throne to a cousin, the Duc d'Orléans.

Although the Southern Netherlands appeared calm in the weeks following the French upheaval, it was not. The veneer of calm vanished when the people of Brussels heard a single song, 'Amour Sacré de la Patrie,' from the opera *La Muette de Portici* by Daniel Auber. The story of a rebel who overthrows a tyrant king, the opera struck a powerful emotional chord. Brimming with pride and patriotism, the lyrics of a particularly poignant duet recalled the anthem of the French Revolution, the *Marseillaise*. The audience couldn't help but compare the opera's tyrant king to Willem I.

On August 25, immediately after the performance, theatergoers wandered the streets of Brussels, wrapped in the afterglow of song and story. The crowd grew in size as people shared the emotion of the moment with bystanders. Together, they became an easy target for students who launched a nationalist demonstration, manipulating their stirred emotions. Soon, the crowd sought an outlet for its tension in violence. They marched to the home of the government newspaper's editor and destroyed everything inside. Next was the home of Director of Police de Knyff de Gontrœul, followed by that of the hated Minister of Justice van Maanen. Violence continued throughout the night, as the crowd coerced gunsmiths into distributing their wares.[3]

Initially, the rebels' demands were modest: more influence on the government and freedom of the press. But when word spread to other cities in Belgium, they rose in revolt, too. The rebels' demands increased from local influence to total independence. Brussels citizens replaced the French flag over the Hôtel de Ville with the red, yellow, and black flag of Brabant.[4]

When news of the riot reached the king, he refused to accept that half the country wanted to tell him how to do his job. He sent his sons, Willem and Frederik, galloping south to Brussels with 6,000 troops.[5] As commander of the armed forces, Prince Frederik's job was to quell the revolt with violence, if need be. Willem was to act as negotiator, using his history of preference for the Belgians to the royal family's advantage.

On August 31, Dutch troops camped outside Brussels. The princes offered to discuss concessions if the rebels removed the Brabant flag, the symbol of the revolt, but if the flag remained, they would have no choice but to remove it by force. The threat incensed the citizens of Brussels. Overnight, they distributed three thousand guns, built barricades, and tore up pavements to prevent the army from rolling in gun carriages.

The next morning, seeing the city's frantic preparations, Willem proposed entering Brussels with only his staff to work out a peaceful solution. Prince Frederik warned against it – why take on an armed and angry populace with no help? – but couldn't change his brother's mind. With only a few officers, including his former governor Constant Rebecque, Willem approached the barricaded city gate. Since the main gate was impassable, he went through the narrow pedestrian gate, wide enough for one man on horseback at a time.

Quickly surrounded by the city's militia, Willem faced an angry crowd armed with the tools of their trade, including butchers' cleavers. As he passed, he heard only a few scattered cheers. Others hissed 'silence' or cried 'Long live freedom!' The French envoy, the Marquis de la Moussaye, described Willem as pale and visibly emotional, looking 'like a criminal being led to the scaffold…'[6] As the surging crowd forced him toward the Hôtel de Ville, Willem reminded onlookers he had fought alongside them at Waterloo and shed his blood for them in battle. But this was a tired trope by now. The faces in the crowd remained tight with tension: no smiles, no cheers, only hisses and growls. Muscles quivered. Fingers tightened on weapons.

The crowd pressed nearer, spooking Willem's horse. The gray Arabian began to kick anyone who came too close, injuring several bystanders. His horse's hooves shattered the fragile balance between the prince and the crowd. Willem and his officers fled to the Place du Palais de Justice, only to find the exits barricaded. Willem urged his horse to a gallop and jumped over the obstacle to escape. His officers attempted to follow, but Constant Rebecque fell from his horse and had to be pulled over the barricade to safety. Pelted by angry bystanders, all five made it to Willem's palace unharmed. There, Willem threw himself into the French ambassador's arms. 'Well, you saw it,' he told La Moussaye. 'I entered without an escort, and as a price for my trust they wanted to assassinate me. But I will not be discouraged. I will stay in Brussels and I will not neglect any means of conciliation.'[7] A nation's peace rested on his shoulders – or so he believed.

Although safe for the moment, Willem and his men were surrounded. Two Belgian delegates brought him a startling proposition: they must separate the two countries. Willem could either be their king or their prisoner; it was up to him. But despite his troubled relationship with his father, Willem refused to betray his sovereign. The soldier prince watched as more rebels, guns, and ammunition flooded into the city. With no authority to make a useful compromise, Willem went to convince his father not to use violence to quell the revolt.[8]

He would never see his palace or the city of Brussels again.

Back in The Hague, Willem couldn't convince his father to keep the peace. The king ordered his younger son to retake Brussels. On September 23, Prince Frederik and his men marched into a quiescent city, fighting brief skirmishes over the Schaerbeek gate and nearby barricades. The Dutch made their way down the Rue Royale and camped in the dappled shade of the city park's lime trees, so recently the site of springtime strolls, picnics, and concerts. But when they attempted to occupy nearby buildings and homes, they triggered several days of fierce street fighting. 'We will live free,' said Belgian journalist Louis de Potter, 'or bury ourselves beneath heaps of ashes.'[9] Leading the rebels was Don Juan van Halen, a Spanish-born adventurer who had served in the armies of Joseph Bonaparte and Alexander I. The Belgians managed to push the Dutch soldiers to the lower ground of the park with their artillery and sharpshooters. The Dutch responded by killing anyone they suspected of resistance, including women and children. About 400 people died in the battle for Brussels, including civilians and soldiers.[10] Facing stronger resistance than expected, Prince Frederik retreated, leaving parts of the city in near-ruins. A report in London's *Weekly Times* described the once-beautiful city park as 'dyed with blood,' littered with 'corpses, horribly mutilated and stripped,' its iron railing and statues 'destroyed by the grape-shot.'[11] Van Halen issued a statement urging the people of Brussels to remain calm and refrain from looting.

Anna and her ladies-in-waiting busied themselves making lint for wounded Dutch soldiers. She asked Nicholas I to send her mother's Triopathy ring to her. She had given hers – one of the most precious items she owned – to Willem when he left to meet the rebels in Brussels. Despite her initial liking for Brussels and its people, she felt they had betrayed her, first by blaming Willem for the theft and now for the revolt.

The Belgian rebels quickly declared a provisional government, announcing their separation from the United Kingdom of the Netherlands. When Prince Willem proposed returning to Belgium to help calm things down, his father refused. But when the Belgian deputies of the States General suggested the same thing, he agreed and named his son temporary governor of Belgium. Willem offered concessions right away, including freedom of language and more voting rights. He begged his father for the power to do more, but the king refused. Then, two days later, his father sent a private letter: he would allow the Belgians to secede if they offered the throne to Willem. King Willem, however, never made this offer public.[12] He preferred to hedge his bets, placing Prince Frederik at the head of his troops once more, ready to attack if needed. He would back whichever son emerged victorious.

The great royal deception was on.

In Antwerp, his new Belgian headquarters, Willem joined the resistance movement and recognized Belgium's independence. In his official statement, he once again described himself as 'one who has shed blood for the independence of your regions…'[13] The result was not what he expected. The Dutch saw it as an unforgivable betrayal, while the Belgians remained unmoved by his reference to Waterloo. Those memories had faded, replaced by new ones that didn't merit the same respect.

To make matters worse, once Willem declared for the Belgians, King Willem I pretended he had no idea what his son was doing. He disavowed Willem's actions and revoked his powers as governor, rewarding his son's earlier forbearance with a dagger between the ribs. 'I'm in a terrible position,' Willem wrote to Nicholas I. '…I'm ready to sacrifice myself if I can thereby pacify these provinces while avoiding a general war.'[14] Even that hope appeared forlorn as skirmishes broke out at the Antwerp city gates. With no hope of retaining his troops and no authority to effect a peaceful separation, Willem had little choice but to flee.

After his very public failures in Brussels and Antwerp, Willem's reputation sank to its nadir. So toxic was his presence that King Willem I refused to allow him to come home. The older man sobbed behind closed doors, but refused to admit he had backed Willem's pro-Belgian stance.[15] Both men believed help must now come from Britain, which had supported the creation of the dual kingdom in the first place. Since Willem couldn't go home, he went to London, where the five Great Powers (Britain, Russia, Austria, Prussia, and France) convened a meeting to discuss Belgium's independence.

Even in the chaos of revolution, the jewel theft remained a subject of court gossip in The Hague. Someone told Anna they suspected a Spaniard – possibly Don Juan van Halen, recent leader of the rebels in Brussels – had been involved. This made sense to Anna, who already suspected the Spanish faction at court, perhaps in league with Machado. Still racking her brain for detail, she remembered the Spanish envoy to the Netherlands, Don Joaquin de Anduaga, acting suspiciously around the time of the robbery.

'Who knows,' she wrote, 'if my diamonds were not kept in his house which, like that of all diplomatic envoys, is inviolable?'[16] Although she didn't want to accuse the palace concierge of anything, she couldn't help but remember he was Spanish, too.

On November 4, 1830, the Great Powers opened their meeting. Of the five, Russia, Austria, and Prussia had long ago sworn to support the monarchist cause wherever it was threatened. Anna's countryman, Prince Lieven, had recently told her, 'We will come to your aid. The army of Poland will form the vanguard.'[17] But when a Polish rebellion forced Emperor Nicholas I to face the possibility of war on two fronts, he had no choice but to focus on the threat closest to home. None of the other Powers were willing or able to help.

Although he wasn't invited to the official conference, Willem campaigned on the London social scene. Once again, he learned just how far his reputation had fallen. The years of gossip, conspiracies, and his recent about-face in Belgium had chipped away at his post-Waterloo reputation. Most negotiators felt he was simply in the way. In the city's drawing rooms, he encountered Princess Charlotte's widower, Leopold of Saxe-Coburg-Saalfeld. Leopold had remained in England after Charlotte's death, since his niece – Princess Alexandrina Victoria, daughter of the Duke and Duchess of Kent – was heiress to the British throne. Leopold, however, had no sway with the Great Powers and was not someone Willem could turn to for help.

Meanwhile, the newly elected Belgian National Congress acted as if the London Conference had nothing to do with them. On November 18, the new country formally declared its independence. Four days later, its Congress chose a constitutional monarchy as their form of government and banned the House of Orange from their throne. 'If you give that family the slightest glimmer of hope, the revolution will persist,' a Belgian representative wrote.[18] Bowing to the inevitable, the Great Powers officially dissolved the United Kingdom of the Netherlands. By the end of January, they had produced a treaty of twenty-four articles that settled the questions of borders, river navigation rights, and deficit share. The Dutch accepted the articles, but the Belgian provisional government disagreed with the division of territory and their share of the former united kingdom's debt. The stalemate continued.

In March of 1831, Willem returned to The Hague to find his family and his country at a low point. His father, fearing a French or Belgian attack, ordered

90,000 men stationed along the border, prepared for defense or offense. But feeding and supplying them cost the country 4,000,000 guilders per month.[19] How long could they keep it up?

During the previous winter and now through the spring, rumors abounded in European newspapers: Anna was going to leave Willem and move back to Russia...permanently. Despite the united front they had worked hard to present, the world knew their marriage was crumbling. Even her brother, Nicholas I, asked about the separation rumors. Anna must have felt a pang of sadness when the artist Jean Baptiste van der Hulst presented her with a new portrait, the one he'd been working on when her jewels were stolen. In it, she wore a blue velvet dress and the grandest of her stolen tiaras. How could she have guessed that, before she saw its completion, her jewels, her palace, and half her adopted country would be gone?

While the Dutch king sobbed and schemed, the Belgians searched Europe for a new ruler, unaffiliated with the House of Orange. A winning candidate emerged at the same time as Anna's missing jewels.

Chapter 6

An American Scandal

An ocean away from the Netherlands, the Huygens family continued to represent their country and their king in America. Back in 1828, they had been grateful to have their three boxes of stolen jewels returned by two Washington police officers, a happy ending to what could have been a painful memory. Their next encounter with American authorities, in the form of President Andrew Jackson and his Cabinet, did not end so happily.

Like Prince Willem of Orange, Andrew Jackson had bled for his country. At age thirteen, he had joined the local militia and fought in the Revolutionary War, where the slash of a British officer's sword scarred his head and left hand. His mother died of cholera not long afterward, leaving him an orphan. When her family took him in as a poor relation, he felt a deep shame that made him desperate to avoid ridicule or embarrassment. That desperation emerged periodically as physical violence. He once tackled and pummeled the governor of Tennessee to avenge a perceived insult. When another man insulted Jackson's wife, he killed the man in a duel.[1] Afterward, Jackson said, 'If he had shot me through the brain, sir, I should still have killed him.'[2] He had been shot twice during a fight that erupted after another duel, in which he was a second. And of course, he was the hero of the Battle of New Orleans in 1815. Outnumbered almost two to one, Jackson defeated Wellington's Peninsular War veterans, reporting only thirteen casualties compared to 2,037 reported by the British.[3] Like Willem, he became a war hero.

As a lawyer, politician, and soldier, Andrew Jackson represented ordinary Americans who succeeded through grit and talent rather than privilege and education. Unlike previous politicians, he was not a gentleman planter who spent his evenings reading books by Enlightenment philosophers. He was a tall, painfully thin man with a wide forehead, long thin nose, and a wild shock of hair that time would turn from red to snowy white. He liked gambling, horse racing, and fighting. He swore frequently, his favorite expletive being 'By the Eternal!'[4]

When he was nominated for president in 1824, he won the popular vote, but not the presidency. This convinced him a conspiracy of enemies had stolen the election. He ran again in 1828, a race that descended into a death match of vituperative mud-slinging. His opponents cast him as a murderer, thanks to his propensity for dueling. Muckraking journalists supporting John Quincy Adams claimed Jackson was British, that he was half Black, that his wife was a bigamist. Jackson's supporters rallied with rumors of their own. The stolen election of 1824 played well, but they also claimed John Quincy Adams had acted as a pimp for Anna's brother, Alexander I, during his time as US minister in St. Petersburg. When the Russian minister in Washington, Baron Paul de Krudener, saw this story in print, he protested to Secretary of State Henry Clay that it was a libel against his sovereign.[5]

To withstand the election's harrowing media blitz, Andrew and Rachel Jackson needed a shoulder to cry (or swear) on. That shoulder belonged to John Henry Eaton, a lawyer and senator from Nashville and longtime colleague of Jackson's. Eaton soothed the couple's frayed nerves, earning Jackson's undying loyalty. Thanks in no small part to his friend, Jackson kept hold of his temper and won the election by a landslide. His victory created a blistering fear in Rachel, who dreaded life in the public eye after the brutal slander hurled at her during the campaign. That overwhelming sense of dread likely became too much to bear. Rachel Jackson died of a heart attack on December 22, 1828, shortly before the couple was scheduled to move to Washington.[6]

About one week later, John Eaton married a 30-year-old widow named Margaret O'Neal Timberlake. Beautiful and precocious, Margaret had married her first husband, Navy purser John Bowie Timberlake, at age 16. During her husband's long absences at sea, she helped run her father's boarding house in Washington, home to many of the country's senators and representatives while Congress was in session. While working in her father's tavern as a barmaid, Margaret enchanted frequent guests Eaton and Jackson with her quick wit. Soon, Eaton's attraction to Margaret prompted gossip about an affair. When Margaret's first husband died by suicide at sea in April of 1828, the scandalmongers blamed her – the affair with Eaton had driven him to it. Now, without waiting a full year to mourn her first husband, she had married another. Instead of silencing rumors, their marriage only amplified them. The American minister in London, Louis McLane, indulged in a verbal assault, referring to Margaret as Eaton's mistress '& the mistress of 11-doz. others!!'[7] Andrew Jackson – who blamed the vicious 1828 campaign for Rachel's death – worried the slander would destroy Margaret like it had Rachel. Still dependent on Eaton for emotional support, Jackson promised him a job in the Cabinet to keep the couple near him. He continued to worry about Margaret as he moved to Washington and took office in March of 1829.

Despite Jackson's landslide victory, not everyone in the political firmament was pleased. Among those who complained was James Alexander Hamilton, third son of former Treasury Secretary Alexander Hamilton. Only sixteen when his father was shot and killed in a duel with Aaron Burr, Hamilton dedicated his life to becoming worthy of his father's memory. His very appearance reminded people of his famous progenitor, as he had 'the tall, slender form of the Hamiltons, with the Greek nose, dashed with Gallic nervousness and decision, and the sensitive mouth of that historic family.'[8] After graduating from Columbia in 1804, he became a lawyer and real estate developer in New York, determined to expose political corruption wherever he found it.

Hamilton met Andrew Jackson in December of 1827, when he represented a group of New York politicians at the anniversary ceremonies for the Battle of New Orleans. Hamilton had traveled to Jackson's home, twelve miles outside Nashville, and joined Jackson's party as it traveled south to New Orleans. Hamilton liked Jackson, praising his self-confidence and decisive nature. 'The whole powers of his mind are more at his command than are those of any other man I ever met with,' Hamilton wrote afterward.[9] The pair even talked about how a president should handle his Cabinet, after which Hamilton was convinced Jackson would be honest and impartial. But as soon as he was elected, Jackson began appointing friends and supporters to public office, often firing long-term government employees in order to do so. This worried Hamilton, who prized experience and education and preferred a government based on meritocracy to one supported by cronyism. Jackson, he believed, had only won the election because of his fame as a soldier. He wasn't a statesman, and despite his good intentions and unquestioned integrity, he was 'wholly uneducated and without talent…'[10] Although he liked Jackson personally, Hamilton began to fear what a Jackson presidency would entail.

One of Jackson's strongest supporters was Martin Van Buren, newly elected governor of New York and a close friend of both Hamilton and the Huygens family. Van Buren compared Jackson to another successful soldier turned politician, the Duke of Wellington. He believed they had the same courage and initiative, with Wellington having more education and experience and Jackson having more 'native intellect.'[11] Van Buren's tact – and his loyalty – earned him a position as Secretary of State in Jackson's Cabinet. As promised, Jackson found a place for Eaton, appointing him Secretary of War. Rounding out the Cabinet were Samuel Ingham (Treasury), John Berrien (Attorney General), John Branch (Navy), and John McLean (Postmaster General). Hamilton found fault with all these nominees, even his good friend Van Buren, whom he felt was unfit for the job because he needed help preparing his reports. 'No thought appeared to be given as to the fitness of the persons for their places,' he complained. It was 'the most unintellectual and uneducated Cabinet we ever had.'[12] Hamilton expected trouble, from the Cabinet and from Jackson.

A presentiment of danger didn't stop Hamilton from accepting a nomination of his own, as District Attorney of the Southern District of New York. When he accepted, Jackson told him, 'Go to the duties of your office, and make as much money as you can; but remember, you are to be always at my command.'[13] Hamilton, who admitted he wasn't a very good lawyer, couldn't muster much enthusiasm for the new job. It required him to work closely with US Customs officials on lawsuits over customs duties, seized goods, and forfeitures. He settled down to work and kept in touch with Van Buren, now based in Washington with Jackson. Van Buren wrote back frequently, asking Hamilton to keep an eye on his son John and let him know when the Huygens family would return to the nation's capital. 'Tell them Washington is the healthiest place in the known world,' Van Buren joked.[14] The Huygenses would have been better off ignoring Van Buren's summons.

❖

In November of 1828, members of the new Jackson administration descended on Washington for the next Congressional session and social season. The two went hand-in-hand, as a scheduled round of formal dinners and parties accompanied each new administration. For the women of Washington, society's unwritten rules dictated that your reputation was only as good as the company you kept. This posed a problem when it came to Margaret Eaton. As the wife of a Cabinet member, protocol dictated she be treated with respect and deference. But she was more than a wife – she was also a woman who had worked as a barmaid, flouted the rules of mourning, and was rumored to have slept with her second husband while married to her first. Those were unforgivable social sins. No matter her husband's rank, Margaret could not be treated as an equal.

To preserve their own reputations, the city's prominent wives promptly snubbed Margaret. First, Vice President John C. Calhoun's wife, Floride, chose not to return the formal visit Margaret had paid her. Following her lead, Jackson's own niece and White House hostess, Emily Tennessee Donelson, ignored Margaret at the inauguration ball. 'War is declared between some of the ladies in the city,' observed Louisa Adams, wife of former president John Quincy Adams, and 'ladies' wars are always fierce and hot.'[15] The social war became the hottest topic in Washington. Van Buren mentioned it to James A. Hamilton by letter, but wrote, 'I would rather pull a tooth than say a word to you…I think you have a little of McLane's fondness for gossip.'[16] From New York, Hamilton proved Van Buren's point by pressing him for more details.

Unsure how to proceed, Margaret confessed her social woes to Andrew Jackson. Her dilemma aroused his protective instinct, spurred on by memories of Rachel. 'I was born for a storm and a calm does not suit me,' he said.[17] But the storm had only just begun. When Jackson investigated the sources of gossip against Margaret, he discovered one of her accusers was the Presbyterian minister of his own church. He left and joined another. When Van Buren, a widower, came down firmly in Margaret's camp, his enemies accused him of currying favor with Jackson. Suddenly, the 'ladies' war' came to represent a dividing line in politics. Those who agreed to socialize with Margaret sided with Jackson and Van Buren. Those who snubbed Margaret sided with Jackson's political opponents.

To lure both sides into a truce, Secretary of State Van Buren threw two lavish parties. At the second, when Margaret Eaton and a prominent military wife bumped into each other, there were words and a scene. A friend went to fetch Van Buren, saying, 'You ought to be above if you wish to prevent a fight!'[18] Nothing, it seemed, could make Margaret Eaton acceptable to the city's society matrons or Jackson's political enemies.

That December, the Russian minister, Baron Paul de Krudener, joined the fray. Named after his godfather, the murdered Emperor Paul I, Krudener was 'a man of excellent talents and amiable manners,' well-liked in Washington.[19] He and Eaton were friends, and he hoped that by throwing an elegant ball, he could help ease Margaret's way into society.

At formal events like this one, custom required the host to offer his arm to the highest-ranking woman present and escort her into the dining room for supper. Each subsequent lady present would then be escorted by a gentleman, all in descending order of precedence. At Krudener's party, the highest-ranking woman was the only Cabinet secretary's wife present, Margaret Eaton. So Baron Krudener gave Margaret his arm and escorted her into the dining room. The next highest-ranking woman present was Madame Huygens, the only diplomat's wife present. She was to be escorted by the next highest-ranking man, Secretary of War Eaton.[20]

What happened next escalated society's war on the Eatons. Unfortunately, neither the eyewitness accounts nor the secondhand retellings agree on what, exactly, that was – if anything. This triggering event is attributed to Madame Huygens. Accounts have her either refusing to enter the dining room, refusing to be escorted by Eaton, being persuaded by Krudener to accept the escort then refusing to sit next to Margaret in the dining room, leaving the party right away, or threatening to hold her own party and not invite Margaret Eaton, indicating the Cabinet wives would follow suit. However, when Andrew Jackson summarized the event as he understood it, he said it was only *after* the party that someone 'stated that Madame H. was piqued at something that took place there...'[21] If anything overt had happened in that dining room, Jackson would likely have known about it.

No matter what actually happened, gossip about the party spread like wildfire, fueled by what Van Buren called 'a conspiracy of excited women and infuriated partisans.'[22] At least part of that gossip was substantiated when the

Huygenses had a party on January 6 and did not invite the Eatons. Cabinet members Ingham, Branch, and Berrien threw parties next and also failed to invite the controversial couple, further substantiating the rumors.

News of the last three parties gave Jackson several sleepless nights. He believed Ingham, Branch, and Berrien had conspired with Madame Huygens to ostracize Margaret. Jackson took this as a great personal insult, 'an attempt to assail my character,' as if he were unfit to choose his friends, let alone his Cabinet members.[23] For Jackson, there was only one solution: annihilation of Margaret's enemies. He would demand King Willem I recall Huygens, and he would fire any Cabinet members whose wives refused to socialize with Margaret. Before he took action, however, he asked Martin Van Buren for advice.

Van Buren, who had been friends with the Huygens family for years, said he didn't believe Madame Huygens would have done such a thing. After all, Constantia was an experienced diplomatic wife who understood the rules of precedence. Breaking them in such an obvious way was completely out of character for her. Van Buren's emphatic defense gave Jackson pause, and he sent Van Buren to suss out the truth. During a visit to the Huygens home, Van Buren wrote, 'Madame Huygens assured me solemnly that she had never used the expressions attributed to her or any of similar import – that she had been too long connected with diplomatic life, and understood too well what belonged to her position, to meddle in such matters...'[24] When Van Buren reported back to Jackson, the president replied, 'I am happy Madame H. has stated they are not true as far as she is concerned.'[25] Van Buren had just saved Huygens's job and Constantia's dignity.

Jackson then turned his anger on the Berriens, Branches, and Inghams. He threatened to ask for their resignations if their wives didn't pay Margaret a formal visit. All three men held firm, insisting their wives' behavior had nothing to do with their jobs. Jackson, however, believed the opposite. Washington society matron Margaret Bayard Smith wrote, 'One woman has made sad work here; to be, or not to be, her friend is the test of Presidential favor.'[26] Each faction became so entrenched that it changed more than the city's social life. The scandal mixed political and personal feuds to the point where it infiltrated political alliances and affected votes and discussions in Congress. And although Jackson had told Van Buren he didn't blame Madame Huygens, the incident was still on his mind that summer. During a trip to Tennessee, he told Eaton he was still prepared to force the Cabinet's resignation if they conspired with 'a foreign lady.'[27]

As summer faded into fall, the Eaton Affair remained front-page news. Jackson refused to back down, effectively banishing his own niece from Washington until she agreed to acknowledge Margaret socially. James A. Hamilton, who came to visit Jackson in Washington, learned firsthand that 'this matter is in greater extreme now than heretofore.'[28] The conflict's staying power unnerved Chevalier Huygens, who understood all too well that a diplomat's top priority was to build relationships and avoid scandal or schism. As it seemed impossible to do that in Washington, he removed his family from the public eye.

The Huygens family spent the winter in Baltimore, where they awaited news about the Belgian revolution and the London Conference. On January 1, 1831, Huygens returned to the capital to pay his usual visit to the White House with the diplomatic corps to wish the president a happy New Year. A Dutch onlooker noted that 'Chevalier Huygens was gaily dressed…in high spirits, (rather unexpected, considering how the kingdom of the Netherlands is torn and distracted.)'[29] Those high spirits wouldn't last long, as the situation in America quickly took a turn for the worse.

In April, weary of the bitter stalemate in the Cabinet, Secretary of State Martin Van Buren volunteered to resign. When told about the idea, Eaton volunteered to resign, too. Using their exit as a catalyst, Jackson then asked Branch, Ingham, and Berrien to follow suit, leaving only the inoffensive Postmaster General in office. Although Jackson had his way, the press lambasted him as an incompetent who couldn't manage his own Cabinet. It was the only time such a dissolution happened in American history. Ingham, Branch, and Berrien took to the press to vindicate their actions, each telling their version of events. America's partisan publishers delighted in printing letter after letter, in which the men accused Jackson and each other of endless missteps and misstatements. Many articles included retellings of the Krudener party and the presumed actions of Madame Huygens. One newspaper even printed statements she had supposedly made, which a rival paper debunked as fiction.[30]

To his horror, Huygens realized his retreat to Baltimore had not been far enough. Although Andrew Jackson reassured Van Buren that he held no grudge against the Huygens family, the Dutch minister felt the need to escape what he called 'scenes of unmatched scandal.'[31] He retreated even further, moving his family to the City Hotel in New York. The nation's capital bemoaned their loss. An article in the *Courier-Journal* plaintively summarized the situation: 'when the Baron and his amiable family resided in this city, their hospitable mansion was the centre for the beauty and fashion of the metropolis. Where are they now? They have left us.'[32] New York, Huygens believed, would be safer – from the press, from the spotlight, and from the nation's divisive politics. Little did he know he had just placed himself and his family in the path of another political firestorm, one that erupted when Anna's jewels were discovered just steps from his new residence.

Chapter 7

A Suspect Emerges

On a moonlit February night in 1831, a dark-haired heavyset man strode through the Brussels suburbs into the countryside beyond. He walked past the ponds and swans of the village of Ixelles, and into the surrounding forest of Soignies, about a mile and three-quarters outside the city. The forest was idyllic, with thick stands of beech trees interspersed with ponds, creeks, and tiny villages. On the far side of the wood, ten miles from the city, lay the battlefield and village of Waterloo.

In the woods, the man veered off the well-worn path, looking for a place he'd been before. He relied on memory and the notches carved into a nearby tree. When he found the notches, he knelt to the ground and dropped the shovel and apron he carried. The man began to dig. His prodigious strength made short work of the task.

The wooden crate was exactly where he'd left it. Its rotted slats disintegrated as soon as he touched them. Inside the crate, a white wooden box had survived intact, its precious contents safe from harm. He transferred them into the apron and gathered the fabric into a loose sack, which he tied onto his shovel. Retracing his steps out of the woods, he stopped at his rented house just outside the Namur gate. As long as he didn't enter the city, no customs agent could examine what he carried. When he finally closed the door behind him near midnight, he fell into bed, exhausted.[1]

He'd been smart to leave the crate in the woods until now. Suspicion had fallen on the prince, Pereira, and Machado. Then the revolution came, and no one wanted the Prince of Orange to return. The time had finally come. America was waiting.

❖

Constant Polari was born to John Polari in 1780 or 1781 in Wicq, a small town in the canton of Ticino in Switzerland.[2] Ticino was the southernmost of Switzerland's thirteen cantons, nestled between the snow-capped Lepontine Alps in the north and Lake Lugano in the south. From its highest peak, the Camoghè, the spires of the cathedral in Milan were visible sixty miles away. Once held by the dukes of Milan, Ticino presented a stark contrast to other Swiss cantons. Its farmers, dairymen, and cattle ranchers spoke Italian, practiced Roman Catholicism, and had dark hair and eyes, unlike their blond, blue-eyed Protestant countrymen.

Constant Polari looked the part, with his muscular 5'8" frame, thick black hair, and dark brown eyes. Like his fellow Ticinesi, he grew up speaking Italian and later learned French, which he never quite mastered. Polari grew up confident in his abilities, both physical and mental. He was uncommonly strong, an attribute noted by nearly everyone who later encountered him. He also had a ferocious temper, a dangerous trait when paired with his strength. A secondhand source later claimed that, in discussing his past, Polari said he had robbed his parents and fled their home, never to return.[3] It may be true, as he doesn't seem to have had further contact with anyone except a brother.

Polari came of age during a time of great upheaval. In 1789, the ideals of the French Revolution began to spread throughout Europe: liberty, equality, fraternity…and violence. From guillotined aristocrats to the Prussian soldiers who fell beneath the revolutionary army's muskets and sabers at Valmy, death became a reality for those who opposed the new order. In the decade after the Bastille's fall, a surprising number of territories fell to the French, including the Austrian Netherlands (present-day Belgium), the northern Netherlands, and northern Italy. When Napoleon reorganized the conquered territory of the latter into the Cisalpine Republic, the people of Ticino had a choice to make. Despite their cultural, religious, and linguistic ties to Italy, they remained loyal to the Swiss, officially joining the Confederation of Switzerland in 1803.

At some point during this turmoil, Constant Polari joined the French army. As a neutral country, Switzerland had no army. Young men who preferred fighting to farming had to become mercenaries. When Napoleon rose to power, he decided to use the Swiss – and other foreign recruits – as cannon fodder. One Dutch recruit complained, 'Unhappy are we…the Emperor's foreign troops, who are invariably employed upon every disagreeable and unprofitable duty!'[4] Napoleon posted four Swiss regiments to Naples, Spain, Marseilles, and Toulon.[5] Polari was likely among them. He later said he rose to the rank of sergeant under Napoleon, but his military career came to a sudden halt in 1809 or 1810, when he was found guilty of desertion. He was tried and sentenced to five years of forced labor. But in 1810, when Napoleon married his second wife, Archduchess Marie Louise of Austria, he issued an amnesty as part of the celebration and Polari was given his freedom.[6]

The experience turned him against Napoleon. He offered his services to Great Britain, Napoleon's most determined enemy, and enlisted in a regiment composed entirely of foreign men. They were garrisoned in the Mediterranean – Malta and Sicily – in 1813 and 1814. According to Polari, his regiment attempted to take Lucca, the Italian city-state where Napoleon had installed his sister Elisa as ruler. On December 9, 1813, a British squadron under Admiral Josias Rowley landed about 1,500 men on the coast of Tuscany, near Viareggio. Under the command of a Sicilian, Colonel Carlo Catinelli, they took possession of a fort. Two days later, they occupied Lucca, but were forced to retreat after only 24 hours. Back in Viareggio, enemy troops continued the attack. The men fled to their British ships, at the cost of several hundred lives. After an attempt to take Livorno also failed, Catinelli's men returned to Sicily.[7]

Polari didn't stay in British service, leaving the military in 1815. He visited the field of Waterloo after Napoleon's defeat, perhaps savoring his enemy's downfall. By April of 1816, he had returned to France and settled in Lyon, a city of commerce that had suffered terribly during the revolution. James A. Hamilton, who visited the city later in life, described it like this:

> The streets of the city are filthy, narrow, and generally without sidewalks. There are one hundred thousand inhabitants - a place of much wealth, from its manufactures of silks, &c. The people have the busy, bustling air which characterizes a commercial people. There are many soldiers and priests (the minions of power and its supporters) and idlers.[8]

Polari was no longer a soldier, but neither was he an idler. He became in turn a tanner, a merchant, and a manufacturer. 'There, with my savings and my diligent work I managed to form an honourable establishment in the industry of skins,' he later wrote.[9] He lived a quiet life as a leatherworker for about ten years.

Then, in 1825, 45-year-old Polari met 18-year-old Susanne Marie Blanche. A fellow Swiss, she came from Sare, in the canton of Vaud. Susanne and her sister had emigrated to Lyon, where she now worked as a seamstress sewing shawls. Lyon was famous for the production of silk, brocade, and other fabrics used in fashion and interior design. When Anna's parents had toured France as a young married couple in 1782, her mother went to Lyon to order silk and fabric wall coverings for her new palace of Pavlovsk.[10]

There is some confusion about the name Polari used in Lyon. Susanne would later say she knew him as Carara, but also as Polari. Polari would later say he never went by the name Carara. In any case, the relationship was troubled from the start. According to Polari, he found Susanne living in circumstances filled with 'misery and dishonor.'[11] He claimed to have saved her life twice, nursing her back to health from diseases that would have ruined her reputation. Susanne never spoke about these circumstances. Polari moved in with her and they lived together for thirteen months. Susanne gave birth to a daughter, Rosine, on December 2, 1826. The new parents baptized Rosine with the last name Polari, even though they weren't married.

But Polari couldn't support himself, let alone a family. He had borrowed a substantial amount of money in an attempt to grow his business. Unable to pay the four to five thousand francs he owed, he went bankrupt in early 1827. That February, he left Lyon, his creditors, Susanne, and two-month-old Rosine behind. He tried to get a passport under the name 'Carara,' but the application required two witnesses. Unable to acquire them, he used the name Polari. He then traveled via Switzerland to the United Kingdom of the Netherlands.[12]

Polari arrived in Brussels in September of 1827, where he found work as a leather merchant. He wrote to Susanne, but never visited or sent money for Rosine. He eventually moved to an apartment in the Rue Montagne de Sion, in the sixth section of the city, near the Leuven gate. There, he ran a liquor and tobacco store near the army barracks.

It was while he lived here that Anna's jewels were stolen. According to Polari, he had been ill with a 'nervous fever' and hadn't left the house in days.

When he felt able, he went to a barbershop down the street. Looking up at the newcomer, the barber joked, 'Here's the one who stole the jewels of the Princess of Orange.'[13] When Polari asked what he meant, the barber explained that someone had just stolen millions of florins of jewels from the royal palace. Polari laughed at the joke. A few days later, he went to an *estaminet* – a popular local café – called Le Petit Paris, on the Rue Ducale, near the palace. There, another patron pointed out the location of the Princess of Orange's apartment within the palace.

That October, Polari moved again, this time into an old bath house. After trying 'various branches of industry,' he started a bleach factory and began to make a decent living.[14] Despite his growing success, he lived a solitary life. His housekeeper, Victoire Desaye, lived with him, but he saw few others on a regular basis. As of yet, he made no move to reunite his little family.

In 1829, Polari learned of a man named Mr. Rey, who ran a painted canvas factory in Forêt, about an hour's walk from Brussels. Polari offered Rey a product demonstration to prove his bleaching process would produce a superior canvas. His first two tries didn't go well. Several days later, Polari walked to Forêt to attempt a third try, but Rey wasn't there. On the way back to Brussels, heavy rain forced him to duck into a tavern. There, a man advised him to try the less sodden west road via the famous farmhouse near Waterloo, La Belle Alliance, and Alsemberg.

Polari took that route on his next attempt, between November 15 and 20. He left Brussels early, hoping to reach Forêt just after dawn. While in the woods, he glanced sideways and saw a large mushroom. He had a 'dominant passion' for mushrooms, so he picked it up and stepped into the forest to look for more.[15]

From a distance, Polari spotted two men keeping watch under a tree. Both held rifles, and he saw a third rifle propped against the tree. Afraid they would shoot him, Polari hid behind a tall bush. They all wore a blue smock, a traditional Belgian working man's garment, and Polari assumed they were hunters. Sure enough, a third man returned to his companions, carrying something heavy in his smock. But then he knelt and began transferring items from his smock to a hole in the ground. He covered them with dirt and hid the spot with dry brush. Then the man picked something up – Polari believed it was an axe – and headed straight for him. Not ten paces from where Polari hid, the man used his axe to mark a tree. Then he picked up his rifle and the three men left together, heading toward Brussels.[16]

Polari breathed a sigh of relief. The men had been too well-dressed in boots and smocks to be thieves, and he wondered what they'd been doing. He found the dry brush marking the spot, sinking his hands into the freshly turned earth. Suddenly, he heard a gunshot. In the distance, a hunter called his dogs. Now was clearly not the time for further investigation. He rearranged the grass and dry leaves over the turned earth and hurried home.

But Polari couldn't stifle his curiosity. He had to know what the men had buried. That day, he bought a shovel, pickaxe, pistols, bullets, and gunpowder. He dressed in a blouse, cap, and the canvas apron he wore when making bleach. Then, after 8 p.m., he left Brussels by the Halle gate.[17] The moon-soaked sky helped him retrace his steps into the woods. When he found the tree notched by the hunters, he dug his pickaxe into the earth. Before long, he heard a thunk.

He picked up the shovel and dug until he revealed the shape of the buried object. It was almost two feet long: could it be a child's coffin? Once he'd revealed the rectangular container, he knelt to pick it up. Something inside rolled around, startling him. It wasn't a coffin, he decided, but a crate. Inside, a white linen cloth covered its contents. To get a better look, he moved the crate out of the shadows and lifted the cloth. Moonlight fell on piles of loose diamonds, colored gemstones, and sparkling jewels straight from a fairy tale. He saw a gilded fan, a bejeweled cross, and a handful of milky stones with a semi-opaque fire glowing green and blue and orange and red all at the same time.

Polari took it all.

Removing his apron, he tied it around the crate and tucked the bundle under his arm. He filled the empty hole in the ground and hid the shovel and pickaxe at the edge of the forest. But when he had almost reached the city gate, he remembered – the customs clerk inspected everything. He turned back into the woods and reburied the crate with the shovel and pickaxe, marking a tree to signal the spot.[18]

The next morning, before daybreak, he went back to the woods to do a better job of concealing the crate. He suspected the stones inside had been stolen from a goldsmith or jeweler, if they were real at all. According to him, he never suspected they belonged to the Princess of Orange. Rumors in Brussels had said '…the stolen items had been returned to the King by a Spaniard named Matsiado [i.e., Machado].'[19] And if the princess had her jewels back, these were fair game.

Polari left the crate buried all winter, when the ground froze to a depth of two feet. Finally, in late spring – May or early June of 1830 – he made plans to check on his cache. One Sunday morning at 2 a.m., he left Brussels on foot. When he located the right spot, he retrieved the buried shovel and pickaxe, whose wooden handle disintegrated in his hands. He switched to the shovel and quickly uncovered the crate. Polari later said he grabbed several stones at random: a diamond, small emeralds, small rubies, two small opals, and an engraved cameo. But this was a lie. He took more than he admitted, including dozens (if not hundreds) of loose diamonds, all between one-quarter carat and five carats.[20] He wrapped them in a handkerchief, put them in his pocket, and reburied the crate.

At home, he hid all the gems but one under his bed. He planned to take what appeared to be a large diamond to an appraiser. Goldsmiths and iron masters often sold objects set with precious stones. But what if he presented the store owner with his own stolen merchandise? Then he remembered his former landlord, a jeweler who had appraised a small diamond Polari bought in Lyon years ago.

Polari made his way to the jeweler's house, rolling the smooth edges of the stone between his fingers. When the jeweler answered the door, Polari asked for a favor and held out the stone. The jeweler pronounced it 'a common rhinestone…not a diamond,' worth eight or ten sous.[21] Crestfallen, Polari began to doubt his find had any value.

He consoled himself with a walk through the famous Brussels city park. There, he saw a Spanish man he knew sitting on a bench. He noticed a ring on the Spaniard's hand and asked if the stone was a diamond. When the man said yes, that his father was a diamond trader, Polari showed him the stone in his pocket. He said he had found it on the ground near the Hôtel des Etats-Généraux. The Spaniard took the stone and polished it with his handkerchief. 'To tell you the truth,' the Spaniard said, 'yes, it is a diamond. It's your lucky day, and if you want to give it to me, I'll give you 200 guilders.'[22]

Two hundred Dutch guilders was the rough equivalent of 415 francs, 830 times what the jeweler said the stone was worth.[23] If the Spaniard was willing to offer that much, Polari assumed it must be worth more. When Polari hesitated, the Spaniard offered four hundred and then six hundred guilders. Polari later wrote, 'This is the moment, gentlemen, that for the first time the idea of the theft of Her Highness's jewels occurred to me.'[24] Because if *this* stone was genuine, so were the others – and who else could they have come from but the richest woman in the kingdom?

Next, Polari played devil's advocate: how could he know it wasn't a rhinestone? After all, imitations were created to look like the real thing. The Spaniard briefly explained cut and polish and clarity. But the simplest way to identify a diamond, he said, was to scratch a window. Only a true diamond would cut glass.

Polari rushed home to test the other clear stones, including one he thought could be as large as eight carats. They all cut glass. 'It was then that, to my great surprise, I realized that I was in possession of jewels of Her Highness the Princess of Orange,' Polari wrote.[25] Dazed, he wandered through the streets of Brussels, finding himself lost in places he knew perfectly well. The gothic splendor of the Hôtel de Ville and its tower topped with a copper statue of St. Michael, wielding a sword and trampling a rebel angel, could have been a lunar landscape. Their familiar glory faded in the face of a single question: could he return the jewels and collect the reward without implicating himself?

He ran various scenarios through his mind, dismissing each one as it revealed the depth of his involvement. If he wrote an anonymous letter asking the Prince of Orange to exchange the reward money for the jewels, they would arrest him when he came to collect the money. Next, he considered paying an errand boy to collect the money. If police arrested the boy, Polari would know he couldn't trust them. He refined this scheme with the idea of using a blind man who would be unable to describe him to the police. Confident in this plan, Polari began looking for blind men in nearby taverns. A few days later, he saw one walking down the street and followed him to a familiar cabaret, St. Elisabet, on the corner of Rue Barlemont and Rue de la Montagne. Once inside, he ordered a beer and struck up a conversation. 'Of all the afflictions a person could have, being blind must be the worst,' he began.

'We have less hassle than people who see,' the blind man responded.

'You are not, perhaps, happy to be blind?'

'No, on the contrary; I would like to see you hanged.'

Surprised at the sharp retort, Polari said that wasn't a very flattering response. The blind man laughed. 'If I could see you hanged, I'd have my eyes…Don't think I'd choose that fate for you: I just said it for laughs.'

Polari made sure to laugh and resumed his questioning. He asked when the blind man lost his sight, if he was married, and where he lived.

This was too much for the blind man. 'For a Mr. I'm Not Curious, you sure want to know everything – but I won't tell you any more,' he said.

Offended by the blind man's sharp retort, Polari decided not to use him.[26] As he left the cabaret, he realized that a blind man – using his sharpened senses of smell and hearing – would still be able to provide identifying information about him. There was simply no way to return the jewels that wouldn't endanger him. And if he couldn't return them, that left only one option.

Chapter 8

The Best Laid Plans

The jewels were his. Every sparkling diamond, every gleaming sapphire, every lustrous pearl. With the promise of more money than he could spend, Constant Polari decided his future lay not in Europe, but in America. He wrote to Susanne Blanche and told her he would meet her soon. Once they were together, all he had to do was convince her to come away with him.

First, he had to convert some of the jewels into cash to pay for their new life in America. He decided to visit Frankfurt, a free city known for its Jewish merchants and bankers, including the Rothschilds. To get there, he had to cross several borders and hide the stones from customs agents. No one, he thought, would suspect a man walking with a cane. He paid a turner to hollow one out and filled it with diamonds, wrapped in paper to keep them silent. With a fresh passport, Polari left Brussels in late July of 1830.[1]

It took him multiple tries to find a goldsmith who spoke French. When he did, Polari pretended to be a customer and purchased a ring. Then, in polite conversation, he said he had found a stone on the steamboat from Cologne to Mainz, and wanted to know if it was a diamond. The goldsmith breathed on the stone several times, cleaned it with a piece of animal hide, and confirmed it was a diamond. Polari asked if he'd like to buy it, and the goldsmith offered 'no more than 600 guilders.'[2] Polari agreed, but the goldsmith seemed strangely reluctant to complete the sale. Before the goldsmith had finished counting out the payment, Polari snatched up the money. At that moment, a young man entered the shop. The goldsmith said something to him in German, and in the young man's response, Polari caught the words 'police commissioner.'[3] He fled Frankfurt on foot.

When he arrived in Lyon in mid-August, he expected a hero's welcome. He didn't get it. According to Polari, when he arrived, Susanne said, 'Ah! It's you,' then sat back in her chair. Polari kissed her, telling her he had traveled

200 leagues to see her. Then he held up his cane and said it was worth 200,000 francs. In a rush, the story tumbled out of him: the well-dressed hunters in the forest, the crate, and the fortune he'd found inside it. The next morning, Susanne asked to see the diamonds. Polari obliged, pulling a few samples from the cane. But when she took the diamonds into her hand, he quickly snatched them back. He warned her never to try to take the jewels from him. If she did, she risked their safety and 'the honour of her infant.'[4]

The next day, Susanne tried to hurry him out of her house. According to Polari, he discovered she had 'a lover whom she loved very much,' which explained why she wasn't excited to see him.[5] His first instinct was to take Rosine and leave her, but now that Susanne knew his secret, there were other considerations. He accused her of talking too much when she drank, and asked her to swear on the Bible not to reveal anything about the jewels, which Susanne did. But when Polari asked for custody of Rosine, Susanne said she would rather they stay together. He agreed not to leave and rented an apartment for them in Lyon. He paid one year's rent plus their family's expenses, including Rosine's nurse and Susanne's debt. He never let her forget that he suspected her of wanting him for the money. 'I told her so many times,' he later wrote.[6]

Having settled his relationship status, Polari turned to a second pressing problem: how to sell the rest of the jewels in the cane. After the fiasco in Frankfurt, he didn't want to approach anyone using his own passport, which identified him as being in Brussels at the time of the theft. Someone else would have to do the selling – and he had just the man in mind.

Roudez was a currier, finishing leather hides for sale after a tanner had processed them. Polari described him as a businessman 'rather skilled in sales' who lived in Lyon at 24 Rue Petits-Souliers.[7] Polari claimed to have known him for 25 years, which made it likely they had met in the army. Roudez, now a married man with a family, was glad to see him but offered a warning: the creditors he had fled years ago still remembered him. It was a convenient segue into the reason for Polari's visit.

Polari assured Roudez he had every intention of paying his creditors, now that he had the means. He showed Roudez the diamonds hidden in his cane, confessing these were the Princess of Orange's missing jewels. He concocted an absurd story about buying them from the real thief, using every penny he owned. Now, he needed to sell them through a front man, since his passport revealed he'd been in Brussels at the time of the theft. He asked Roudez to be that man, for a commission. Roudez took the job, instantly concocting a viable backstory. Newspapers had reported the recent French capture of Algiers, during which valuable jewels went missing from the Bey's palace. It was the perfect cover: they would claim one set of stolen jewels was actually another. Roudez consulted a book about diamonds, learning they could get about 96 francs per carat.[8] Another book warned that the slightest imperfection greatly reduced the value of a stone. 'To hear Roudez,' he wrote, 'diamonds could sell like cherries, a price per pound…'[9] He thought Roudez was wrong, but didn't press the issue.

Polari gave Roudez 49 carats of diamonds to sell, ranging in size from three to five carats. It was the first of five such batches. Each time, Polari demanded a certain number of francs in return. By the time he handed over the fourth batch, Roudez had brought him 24,000 silver francs, an average of 110-120 francs per carat, well above the book's suggested 96 francs.[10] How, he wondered, was it so easy for Roudez to sell the stones at values above average?

Before they ran out of diamonds, the two men planned to go to Algiers to back up their cover story. To pay for the trip, Polari gave Roudez a fifth batch of stones, totaling thirty carats. When Roudez brought back a pitiful 600 francs, Polari began to suspect he was only selling enough diamonds to get the amount Polari demanded and pocketing the rest.[11] For the moment, however, he kept his suspicions to himself.

The pair left Lyon in early November of 1830. They sailed down the Rhône to Toulon, where they learned all ships bound for Algiers had orders not to admit civilians. No matter, said Roudez. Toulon was close enough to say they'd bought the jewels from someone who *had* been in Algiers. He asked Polari to give him more diamonds to sell. This time, Polari hesitated. Most of the diamonds from the cane had already been sold, and after paying his old debts, he only had 24,000 francs left. He did as Roudez asked, but for these last fourteen carats, he wanted double the cash Roudez had brought back previously.

The pair set out for home, traveling north. Polari gave Roudez a slightly colored six-carat diamond and told Roudez he wanted at least 4,000 francs for it. They found a broker willing to help in Bordeaux, a man named Paglianti. After introducing Polari as his uninvolved traveling companion, Roudez got Paglianti to agree to pay 4,000 gold francs. When Polari left to allow Roudez to complete the sale, Roudez and Paglianti set out together to find a buyer. But when Roudez tried to sweet-talk a goldsmith, he bragged that the six-carat stone was nothing compared to what else he had. The boast didn't entice the goldsmith, who passed. Eventually, Roudez and Paglianti sold the six-carat stone to a merchant, agreeing that the final exchange would take place the following day. And then, by chance, that merchant visited the goldsmith who had just refused to buy the same six-carat stone. The men realized they'd been shown the same stone, and the goldsmith told the merchant Roudez was holding out on them: he had bigger, better stones. The next day, the merchant balked. He would only complete the purchase of the six-carat stone if he could pick the best of the batch.

Roudez was now caught in his lie. He fled the merchant's shop and dashed to Polari's hotel to ask for more stones. But Polari wasn't there – he had gone for a walk. And while strolling through the Place de la Comédie, who should Polari run into but the angry broker, Paglianti. 'Your friend is a simpleton,' snapped Paglianti. 'He doesn't know how to do business.' Roudez's boasting, he complained, had killed their deal for the six-carat stone. Now their best prospects would have nothing to do with him – it was a waste of the 28 or 30 carats Roudez had to sell. 'I think, for the present, it's all over,' moaned Paglianti.[12]

28 or 30 carats.

Now Polari's suspicions were confirmed. He had only given Roudez fourteen carats, which meant his friend had been skimming the entire time. When he confronted Roudez, his friend denied it, but the incident effectively broke up their partnership. They arrived in Lyon at the end of December, parting as friends on amicable terms. Roudez returned the unsold carats to Polari, but kept a cameo he had been unable to sell.

❖

Despite the rocky start to their reunion, Polari and Susanne appeared on better footing as 1830 came to an end. On January 1, 1831, Polari gave Susanne a ring made from Anna's diamonds. At its center lay a glittering brilliant, surrounded by four smaller diamonds.[13] He was also able to sell the fourteen carats Roudez had returned, plus a few more from the stash he had brought to Lyon. That money helped him create something he needed for the next stage of his plan. Since the hollow cane had worked so well to elude customs on the way to Frankfurt, he now commissioned a hollow umbrella shaft. Topped with ordinary brown silk, the umbrella's screw-on hook could be opened, revealing a hollow pipe inside.[14]

With their props ready, it was time to retrieve the rest of the jewels and leave for America. But when he asked Susanne to come with him to Brussels, she hesitated. He tried to reassure her, telling her he would kill anyone who got in their way. This frightened Susanne even more, and she refused to be present when he unearthed the remaining jewels. There was no choice but for Polari to return to Brussels alone. Before he left, he gave Susanne everything she might need if anything happened to him. All the diamonds he had left – worth about 40,000 francs – lay hidden in a tin case under the foot of Susanne's bed. He also left her a map showing where he had buried the jewels in Brussels. If he never returned, he told her to contact his brother, a musician in Piedmont, and dig up the remaining jewels with him.[15]

At the end of January, Polari left Lyon. In Brussels, he rented a room in the Rue St. Anne and a small house outside the city's Namur gate. The house was near the path that led into the woods where the rest of the jewels were buried. It would function as his safe house during the retrieval effort. For a few weeks, he kept to a regular schedule: paying his debts, visiting taverns, and doing small errands to reassure anyone watching he was simply there to transact business.

His caution paid off. On a moonlit February night, he retrieved the jewels without incident. The next morning, he set to work evaluating what he had. As he studied the stolen grandeur that a grand duchess might have taken for granted, he noted 'pieces in the shape of an animal which seemed to have been a serpent, as well as the pieces of a fan…'[16] Even in ruin, the fragments were beautiful. His first instinct was to disassemble everything. Prying out the gemstones would make them easier to transport and harder to identify.

A single piece, if recognized, could land him in jail. But, he wrote, after 'reflecting to whom they belonged, I was filled with a certain respect which [meant] I did not dare.'[17] He decided to leave behind the most damaged and least valuable jewels, including the broken settings, a parure of cameos, the fan, and engraved stones, including one with a portrait of Anna's brother, Nicholas I. To this collection he added the small portraits of the Russian imperial family.

All these objects went into an iron pot, which Polari decided to bury. But when he surveilled his first choice, the cemetery of St. Giles, it was too dangerous – a busy path ran alongside the cemetery wall. Instead, he opted for the quieter cemetery of Saint-Josse-ten-Noode, outside the Leuven gate. He placed the iron pot in a wooden case and buried it at the foot of the cemetery wall.[18] Now, without the most incriminating items, he could focus on smuggling the rest of the jewels across the borders of two countries.

That April, Susanne and Rosine set out to join Polari in Brussels. On the way, she deposited a trunk at the Hôtel de Mars in Paris. It contained a corset sewn full of the diamonds Polari had left her, to be retrieved on their way to America. When she arrived in Brussels, Polari placed her in the Hôtel de la Paix in the Rue de la Violette, a comfortable hotel recommended in guidebooks. But distance, as it turned out, had not made the heart grow fonder. The couple quarreled and neither trusted the other. Later, Susanne claimed Polari 'had often threatened to murder her.'[19] Once, he drove her to La Belle Alliance, the farmhouse near the woods where he had found the jewels. He wanted to show her the exact spot, but she told him she was too tired to go on. It was a lie. She was afraid to go into the dark woods alone with him.

Another time, Polari took her and Rosine for a walk in the Brussels park. As if drawn to locations tied to the theft, Polari sat on a bench facing the Prince of Orange's palace. He pointed at a window. 'That,' he said, 'is the window they removed the stolen items through.'[20] Then, when they walked past the palace, Polari pointed out the side street where the thieves had propped a ladder against the garden wall. Although he later denied it, Susanne remembered him saying one of the thieves had been in the palace, a second on the terrace, and a third on the ladder or wall, implying these were the men he'd seen in the forest. To get into the room where Anna's jewels were stored, he said, one had to 'pass another room where there were large gilded candelabra and other precious furniture.'[21] Polari had never said the jewels he'd found belonged to the Princess of Orange, but what else was she to think?

He did, however, show her the jewels. Spread out on a table in his rented house, they included diamonds, pearls, a square emerald, and several amethysts. She remembered seeing 'a gold necklace which included a knot… turquoise and ruby earrings…a gold buckle, the tongues of which were adorned with diamonds…a bracelet in the shape of a snake…and watch seals adorned with small turquoises…'[22] The trick now was in making sure no one *else* saw them. First, Polari purchased a barrel of lard, something no customs agent would be eager to inspect. He removed a bit of lard, nailed a jewel–filled box to the side, and shipped the barrel to a general delivery post office in Paris, under the name of Delpeche.[23] Next, he filled the hollow cane and umbrella shaft with diamonds, but still had a number of pearls and other gemstones. To hide these, he commissioned a trunk with hidden side compartments, a hollow crossbar, and four boxes that fit into the crossbar, all stuffed with pearls. The colored stones, wrapped in paper, filled the side compartments. When he was still left with a large sapphire and some topaz, he bought a cardboard poodle for Rosine. He slit a hole in the underside, stuffed the gems inside, and sealed the hole with glue and varnish. If all went well, Rosine would carry the toy through customs, leaving agents none the wiser.

As they finalized their travel plans, Polari's conscience began to whisper words of guilt – or so he later claimed. He bought one of the many cartoons that showed Willem stealing from Anna's jewelry box and showed it to Susanne, confirming her suspicion that he knew where the stolen jewels had come from. 'Look, see how these scoundrels are destroying the reputation of this poor prince,' he said. 'But he is innocent and it is I who have the jewels someone stole from him.'[24] Polari's conscience did not, however, protest loudly enough to dissuade him from keeping the jewels. Instead, he took Susanne to the cemetery where he had buried the last of the gems and broken settings. He gave her an exact location and a precise depth – four feet – to dig for the jewels. After his death, he told her, 'wherever you are, come to Holland and give them to the prince; this will at least repair his reputation.'[25] Susanne didn't like the idea. She feared being arrested, but Polari assured her she was safe because she could prove she was in Lyon when the theft occurred. All she had to do was tell the royal family a recently deceased good friend had given them to her. He made her promise to do this, and Susanne obliged.

Even with all the items Polari created to hide the jewels, there were still more than would fit. He and Susanne realized at least one of them would have to make two trips. Toward the end of April, Susanne and Rosine took the jewel-laden trunk to the Rue de la Madeleine stagecoach departing for Paris via Valenciennes. Polari took a different coach from the Rue de la Montagne, also bound for Paris. They all got off at Cambrai to spend the night, where Polari emptied the cane and umbrella of 'about half the diamonds.'[26] They wrapped these stones to protect them, and inserted them into the pockets Susanne had sewn into her corset. Dripping with unseen diamonds, Susanne took Rosine to Paris, while Polari returned to Brussels to refill the cane and umbrella. When Susanne arrived, she checked into the Hôtel de Mars on the Rue du Mail – the same street where a young cash-strapped Napoleon Bonaparte had lived in 1795.[27] The trunk she'd shipped while en route from Lyon to Brussels had arrived as expected. She and Rosine duly waited for Polari, who arrived three days later.

They remained in Paris for about two weeks, while Polari made a belated attempt to learn more about diamonds. He discovered the current value per carat was 250 francs, a far cry from the 96 francs Roudez had claimed was correct. Later, Polari would write, 'I very much suspected that Roudez was fooling me; but I did not know how much…he must have made his fortune.'[28] In the course of his research, he visited a well-known jeweler, Daux, in the Galerie Montpensier at the Palais Royale. Daux had the best stock in Paris and would later become a supplier for Cartier. To blend in with the clientele, Polari bought a wedding ring for ten francs. Then he pointed out a ring with a large blue stone, similar to the one hidden in Rosine's toy dog. Polari asked if it was a sapphire. 'Yes,' Daux said, 'and the most beautiful.'

The jeweler removed the stone from its case and put it in Polari's hand. 'Are there any bigger than this?' Polari asked.

'Yes, certainly,' Daux replied. 'The bigger they are, the more expensive they are.' He launched into a story about a very large sapphire he had once acquired, absolutely enormous, unique in all of Europe. The Princess of Orange had bought the stone, which was later stolen from her. Daux pulled out the Belgian court jeweler's drawing of the stolen stone, sent to renowned jewelers all over Europe after the theft. Polari recognized it instantly. It was the big blue stone inside Rosine's cardboard poodle. He dashed out of the jeweler's shop and ran to the hotel, worried about the housekeepers who made the beds while the guests were out.

When he arrived, he was relieved to see Susanne still in the room. He asked her to keep the toy under lock and key. Based on what Daux had showed him, the blue stone in Rosine's poodle was an incredibly valuable sapphire. He told her about the drawings, which revealed what some of the damaged jewels had originally looked like. 'I would have been very curious to see that, too,' Susanne replied, calmly removing the cardboard dog from view.[29]

If Polari had any doubt, none could be left now: the jewels in his possession were Anna's. It was time to leave – permanently. He took the last banknote from his Lyon banker to André et Cottier and deposited the 8,000 francs. He withdrew 3,000 gold francs and requested a bill of exchange for a New York bank, De Rham & Moore, for the remainder.[30] Laden with cash, Polari, Susanne, and Rosine left Paris for the port city of Havre-de-Grâce in Normandy. There, he paid 2,750 francs for three fares, using the name Palarrio. They departed on May 18, 1831 aboard the ship *François I*, bound for New York City.[31]

While Polari and Susanne finalized their travel plans for America, four diplomats in Brussels planned a trip of their own. They crossed the English Channel and went to London to make a prince an offer they hoped he couldn't refuse. On April 20, 1831, they asked if he would accept their new country's crown.[32] That prince was Leopold of Saxe-Coburg-Saalfeld.

Leopold was now a wealthy man. Princess Charlotte of Wales's death in 1817 had left him with a £50,000 per year allowance from the British government and a country home, Claremont House.[33] Since Charlotte's death, he had played the role of mentor to his sister, the widowed Duchess of Kent, and his niece, Princess Alexandrina Victoria. He had gladly remained in the background during the previous fall's London Conference, when Prince Willem of Orange clung to his status as a potential candidate for king of an independent Belgium. Dutch ambassador Anton Reinhard Falck remembered with no little amount of spite that whenever the two men met at court or a party, Leopold appeared 'as if in the shadows' beside Willem, who took the leading role.[34] But Leopold proved the superior tactician. By playing coy, he ultimately earned himself the nod from the British Prime Minister, Charles Grey.

Leopold was not most Belgians' first choice. Due to a shared language and religion, they preferred a French prince. After all, Leopold was Protestant while the majority of his subjects would be Catholic. But the British had blocked the French prince's nomination, unwilling to give King Louis Philippe too much influence over a territory originally intended to be a buffer state against French aggression. They pressed for Leopold, with the stipulation that he marry a French princess. Russian diplomats worked against Leopold in favor of Willem, but faced surprising opposition from Willem's own father. The old king 'withdrew his son's permission to accept the crown of Belgium and openly acknowledged that he preferred Prince Leopold,' wrote Count Matuszewicz, a Russian diplomat.[35] Leopold, therefore, topped the list of candidates largely because no one could find a better solution.

But Leopold was nothing if not cautious. After all, some Belgians said they didn't want *any* king. Why pick a compromise candidate? Why not declare a republic, even if it angered the Great Powers? To avoid committing himself, Leopold stalled for time. First, he asked the Conference to draw up the country's final borders. Then he decided he wanted the Belgian National Congress to elect him. If he accepted the throne without complete approval from Congress and the Powers, he said, it 'would be tantamount to placing myself…in a state of war with the whole world…'[36] But his modest act didn't fool everyone – not Willem, at least. 'I personally believe he will end up accepting,' Willem wrote to Nicholas I. He predicted that France and England would recognize the new sovereign immediately, followed by Austria and Prussia. 'Then you will do the same and he will be King of Belgium by the confession of all Europe, and my father frustrated of the good half of his Kingdom.'[37] Willem's bitterness seeped through his ink onto paper.

Finally, on June 4, 1831, the requested election took place: Leopold received 155 votes in his favor, with 44 against.[38] It was enough to guarantee him a crown. The wife of the Russian foreign minister, Countess Nesselrode, was surprised Leopold accepted. His own brother, she reported, had come to London to beg him to refuse. 'When our descendants read the history of these events,' she wrote, 'they will have a thin opinion of the rulers…I, for my part, live in endless astonishment.'[39] At the end of June, the Great Powers produced a second draft of the treaty of separation, called the Eighteen Articles, to officially recognize Belgium's independence. With no further reason to delay, Leopold accepted the crown on June 26, 1831. But two days before he left London for Brussels, Leopold received unwelcome news. King Willem I of the Netherlands had refused to sign the Eighteen Articles. As a result, Russia, Prussia, and Austria postponed their formal recognition of Leopold as sovereign. His support was slipping before he even mounted the throne.

Leopold set out for Belgium with no military escort to protect him. Once he reached Brussels, the Dutch king retaliated. On July 23, 1831, King Willem I, Prince Willem, Anna, and their three sons reviewed their troops at Breda. The troops raised a cry – 'Long Live the King!' – soon echoed by thousands of spectators.[40] The Belgian revolution had wounded Dutch pride, and the country was spoiling for a fight. The world saw their king as a bitter, stubborn, deluded old man. But he had stood up for his people, for *them*, refusing to let the Great Powers ignore their interests. If he asked them, they would fight.

Chapter 9

Welcome to New York

As Europe threatened to descend into war, the *François I* carried 35 passengers from the old world to the new. Packet ships like this one were fast and big-masted, carrying travelers, textiles, wine, mail, and newspapers to America's largest port cities. Most passengers were businessmen and army officers, along with a handful of immigrants. The routes were so popular that, in 1829, two companies had dedicated twelve ships to a scheduled service between Havre-de-Grâce and New York City on the first, tenth, and twentieth of every month. *François I* was one of them, sailing under Captain William T. Skiddy. Captains were responsible not only for their passengers' safety, but their comfort during ten-day doldrums or stomach-churning storms. Good captains earned effusive thank-you notes, as Skiddy had for his 'polite deportment' and attention to passengers' 'comfort and convenience.'[1]

The more elegant ships offered luxurious common areas with mahogany furnishings, plush sofas, Turkish carpets, a library, and perhaps a piano. Men and women had separate cabins to maintain propriety, equipped less comfortably than the common areas. Food was plentiful, as captains hired chefs and sailed with cows, chickens, geese, and sheep on board. Aside from mealtimes, passengers entertained themselves by playing cards or shuffleboard, watching for whales, stargazing, dancing, strolling, talking, drinking, or fighting seasickness.[2]

Polari found a different way to entertain himself. He told anyone listening he was traveling with a fortune in diamonds. No one could see it, of course, but Susanne strolled the deck daily wearing a corset sewn with loose diamonds, while Rosine played with her cardboard dog, concealing one of the largest sapphires in the world.[3]

On June 21, just over a month after departure, the *François I* reached New York. The city greeted Susanne and Polari 'with its pointed spires and forest of masts' as ships rolled gently in the East and North rivers.[4] In the bay itself, they saw numerous small islands dotted with brick forts, including Ellis Island and Castle Garden. The packet ship docked at a wharf in the North River, where passengers debarked with their luggage and a ship's representative took the manifest to the Customs Collector.

Once on shore, Polari switched from his birth name to an alias, Charles Dominique Carara. Confident in his preparations, Polari made no effort to avoid port officials. He, Susanne, and Rosine sailed through Customs without declaring any of the jewels hidden in the trunk, corset, cane, umbrella, or dog.

New York City was the busiest port in North America, with wharves of workers hauling cargo to and from the ships that made their city's fortune. Beyond the harbor lay long, straight streets lined with marble public buildings, sturdy brick houses, and a few old wooden houses from the Dutch colonial days. At the time, the city had a population of almost 250,000 people.[5] Jacob de Brauw, an unemployed Dutch mill worker who arrived six months after Polari, described the city as diverse, with a 'great variety of persons…those of European and American nations, as well as a multitude of coloreds and African negroes, formerly slaves, now free people…'[6] Close to the harbor, in the lower town, the city thrummed with energy. There, new arrivals found the Customs House, the stock exchange, the Bank of the United States, and offices for newspapers, merchants, lawyers, and real estate brokers. An omnibus connected the lower town with the upper town, containing restaurants, hotels, and boarding houses. At night, flickering gas lamps cast their warm glow over Broadway, Maiden Lane, Wall Street, and Pearl Street. Other streets used only oil lamps, their dim output leaving passersby vulnerable to pickpockets.

Polari steered his little family away from the harbor into the safety of a nearby inn. The next day, they moved into a boarding house owned by a French wine merchant, Joseph Collet, at 133 Greenwich Street. According to his newspaper advertisement, Collet offered 'French & Spanish Boarding' in an elegantly furnished home that included baths, 'a well furnished table and the best qualities of wine, at moderate terms.'[7] At boarding houses like Collet's, staff served coffee and breakfast in the morning, a midday meal at

2 or 3 p.m., and a light supper with tea at 6 p.m. Afterward, residents often remained in the common areas until 10 or 10:30 p.m.[8] Those shared meals made it difficult for Polari to keep a low profile. Like on the *François I*, he had trouble holding his tongue.

At the boarding house, Polari and Susanne met a 52-year-old Frenchman named Jean Roumage. Friendly and full of Gallic charm, Roumage showed them the city's most popular promenades. No physical description of him exists, but Roumage's lawyer described him as 'a man of education and gentlemanly bearing, possessed of an astute and penetrating mind, but of no moral rectitude.'[9] That penetrating mind quickly became suspicious of Polari, who veered from moments of levity and braggadocio to outright hostility. Residents whispered that behind closed doors, Polari beat Susanne. Roumage confided in the boarding house's senior resident, 72-year-old Jonathan Schieffelin, only to discover Schieffelin shared his suspicions. The newcomer, they feared, was up to no good.

Polari did nothing to counter their suspicions. He carried precious stones in his pockets and showed them to everyone at the dinner table. He flashed Roumage a small handful of diamonds, saying he bought them in Algiers. Once, in Roumage's room, a small sapphire fell out of Polari's pocket. Roumage picked it up and Polari told him to keep it. One day, Polari asked Roumage to find him a workman who could make a small padded case. Roumage took Polari to a shop where Polari ordered a case to store a large sapphire and large yellow stone he claimed was from Siberia. 'Don't you admire that?' Polari asked the workman. 'It's worth six thousand piastres!'[10] Roumage became convinced that Polari had something to hide.

After a few days in the boarding house, Polari noticed Susanne's behavior changing and suspected it had to do with the overly solicitous Frenchman. He was relieved when Roumage left on a planned trip to Philadelphia and Baltimore. While the other man was away, Polari set about finding a more permanent place to live. He hired an Italian man, a commercial merchant named Eugene Bergonzio, to act as his interpreter, business agent, and broker. Bergonzio helped Polari rent a small house at 566 Pearl Street, between Elm and Broadway.[11] When Jean Roumage returned to the boarding house, he found his new friends had gone.

But Roumage wasn't put off so easily. He began wandering the nearby streets, hoping to discover where the couple had gone. When he found them, he presented himself at their door, offering to help the non-English-speakers get their household up and running. But although he ascribed no ulterior motive to his offer, Jean Roumage was lying. On one visit, he'd seen Rosine playing with what looked like two large gemstones. This time, he decided to investigate.

The Frenchman began looking for people who had spoken with Polari. Two weeks after Polari's arrival, he located Captain Skiddy of the *François I*. When Roumage asked about passengers who had bragged about their riches, Skiddy remembered one right away. 'I had a millionaire with me,' Skiddy told him. 'One day he said to us on board, "You have a rich cargo, for my wife's corset alone is worth more than two million."'[12] Roumage instantly recognized Polari's careless braggadocio. But two million was a far cry from the handful of stones he'd seen Polari handle. What had happened to the rest of them?

Jean Roumage wasn't the only one acting on his suspicion. Polari, believing the Frenchman had designs on Susanne, also asked around and learned Roumage had a criminal past. Born in Cognac, France on December 8, 1779, Jean Roumage was the eldest of seven children. The well-known merchant family 'lived in affluence, and enjoyed a good reputation.'[13] Roumage and his brothers grew up industrious and ambitious. As a teenager, Roumage worked as a traveling salesman to support his unmarried sister, Anastasie. When sales boomed during the Napoleonic Wars, Roumage used the cash to send his brother Victor to New Orleans, where he became a successful importer. Another brother, Frédéric, also moved to the United States, where he patented a machine for dressing flax. In 1821, Roumage opened a financial firm with another brother, Constant, headquartered in Paris and Havre-de-Grâce. But in the early 1820s, Roumage became careless. Distracted by the stock market and lottery schemes, he began speculating and lost money rapidly.[14]

The final blow fell in June of 1824, with a bond purchase gone horribly wrong. A middleman, Banès, brought Roumage 700 Spanish loan bonds, for which Roumage had agreed to pay 454,100 francs. According to Roumage, he paid Banès and completed the deal. According to Banès, Roumage hid in the bathroom then fled, returning hours later to insist he had already paid Banès. It was one man's word against the other. At Roumage's trial, a parade of character witnesses, former employers, servants, and acquaintances painted the picture of a man who, although honorable and well-intentioned, had lost his fortune and propped up the family business with high-interest loans. Roumage, however, stuck to his story. 'I answered what my conscience and the truth dictated to me,' he testified. 'I cannot answer anything else.'[15]

The court did not believe him. It sentenced Jean Roumage to five years in prison and ordered him to return all 700 bonds to Banès, with interest. Roumage listened to the verdict and replied softly, 'Your error, Gentlemen, cost me 450,000 francs.'[16] He appealed four times in six months to no avail.

In mid-July of 1825, Roumage began his prison term in Orléans. On July 29, his wife and niece came to visit, accompanied by a priest. Some time later, the priest emerged, weeping. About 15 minutes later, Madame Roumage, her niece, and the priest left the prison. The jailer didn't notice (or was bribed not to notice) that too many people had left the cell. Roumage and his male accomplice, likely a brother, rode hell-for-leather to Chevilly, where they separated. Roumage fled to Antwerp, using the name Jean Robert to elude police, creditors, and the press (his trial had been well covered by European newspapers). Ever the gentleman, he chose an alias that would match the initials embroidered on his linen.[17]

Nine months later, in November of 1826, Roumage arrived in New York City. But although he had a fresh start, he couldn't stay out of trouble. In 1829, he was accused of setting fire to a building he occupied to claim the insurance money. He hired four lawyers to defend him: Price, Maxwell, Knapp, and Seely. After a seven-hour trial, the jury found him not guilty due to a lack of evidence.[18]

Polari's informants told him about Roumage's conviction for fraud in France and his purported insurance fraud in New York. They told him that 'no one knew what Roumage lived on, but that he had deceived several people, and that he did not enjoy at all a good reputation among the citizens of New York.' That settled the matter for Polari. He told Susanne he no longer wanted Roumage in the house. According to Polari, her response was simply, 'Ah! ah!'[19]

Susanne's guarded reaction was an act of self-preservation. As others in the boarding house had suspected, Polari unleashed his violent temper on Susanne behind closed doors. Once, when Roumage had visited the Pearl Street house, he found Susanne alone, sewing. She complained about Polari's brutality towards her. Polari, she said, 'never left her side and always carried a stiletto in his sleeve.'[20] Frightened and alone, she feared for the future. On another visit, Roumage found Susanne crying, her eyes red and swollen. When he asked why, she said it was, once again, because of Polari. He no longer wanted Roumage as a visitor, a rule neither Susanne nor Roumage wanted to obey. They agreed to meet in secret using a signal, a handkerchief in the window, to indicate Polari's absence.

While Roumage comforted Susanne, Polari found his financial footing. His business agent, Bergonzio, opened a bank account for him with De Rham & Moore. He found a French jeweler, Joseph Deguerre at 30 Reed Street, willing to buy his diamonds. He sold twenty diamonds, each one carat, for 140 francs per carat, followed by one four-carat diamond.[21] Although the transactions went smoothly, a sliver of doubt remained in Polari's mind. He asked Bergonzio to learn more about US customs duties. Could agents seize items that had not been declared?

Bergonzio researched his client's question, then visited the house on Pearl Street to make a full report. Seated on the couch next to Susanne, he told the couple what his lawyer – 'one of the best' – had told him. Customs agents could seize items at any time, even decades after the fact. They sold the seized items, with half the proceeds going to the whistleblower. Polari asked what happened when the person whose goods were seized found out who the informant was. 'This country isn't like Europe,' Bergonzio replied. 'When the customs collector takes their statement, it's over; the informant is never revealed.' Bergonzio and Polari then discussed other differences between American and European laws. Bergonzio told him that 'women have great rights and great privileges over men in this country,' and shared several examples.[22]

Susanne listened closely to Bergonzio's words. Could American laws help her escape Polari? She asked Roumage to consult a lawyer on her behalf.

But Roumage's lawyer, William Austin Seely, destroyed her hopes when he told Roumage that unless the couple was legally married, the woman had no right to the man's property. Susanne and Polari had never been married, even though Rosine had been baptized with his last name. American law, she realized, couldn't help her.

As the hot July days wore on, Susanne despaired of ever escaping the house on Pearl Street. Polari noticed her darkened mood, but didn't realize he was the cause. One day, he asked, 'What does this arrogance and change of character mean, that you wanted to steal the jewels, that you wanted to leave with someone?' Susanne said nothing, according to Polari. He called her 'insipid' and claimed 'I could not live with her without always arguing…'[23] The feeling was mutual. During a moment of clarity, the couple agreed to separate.

According to Polari, Susanne asked him for 60,000 francs as alimony, which he agreed to pay as soon as he could gather it. He told Susanne he would always help her, including advising her how to spend her separation money. He promised to marry her one day, and offered to put that promise in writing.[24] In his mind, he was a loving and loyal partner who had given everything he could. In all his letters and interrogations, he said nothing about the emotional and physical violence he regularly unleashed on her, or the effect that violence might have had on Rosine. Blameless in his own mind, he laid the guilt for what happened next entirely at Susanne's feet.

Despite their impending separation, Susanne and Polari kept up appearances. She continued her English lessons with a tutor, using the French-language textbook *Élémens de la langue anglaise*. In the evenings, they walked together in Castle Garden, an entertainment center at the southernmost tip of Manhattan featuring art exhibits, promenades, vendors, a restaurant, and the adjacent Battery Park. Most evenings, there were fireworks and music, with ice cream available for a few cents. The band, noted Dutch immigrant Jacob de Brauw, usually played 'the well-known song from the Mute of Portici.'[25]

For Susanne, these walks were more than exercise and fresh air. They were a lifeline. She and Roumage chose locations in Castle Garden to pass notes.

One night in late July, she left a note begging him to come see her; she felt threatened and unsafe with Polari. Roumage showed it to Jonathan Shieffelin and asked for advice. The gallant old gentleman urged him to help a woman in need. So Roumage went to the house on Pearl Street, where Susanne poured out her grievances against Polari. In despair, she told Roumage about the violence, the fear, and – as Roumage had suspected – Polari's source of wealth. Susanne told him Polari had valuable gemstones here in America, as well as in Brussels. Roumage replied that if Polari hadn't declared the jewels when he entered the country, he had broken the law.

For Susanne, this confirmed what Bergonzio had told Polari. But now that Roumage knew it, too, she had to make a choice. If she didn't work with Roumage to exploit that information, it was possible he could do it without her. Could she trust him? At that moment, it seemed her odds were better with Roumage than Polari. After all, Polari had created the trap for himself. All they had to do was spring it.

But until they did, she had to live at the side of a man she feared. Her despair and his suspicion clouded the atmosphere in their home. Polari sparked a storm on Wednesday, July 27, when he scolded Susanne for a lack of progress in her English lessons. She wasn't working hard enough to justify the money he spent on them, he said. The scolding turned into a bitter fight about money. Polari later said that Susanne pointed toward the sky, raised her eyes to heaven, and said, 'I want God's thunderbolt to crush me if you don't pay.'[26] For Susanne, the cash he promised represented safety for herself and Rosine – a life without fear. But Polari saw only a greedy, ungrateful woman, draining him of every cent he possessed. His anger rose, hot and fierce, as he closed the distance between them. In a red haze of anger, his fingers curled around her neck and squeezed. Polari choked her until blood poured from her mouth.[27]

When he felt she had learned her lesson, he flung her to the ground and locked himself in the bedroom. Susanne slept on the sofa, too afraid to move. When she woke the next morning, she tried to summon the strength to rise. But then she saw something under the table nearby, something that sparkled in a shaft of morning light. Crawling from the sofa, she reached out and closed her fingers around seven small diamonds. With a glance at the bedroom door, she quickly wrapped them in paper and hid them in her dress.

Chapter 10

The First Betrayal

With seven diamonds hidden in her dress, Susanne Blanche began to move around the house, dressing and then waking Rosine. Remnants of the previous day's stagnant heat choked the early morning air. When Polari heard her, he emerged from the bedroom and ordered her to spend the day in Brooklyn, away from the house.

Susanne acquiesced. She told Polari she'd take Rosine to Du Flon's Military Garden. But once they were out of the house, Susanne didn't head toward the ferry. Instead, she went straight to 133 Greenwich Street – Joseph Collet's boarding house – to see Roumage. She told him about her fight with Polari. 'Last night,' she said, 'Polari tried to strangle me; blood was coming out of my mouth…what course must I take to escape his brutality?'[1] She showed Roumage the marks he'd left on her body, and said she believed her life was in danger. Roumage advised her to ask the authorities for protection, but she was too afraid to do that. Susanne then removed the paper-wrapped bundles from her dress and placed them in Roumage's hands. She asked him to keep the diamonds safe, in case she needed them. He told her she'd done well. So well, in fact, that he asked her to steal more, preferably stones 'worth a hundred thousand francs.'[2]

If his suggestion angered or frightened her, she didn't show it. She told Roumage where she planned to take Rosine, and he volunteered to escort them to Brooklyn. On the way, Susanne realized she might never have another opportunity to confide in Roumage, away from Polari. She let the story tumble out of her, beginning with Polari's bankruptcy in Lyon, his flight to Brussels, and his return last autumn when he'd promised to share a great fortune with her. She told him about Polari's mushroom hunt, how he'd stumbled onto a cache of jewels, and how he'd smuggled them into this country. If she wanted revenge for his brutality, all she had to do was tell the Customs Collector what Polari had done. Here she paused, perhaps to draw Rosine closer. Polari was still her child's father, she said, and Rosine bore his last name. She couldn't bring herself to do it.

Still clinging to the tatters of his former wealth and status, the Frenchman realized he'd just been given a gift. A woman and child in danger, in need of protection from a violent man – this wasn't greed, it was chivalry. And thanks to the details she'd just provided, Roumage had everything he needed to spring the trap. There was just one more step, perhaps required by his conscience. He left Susanne and Rosine to amuse themselves in Brooklyn, while he returned to the city.[3]

His first stop was the house on Pearl Street. On the pretext of needing a word about a servant, he talked his way in, only to discover Polari's house was a mess. He saw a large trunk and suitcase, packed and waiting. Suspecting Polari was about to abandon Susanne and Rosine, Roumage made the decision to move forward with his plan. Blameless in his version of events, Roumage claimed he only wanted 'to save Madame Blanche from the dangers which threatened her, to ensure her existence and himself an honorable reward.'[4] He excused himself quickly and went straight to the Customs office, on the corner of Wall and Nassau. He told the Collector, Samuel Swartwout, that a man he knew had failed to pay import duties on precious gems he planned to sell. He provided Polari's address, anticipating the 25% bounty paid to informers when their tip led to the capture of smuggled goods.[5] What he could *not* anticipate was the political and bureaucratic firestorm he had just unleashed.

Andrew Jackson had appointed Samuel Swartwout as Collector of Customs at the Port of New York when he took office in 1829. The nomination sent ripples of panic up and down the Eastern seaboard. 'Swartwout was odious in New York,' wrote James A. Hamilton. 'He had not a single quality of mind, education, or character, to entitle him to the office.'[6] It was a sentiment he shared with Aaron Burr, the man who had shot and killed his father. Upon learning that Jackson wanted to appoint Swartwout, Burr said it would be 'the most outrageous thing that had yet been done in any part of the United States…'[7] Martin Van Buren was against Swartwout, too, referring to his appointment as a 'great evil.'[8] Although Van Buren knew Swartwout personally and vouched for his friendliness, he told Jackson that Swartwout's appointment was a mistake. Additional letters poured into Jackson's office, begging him to change his mind. But why?

Born in New York in 1783, Samuel Swartwout became a close associate of Aaron Burr. His brother, John, had been the one to arrange the fatal duel between Burr and Alexander Hamilton. Swartwout supported Burr when, in 1806, Burr plotted to carve a new country out of the American southwest. Burr tried to sway Andrew Jackson as well, but upon learning that Burr's plan involved annexing the western portion of the United States, Jackson wanted nothing to do with it. When one of Burr's co-conspirators got cold feet, he arrested Samuel Swartwout; both Swartwout and Burr were charged with treason. Swartwout testified that Burr had intended to take territory from Mexico, not the United States, and the Supreme Court acquitted both men.[9] When Swartwout challenged his accuser to a duel, his confidence impressed Jackson. The two men became friends, remaining close even as Swartwout's career devolved into ruinous stock and land speculation.

When Jackson won the presidential election in 1828, Swartwout hoped to gain from what he called 'the general scramble for plunder.'[10] Men like Van Buren, Hamilton, and even his former co-conspirator, Aaron Burr, hoped he would not. The New York Customs House brought in $15,000,000 in revenue per year, between 50% and 75% of the entire US Treasury's funds. The job required someone with unimpeachable ethics, a spotless criminal record, and a history of positive financial transactions. Swartwout had none of these things. As one opponent put it, no one who had engaged in 'large and unfortunate speculations' for more than a decade 'can be a proper judge of the responsibility of principals and sureties to bonds to the amount of more than two-thirds of the whole revenue of the Country.'[11] The appointment reeked of cronyism.

But as with Margaret Eaton, Jackson proved unshakeable in defense of a friend. Jackson described Swartwout as 'strictly honest and correct in all his dealings and conduct.'[12] In thanking Jackson for the job, Swartwout told him nothing had ever given him so much happiness. James A. Hamilton, however, believed there was more to the appointment than friendship. Swartwout, he said, had bragged that if Jackson failed to give him the job, he would reveal the true extent of Jackson's participation in Burr's treasonous empire-building scheme.[13] Blackmail, however, proved unnecessary. The force of Jackson's personality ensured Swartwout was confirmed as Collector in 1830.

On the job, however, Swartwout quickly revealed his ignorance. Hamilton complained that Swartwout summoned him to the Customs House every morning for help with the legal aspects of assessing duties. One morning, Hamilton saw Swartwout slip a check for $5,000 to a man standing near his desk without creating a receipt or ledger notation to indicate what it was for. Convinced Swartwout was stealing public funds for private use, he told Jackson. The president agreed that Swartwout should be investigated, but nothing was ever done.[14]

This was the man Roumage had sent after Polari and his smuggled cache of gemstones. But something – local gossip, or perhaps instinct – warned Roumage that Customs agents were not to be trusted. And although Susanne had never hinted that Polari's jewels were the ones stolen from Anna in Brussels, Roumage had already guessed the truth. Instead of waiting to see what Customs would do with his tip, Roumage played his hunch. He took the same information to the Dutch consul in New York, John C. Zimmerman. He went to Zimmerman's home at 96 Leonard Street and asked who he could speak to about a matter of great interest. Zimmerman escorted him to their senior official, the Minister Plenipotentiary and Envoy Extraordinary: Chevalier Christiaan Bangeman Huygens.

Since leaving Washington in the wake of the Eaton scandal, the Huygens family lived at the City Hotel, a luxurious residential inn occupying a full city block on Broadway. When Zimmerman and Roumage arrived, Huygens invited them in and Roumage quickly explained why he'd come: he had found the jewels stolen from Brussels in 1829. They were with a man named Carara (the name by which he knew Polari), who had shown him a 'magnificent sapphire' and 'other jewels of great value.'[15] When Huygens appeared skeptical, Roumage described the stones in a way that convinced Huygens he could be telling the truth.

Now that he had Huygens's attention, Roumage pulled out the small handful of diamonds Susanne had given him that morning. Huygens looked at the stones, all one to two carats, and judged them to be of very high quality. Roumage returned the stones to his pocket 'so as not to arouse suspicions in Madame Blanche.'[16] He volunteered to use Susanne to uncover more of the thief's secrets. To that end, he asked Huygens for details about the theft and the reward. Huygens showed him drawings of the missing jewels, after which Roumage extracted two promises from him: to keep his identity secret and to guarantee him the full reward in writing. Huygens agreed, promising the full 50,000 florins (about $20,000 at the time, or about $674,622 today).[17] Satisfied, Roumage provided Polari's alias and location, urging Huygens not to waste a moment in detaining him.

After Roumage had gone, Minister Huygens and Consul Zimmerman debated what to do. As diplomats, they weren't authorized to conduct an arrest or search. Zimmerman warned Huygens not to trust Roumage; he had a 'suspicious appearance' and 'bad reputation.'[18] Instead, he suggested they hire someone to help them proceed within the boundaries of American law: a local lawyer with an excellent reputation, William Austin Seely. That evening, Huygens and Zimmerman went to Seely's office with a unique proposition. They asked him to take them on as his sole client, working exclusively to capture Polari, prove his guilt, and recover Anna's missing jewels.

Seely agreed. It would be the worst decision of his life.

William Austin Seely was born in New Jersey on August 28, 1787, one of three surviving children of Joshua and Bethia Seely. While he was a toddler, the family moved to Orange County, New York and later to New York City. His father died there at age 41 in 1803. In his will, his father nominated a guardian for each of his underage children. For 15-year-old William, he selected a New York lawyer, Benjamin Ferris.[19] The choice likely influenced Seely's decision to follow in his guardian's footsteps. He studied law and became fluent in French. In 1813 at age 25, he married 28-year-old Hannah Fountain of Staten Island.[20]

That October, Seely was licensed as a solicitor by the Court of Chancery in New York City. He set up shop in the Financial District and began to make a name for himself, in no small part because of his foreign language skills. He worked as a translator in an 1817 case against three men accused of sinking a ship to collect the insurance money. Over the next few years, he handled cases ranging from estate administration to criminal defense. Seely's stock in trade was unflagging enthusiasm for his clients. In 1825, he was one of three lawyers defending a pair of Swiss immigrant brothers accused of murder. When the jury acquitted the brothers, a local newspaper praised Seely, who 'evinced from the commencement the most untiring zeal and talent in the cause of these helpless foreigners...'[21] In 1829, he had successfully defended another immigrant, Jean Roumage, from a charge of arson.

During nearly two decades of work in New York City, Seely had developed what he called 'peculiar and very general local information, especially among all Europeans and foreigners resident there...' As a result, he was a highly recommended attorney and brought home $8,000 - $12,000 per year ($269,849 - $404,773 in today's money). At age 43, he was as enthusiastic and determined as ever, but the years were beginning to show on his 5' 10" frame. His hair had turned mostly silver, but his gray eyes were still alert.[22] When Huygens and Zimmerman appeared on his doorstep that Thursday night and asked him to take their case, he hesitated.

The Dutch men pleaded the political importance of their case. While the missing jewels were incredibly valuable, the Dutch government's main concern was proving Prince Willem wasn't the thief. Seely's job, Huygens explained, was to prove beyond a shadow of a doubt that someone else was responsible. That person must be apprehended and extradited for a public trial and punishment in The Hague. Huygens promised his government would help in any way possible. Money, he said, was no object.

Seely accepted the case.

Only then did Huygens tell him about his meeting with a French informant that morning. But when Seely asked to interview the informant, Huygens politely refused. He had agreed to keep the informant's identity a secret and would not break his word. Suspecting the informant was one of his many contacts, Seely asked Huygens to describe the man without naming him. Based on the description, Seely immediately recognized Jean Roumage's 'character and manner of acting.'[23] He remembered that Roumage had come to him twice recently, asking first about women's rights in the United States and then about 'a commercial matter concerning the possession of some objects.'[24]

Seely warned the Dutch minister not to trust Roumage. Well aware of his past, peppered with accusations of fraud, Seely guessed the Frenchman wouldn't be able to resist claiming both the Dutch reward and the US Customs bounty for informants. The good news, Seely said, was that Roumage owed him a favor after exonerating him from the 1829 arson charge. If anyone had moral leverage over Roumage, it was Seely.

Since Roumage had provided a name and location for the thief, Seely's first task was making a legal arrest. That required a warrant authorized by the district attorney and the presence of a police judge. Despite the late hour, Huygens and Zimmerman asked Seely to organize this as quickly as possible. Seely assured them he wouldn't let the culprit slip away.

That afternoon, while Huygens and Zimmerman had debated how to proceed, the Customs Collector took full advantage of his head start. After Roumage left his office, Samuel Swartwout approached James Hopson, a police magistrate, to request a search warrant. A mainstay of the city's police force, magistrates were judges with limited jurisdiction, able to try minor offenses including a customs violation. Judge Hopson granted the warrant and set out with Swartwout for Polari's home, trailing an entourage that included Thomas Morris, the US Marshal of the Southern District of New York, High Constable Jacob Hays, and several policemen. Accounts differ as to when they arrived. Roumage placed their arrival at 3 p.m., Polari timed it at 6 p.m., and a newspaper account described these events as taking place 'on the night' of July 28.[25]

When Swartwout and the police arrived, Polari was upstairs, with a housemaid tidying downstairs. On the table beside him lay the hollow cane and umbrella shaft, both open, still stuffed with diamonds and pearls. The knock on the door surprised him and Polari looked out his window. When he saw a handful of uniformed policemen, he slammed the openings of the cane and umbrella shut. Before dashing downstairs, he grabbed a tin box full of pearls and colored stones that he hoped to hide in the cellar. But it was already too late – the police had broken through the door. Rushing into the house, they stormed up the stairs, halting him on his way down. Polari did his best to stall, expostulating in French as he held the tin box behind his back. Using sleight-of-hand movements, he slid a large sapphire into his watch fob. He palmed a boxed sapphire, followed by two smaller boxes of pearls, and waited for an opportunity to hide them.[26]

US Marshal Thomas Morris stepped forward. He had come, he said, to search for the jewelry Polari had failed to declare and pay for at Customs. Polari's protests carried no weight and the policemen spread out to search his house. He followed them upstairs, where they stripped his bed, pulling straw out of the mattress and tossing it on the floor. Polari saw his chance and hid a box of pearls in the discarded straw.

On the way downstairs, Polari passed his housemaid. He slipped her the boxed sapphire and asked her to hide it upstairs. She attempted to do so, but a constable named Steveson followed her, found the box, and put it in his pocket. The housemaid was able to get close enough to Polari to tell him what had happened. Polari protested to Morris, who spoke French, and the box was returned with an apology. During the search, Polari saw Samuel Swartwout pick up the cane and umbrella. He set both of them down, never suspecting they were filled with pearls and diamonds. When Morris looked inside a green box and saw handfuls of diamonds, Polari claimed they were fakes, worth maybe six francs each.[27]

The raid lasted for at least one hour, and possibly as long as three. Swartwout seized every jewel they found, a list that filled 35 lines in a column of *The Evening Post*. Among the items seized were dozens of loose diamonds, sixteen large round pearls, a nineteen-carat sapphire, 63 amethysts, a 61-carat sapphire, a large square emerald, two large Brazilian topazes, and rare drop pearls. For safe keeping, they were all placed in Mechanics' Bank. In addition to jewels, the officers seized about $4,000 found in Polari's wallet, as well as a handful of books and documents.[28]

After the seizure, Swartwout went to see District Attorney James A. Hamilton, who was home sick in bed. He asked Hamilton to arrest Polari and 'institute the necessary proceedings to condemn the jewels as forfeited to the United States.' Once the jewels had been declared US property, they could be sold. Half the payout would go to the United States, and half would go to three Customs officers, including Swartwout.[29] The Collector's priority was obvious: himself.

Chapter 11

Buried Treasure

Back in Pearl Street, Polari knew the raid wasn't the end of his troubles. Once Swartwout and the police left, he collected all the jewels left to him – from the cane, umbrella, and a few other boxes he'd managed to hide – and fled over the river into Brooklyn. He made his way toward Du Flon's Military Garden, where he met Susanne and Rosine on their way home for the night. Visibly agitated, he told Susanne to turn around. He needed her help and that of his friend, Du Flon.[1]

Located at the corner of Joralemon and Fulton, the Military Garden was a much-loved recreation area. Since 1822, it had been owned and operated by a Swiss immigrant, Jean François Louis 'Poppy' Du Flon. He and his wife maintained a lush garden with seating nooks tucked into arbors, perfect for relaxation and people-watching. The resort also included a small outdoor theater, a hall that hosted private parties, and a hotel. Years later, Walt Whitman would remember the Military Garden and its proprietor as part of old New York, vanished in all but memory. In 1831, however, 'Poppy' Du Flon was beginning a gradual slide into bankruptcy, which may explain his family's actions over the next few days.[2]

After a quick word to explain the situation to Du Flon, Polari checked himself, Susanne, and Rosine into the Military Garden's hotel. Finally safe behind closed doors, he told Susanne about the Customs raid. 'If they had looked in my umbrella and my cane,' he said, 'I would have suspected it was you that had caused me to be denounced.'[3] Had she betrayed him, he added, he would have killed her. Polari locked the remainder of the jewels in a chest of drawers in the hotel room and pocketed the key. He had to go back to Pearl Street, but ordered Susanne to keep the jewels in her sight until he returned in the morning.

As darkness fell that Thursday night, Polari walked home, his fingers thrust deep into his pockets. There, he found 'the biggest pearl of all' – likely fallen out of a box he'd pocketed during the raid.[4] When he arrived home, he hid it under a candlestick. Then he turned to survey the afternoon's damage: empty drawers, overturned boxes, opened trunks, and his family's meager possessions strewn across the floor. Would the police come back the next day? How many times could they use the same warrant to terrorize him? That night could be his last chance to search the house for jewels overlooked in the afternoon's chaos. With a glance at the candlestick, he set to work.

That evening, William Austin Seely and his two Dutch clients began the paperwork needed to arrest Polari and search his premises. Between 9 and 11:30 p.m., Seely reached Judge Hopson. He explained the situation and asked for a warrant. To the lawyer's surprise, Hopson said they were too late. He had already gone with Swartwout to Polari's residence to seize the jewels that afternoon. But since no one had mentioned a possible tie to the stolen Dutch jewels, they had left Polari at liberty. With this new information, Hopson immediately granted an arrest warrant.[5]

Neither Huygens nor Zimmerman wanted to wait until daybreak to arrest Polari. The Customs seizure would have put him on edge, and without the element of surprise, a quick reaction time was all they had. With three officers and the chief of police as backup, Seely and the Dutch officials headed for Polari's home. Before they arrived, Seely suggested one of the officers cover the back. No one moved. When an officer knocked on the door, Polari poked his head out a second-story window. When they asked to be let in, Polari replied, '*Dans le moment, Messieurs!*'[6]

But *le moment* never arrived. When nothing happened, the policemen forced the door open a second time that day, only to find it barricaded with furniture. Seely realized Polari had been expecting them – if not tonight, certainly tomorrow morning. A quick search of the house revealed he had already fled, likely with any remaining jewels or incriminating evidence. Seely and Zimmerman blamed police negligence in leaving the back unguarded and allowing Polari to escape. The mistake seemed so egregious that Huygens wondered if perhaps the 'connivance of the chief officer' had anything to do with it.[7] A disappointed Seely posted one of the officers, Benjamin J. Hays, inside the house. Hays remained there for over 24 hours, but Polari would never return.

Polari had to consider his next move carefully. Having fled from the police, he must have known they wouldn't simply give up. Anyone he turned to from this point forward had the potential to become a witness who might testify against him. Who could he trust?

He chose the very man who had betrayed him. Around midnight, carrying his hollow cane and umbrella, Polari went to Collet's boarding house and knocked on Jean Roumage's door. He told Roumage he had fled from the police over a customs misunderstanding and asked to stay the night. Roumage let him use the sofa. But while Polari slept, the Frenchman went through his wallet. He took notes on the contents in Latin so Polari wouldn't understand if he discovered the note while Roumage slept.[8] The precaution proved unnecessary. Roumage woke first, before sunrise, and insisted Polari leave. Polari obliged, reaching for his wallet. He gave Roumage some money, asking that half go to Bergonzio to pay for a lawyer and half to Susanne, in case she needed anything.

Like a jailer escorting a prisoner, Roumage accompanied Polari to the ferry that crossed the East River. There, he couldn't resist having the last word. 'I let you go,' he said to Polari. It was a lie. Once the ferry departed, he proceeded to inform on Polari to as many people as possible. He started with Seely at 6 or 7 a.m., telling him Polari had gone to Brooklyn. He promised to return with a more precise location, if possible.[9] He delivered the same information to Huygens, along with his note about the contents of Polari's wallet, which included a birth certificate for one Charles Dominique Carara, born on September 13, 1781 and baptized in Strambini.[10]

Meanwhile, Polari stepped off the ferry in Brooklyn. He made his way to Du Flon's hotel, where he woke Susanne. The police were looking for him, he said, so they must hide the remaining jewels in the woods as soon as possible. Susanne dressed herself and Rosine while Polari stole a spade from Du Flon's garden, cutting the handle so it could be hidden under his jacket. Once she and Rosine were ready, Polari unlocked the drawer in their room. They tied all the gemstones in handkerchiefs, shoved deep into their pockets. Carrying hundreds of thousands of dollars of stolen jewels, the little family made its way downstairs into Du Flon's pleasure garden. As they hurried toward the street, Jean Roumage arrived, panting and out of breath. He had come from the city, where a manhunt was in effect. 'They're looking for you everywhere to arrest you both,' Roumage said. 'You, madame, you have been described as being with an infant, and a constable has been sent to the promenade to see if you are there.'[11] Susanne clutched Rosine and grew pale with fear, but Polari assured her she wouldn't be arrested. Roumage fled as quickly as he had come, returning to New York to confirm Polari's location to Seely.

Polari waited until Roumage had gone, urging Susanne to stay calm. Then they walked 'about a good league of road' (approximately three miles) behind the South Ferry before they found a convenient spot to hide the remaining jewels. Later, Susanne remembered they passed an inn, a meadow, and a house. To the left of that house, Polari selected a spot to dig in 'an almost inaccessible thicket' full of trees.[12] Using the stolen spade, he dug a one-foot hole, buried the jewels, and marked nearby trees with crosses.

But haste had made Polari less thorough than usual. As they walked back to the road, he found more jewels in his pockets. The first time, they turned around and buried a cardboard box with some of Anna's largest pearls and a sapphire near the original cache. On the way out a second time, Polari found more small diamonds in his pockets. Rather than return again and risk being spotted, Polari gave them to Susanne, who put them in her handkerchief. The longer they walked, the more jewels he pulled from his clothing, including the large pearl he'd hidden in the candlestick, grabbed in haste as Seely had banged on his door the previous night.[13]

They returned to Brooklyn and their room in Du Flon's hotel without incident. According to Polari, he stayed there, out of sight, and sent Susanne into New York to gather information and contact Bergonzio. If he had known how closely he was being tracked, he might have chosen to go with her.

At about 10 a.m. that morning, Seely and five police officers made their way to Du Flon's hotel in Brooklyn. Their informant, Roumage, had confirmed

Polari would be somewhere on the property. Seely suggested they start with the hotel, then search the nearby theater and hall. He stationed four policemen around the building before he and the chief officer went inside.

When Seely arrived, Polari was upstairs shaving. Aware that something like this might happen, Du Flon (or one of his five sons) hurried to tell Polari they were surrounded.[14] There was no time to think. As Seely's footsteps shuffled on the staircase, Polari made a split-second decision. He climbed out the window onto the roof, three stories above the streets of Brooklyn. From Du Flon's roof, he leapt onto a neighbor's, then onto a shed whose roof lay hidden beneath the downcast branches of a willow tree. He remained out of sight while the police searched the hotel. Once more, Seely went away empty-handed.

When they had gone, Polari retraced his steps and climbed back into his room. According to the residents of Monsieur Collet's boarding house, several of whom later spoke to Polari, he offered 100,000 francs to one of Du Flon's sons to help him continue to evade the police.[15] The younger Du Flon obliged, escorting Polari out a window and hiding him in a nearby Freemason's lodge.

Polari's second escape was not without consequences. The Du Flon family now found themselves under suspicion. When their search turned up nothing, the police took Poppy Du Flon into temporary custody to interrogate him before a magistrate. When Du Flon refused to tell them where Polari was, the magistrate threatened to send him to prison. The Du Flon family needed a solution – and fast. That solution arrived in the person of Jean Roumage. Still trying to engineer Polari's arrest, he advised the Du Flon family to speak to Minister Huygens.[16] The Dutch minister, he said, would likely offer a cash reward for the person who delivered Polari into his hands. It was a tempting offer for a man slowly sinking into debt with many mouths to feed.

While Polari ran from the police, Susanne returned to the city and sought out her confidante, Roumage. She told him about the morning's trip, the thicket, and the buried gems. She also told him about Polari's threat to kill her if he thought she'd betrayed him. In every word she said, Roumage saw another opportunity. He convinced Susanne her future depended on protecting the buried jewels from Polari. After all, what was to stop Polari from digging them up alone and abandoning her and Rosine? Those jewels were her leverage over him, the key to an independent future. He made her promise they would retrieve them the following morning. Susanne agreed, on one condition: the jewels must go back to their rightful owner.[17]

Gallantly accepting Susanne's stipulation, Roumage asked her to describe where the jewels were buried. But although she was frightened, Susanne hadn't lost her wits. She refused to provide the exact location beforehand. If they dug up the jewels together, he must promise not to dispose of them without her consent. She was desperate to escape Polari, but it didn't mean she wanted her child's father imprisoned for the rest of his life. If it were possible to use the jewels to obtain a pardon for Polari as well as return them to their rightful owner, she preferred to do that. As for the hundred or so loose diamonds tied in her handkerchief, she gave them to Roumage for safekeeping. When she left, she had no jewels with her – which was likely her plan all along, in case the police stopped her.

Her caution was not out of place. Later that day, while she was in a carriage in Brooklyn, a messenger caught up with her and thrust a note into her hand. Sent through Du Flon's son, it was a request from Polari. He asked her to go back to their house and check for more jewels in her trunk and the kitchen pots. She decided to wait until the next morning, perhaps hoping their situation might change overnight. Susanne and Rosine settled into their room at Du Flon's hotel for a long, restless night.

Meanwhile, Polari hid in the safehouse chosen by one of Du Flon's sons. A mile away from the hotel, it was near enough for the Du Flon family to get word to him if needed, but out of sight of any lingering police officers.[18] With nothing to do but think, he wondered how he had ended up in this situation. Someone must have informed on him. Who had seen him with the jewels? Who had been inside his house? Susanne, Bergonzio, the housemaid and…Jean Roumage. But the stakes were higher now. Instead of fighting the Frenchman for Susanne, he was now fighting for his life.

Chapter 12

The Second Betrayal

On Saturday morning, Susanne took Rosine by the hand and set out from Du Flon's on the mission Polari had asked her to complete. When she arrived at the Pearl Street house, police officers were still inside, hoping their suspect would make a mistake and return.[1] They let her in, but she found nothing in the places Polari had indicated. Next, she met with Roumage and steeled herself for the task at hand: digging up the jewels. The idea terrified her. Polari was still free, last seen in Brooklyn. What if he saw them together? What would he do to her then? Roumage assured her that Polari had bigger problems than following her or keeping an eye on the buried jewels.[2]

Later that morning, Roumage hired a carriage to take the three of them to Brooklyn. As they neared the burial site, Roumage stopped the carriage. Susanne took Rosine to a nearby inn and left her inside to keep her out of sight. By the time she rejoined Roumage and located the exact spot, it was about noon. Under the high summer sun, Roumage began to dig with his hands. Susanne kept watch as he shoveled away the earth. But when she looked across the road, she spotted a familiar figure: Rosine, walking straight into the middle of the road. She ran to scoop up her child while Roumage retrieved and pocketed the jewels. With an estimated $200,000 of diamonds and pearls in their pockets, the bedraggled trio left the Brooklyn countryside.[3]

Having successfully eluded Polari, Susanne felt confident enough to make two more confessions to Roumage. She told him that not only were these the famous jewels stolen from the Princess of Orange, but that there were more buried outside Brussels. Roumage, of course, had already guessed their origin, but details of another cache must have piqued his interest. He asked several questions, but none about the exact location. Mindful of the promise Susanne had exacted, he insisted on keeping the Brooklyn cache until they could find a safe way to return the jewels to the royal family.[4] He placed them in a sealed box in his room at Collet's boarding house.

Roumage now realized he had another way to ingratiate himself with the Dutch minister. He went to Huygens and told him about the jewels hidden outside Brussels. Using information extracted from Susanne, he detailed the cache's contents, including cameos, a portrait of Emperor Nicholas I carved onto a gemstone, and gold and silver jewelry mounts.[5] To demonstrate his worth as a source, he offered Huygens several of the stones he had just dug up: two pear-shaped pearls, an emerald, and two diamonds.[6] But at that moment, the Dutch were more interested in Polari – and Roumage had no further information on his location.

With nothing to be gleaned from Roumage, Huygens and Zimmerman turned to the press. The police had already released a statement referring to Polari by his alias, Charles Dominique Carara. Consul Zimmerman provided Polari's birth name and requested the original list of missing jewels be reprinted in Saturday night's *The Evening Post*. He asked for the public's help tracking a 'short stout man, of swarthy complexion, large black whiskers, and a face broad and flat. He was dressed in a blue roundabout, grey trowsers [sic] and straw hat.'[7] The article also included the text of the original reward offer.

While Zimmerman dealt with the press, Huygens went to look at the jewels Samuel Swartwout had seized the previous day. Retrieved from temporary storage, they were laid out for his inspection. He compared them to the drawings the court jeweler had made in 1829. Although the settings were gone, he compared the size and shape of the stones themselves. He found enough matches to confirm these were indeed Anna's jewels. Huygens estimated the value of the stolen jewels to be 'several hundred thousand dollars,' consisting of 'thirteen thousand four hundred and sixty-two' individual stones, including 'two thousand and ninety one carats of diamonds.'[8] Now that the seized jewels had been matched to the drawings, the case seemed to be shaping up nicely. Consul Zimmerman wrote to a friend, 'I do not believe that the Government of the United States will find it difficult to extradite them [i.e., the jewels] in due time, after sufficient evidence.'[9] He could not have been more wrong.

After near-misses on Thursday and Friday, William Austin Seely believed Polari's luck had finally run out. To save their patriarch, the Du Flon family had brought him an offer: $2,000 to deliver Polari. That was exactly what Seely and Huygens wanted to hear. After two failed arrest attempts, Huygens had come to believe 'that the police wanted him [Polari] to escape.'[10] He instructed Seely to take the deal and set up the capture.

To bait the trap, a Du Flon son visited Polari in the safehouse. That night, Du Flon said, he would arrange for a boat to carry Polari from the Brooklyn shore to Hoboken, New Jersey – out of the jurisdiction of New York. If Polari was interested, he was to meet Du Flon at a certain tavern near the South Ferry that night.[11]

Just before 9 p.m. on that moonless night, Seely led the sheriff of Kings County and several New York City police officers toward the South Ferry terminal and the shoreline. They crouched on the side of a nearby hill, about twenty feet from the water, and waited. They were almost too late. As Seely and his men ducked out of sight, Polari followed Du Flon's son out of the nearby tavern. The pair walked toward the East River, its gently rippled surface cloaked in darkness. But as Polari's eyes scanned the shoreline, he realized something was wrong. 'Where is the boat?' he asked in French.

It took only a moment for Polari to realize the truth. He rounded on Du Flon and shouted, 'Brigand, thief, you have betrayed me!'[12] He sprinted away from the river and up a hill, toward a local distillery. Seely and his men sprang from their hiding place and gave chase. As he pumped his legs to close the gap between them, Seely saw Polari look over his shoulder. It was clear that Polari recognized Seely, who had come to arrest him the night of the Customs raid. Anger fueled Polari's already powerful legs, giving him a frantic burst of speed.[13]

Seely chased Polari up the hill, unwilling to lose his quarry a third time. Suddenly, Polari changed direction and ran toward a ditch, into which he either dove or fell. In the heat of the moment, Seely jumped in after him. Polari fought as if for his life, flailing, punching, and kicking. His extraordinary strength heightened the impact of every blow. But Seely was strong, too, and eventually got his arms around Polari. Officer Homan was next to jump into the ditch to help subdue Polari, who punched him in the face. Both Polari and Seely emerged dripping blood, with multiple blows to the face and head, but in the end, Seely and his men triumphed. They arrested Polari and placed him in irons. Years later, Seely was still haunted by Polari's explosive temper and incredible strength. Shuddering at the thought of a foe who could have killed him with his bare hands, Seely swore 'nothing would tempt me to encounter such a hazard' again.[14]

Polari claimed he had 'offered only a feeble resistance.' As was his habit, he blamed someone else for the violence of his arrest. 'I had the honor to be arrested, garotted [sic] and searched by a lawyer,' he wrote, 'and you will see, Sir, by what quality of person the honorable profession of lawyer is practiced in this country.'[15] The arresting officers escorted Polari back to the city and placed him in the Watch House, a temporary prison, where he would remain for three days. From the Watch House, Judge Hopson sent for Huygens and Zimmerman. Although it was around 11 p.m., both men obeyed the summons immediately. Huygens swore before Hopson that the confiscated jewels belonged to the Dutch royal family, which allowed Hopson to detain Polari for further questioning.

From that moment, however, the case began to spiral out of control. Who controlled Polari's fate: the state of New York, or the federal government? As of 1830, New York law stated that thieves who brought stolen property into the state could be punished as if the theft had taken place in New York.[16] But Polari had also violated US Customs law, which gave Collector Swartwout a personal financial stake in the case.

The Dutch didn't care which laws Polari had violated. Their mission was to clear Prince Willem's name, and if possible, recover the jewels. To convince the public Willem had never been to blame, only a full public confession would do. To get it, Huygens offered Polari a conditional pardon that very night. If he would travel to the Netherlands, confess, name any accomplices, and explain where the remaining jewels were hidden, they would set him free to return to the US. Polari refused, preferring to take his chances with the American legal system.

Lacking Polari's cooperation, Huygens asked his old friend, Martin Van Buren, for advice. Van Buren said he believed either the president or Congress would have to grant the Dutch custody of both the prisoner and the jewels.[17] Since he was no longer Secretary of State, however, all he could do was refer Huygens to his replacement.

❖

Born in 1764, Edward Livingston had studied law in Albany with Alexander Hamilton and Aaron Burr. After a stint as a Congressman, he became the district attorney of New York. There, he trusted a colleague to hold approximately $100,000 of government money. But when it came time to return the money, Livingston found it had mostly vanished. His colleague, it seemed, had 'appropriated a very large proportion of the sum...'[18] Scrupulously honest, Livingston agreed to pay it back, with interest.

Now in six figures of debt, Livingston moved to Louisiana to economize and seek out new opportunities. He became Jackson's military aide in 1814, in part due to his fluency in French, and earned the general's friendship and trust. But Livingston's greatest achievement was the work he did on Louisiana's criminal code. He took the existing Spanish laws, which still included burning at the stake as punishment, and turned them into a modern masterpiece of forward-thinking ideals: prevention rather than punishment, rehabilitation rather than revenge. Despite commissioning his work, the Louisiana legislature didn't act on it. But once it was published outside the US, Livingston became a celebrity praised by Jeremy Bentham, Victor Hugo, King Karl XIV Johan of Sweden, and Anna's brother, Emperor Nicholas I.[19] In 1826, Nicholas praised Livingston's 'insight and profound education' and said he had given the code to his own lawmakers as an example of 'judicious ideas, [and] useful materials.' Even King Willem I of the Netherlands sent Livingston a gold medal inscribed with praise.[20]

Now, as Jackson's second Secretary of State, Livingston was responsible for America's diplomatic correspondence. After Polari's arrest, Minister Huygens asked him to ensure the jewels were returned to the Dutch royal family. He also requested Polari be extradited for trial in the Netherlands. The request presented Livingston and Jackson with a quandary the government had never before faced: what should happen when a foreign monarch wanted a US resident extradited for a crime that hadn't been committed on American soil? Obliging the Dutch would set a dangerous precedent that a young, isolationist America did not want.

Meanwhile, the Dutch representatives continued to interrogate Polari. Consul Zimmerman returned to the Watch House at 7 a.m. on Sunday morning, but learned nothing. 'He does not want to confess anything yet, he is terribly stubborn,' Zimmerman wrote.[21] Whether out of compassion or strategy, he asked police officers to stop treating Polari so roughly. After this show of kindness, Polari obligingly fed Zimmerman the cover story he and Roudez had concocted in France. In a matter of hours, he changed the story and said he bought the jewels not in Algiers, but at the Café de la Victoire in Paris for 28,000 francs. Over the next few days, small details of the story changed again. Polari told Seely he had bought the jewels in Paris for 30,000 francs. He told a police officer he had bought them in the Palais Royale, and told someone else he had bought them in Brussels during the revolution.[22]

Seely and the Dutch had done the hard work of pursuing Polari physically. Now, the federal government pursued him legally and financially. Two days after his arrest, a *capias* warrant was issued against him, allowing the government to hold him until he paid the penalty for his Customs fraud. Seely remembered the penalty as $200,000, but James A. Hamilton remembered it as $50,000.[23] Either way, Polari didn't have the money. Anticipating trouble, he hired two lawyers, William H. Maxwell Esq. and William M. Price Esq., both of whom had previously defended Roumage.

On Sunday, July 31, the day after his arrest, Polari asked to see Susanne, a request the authorities allowed. He asked her to give the buried jewels to Huygens, believing that would set him free. Neither Susanne nor Polari paid attention to the nondescript prison guard standing inside the cell – but they should have. That guard was an undercover police marshal named George B. Raymond. Selected by Seely because he spoke French, Raymond would remain in the cell during all of Susanne's visits.[24] The French-speaking prisoner and his visitors never suspected that Raymond reported every word they said to Seely and Huygens.

After Polari's arrest, Roumage moved Susanne and Rosine from the Military Garden to a hotel on Barclay Street. He didn't want her to soften against Polari, so he made himself indispensable to her. When Polari's lawyers 'tormented' her to pay their fees, he offered to help.[25] And when Polari wrote to remind her that she had agreed to help him, he tore up the letter before she could read it. He watched constantly to make sure neither Seely nor Huygens ever spoke to her alone. It didn't take long for Susanne to realize what he was doing, but she allowed it, fearing the Dutch minister wanted to arrest her as an accomplice.

Later, when asked why he involved himself in the case, Roumage framed it as a quest for redemption. 'I saw in it both the means of rescuing her from the hands of this monster, of providing her with an honest existence, and for myself the opportunity of repairing terrible misfortunes.'[26] The chance to build a new life with a ready-made family appealed to him. He would be the hero in Susanne's story, finally able to close the chapter on his criminal past. Once, that is, he had committed a few more crimes in the name of their impending salvation.

Since the Dutch reward would take them one step closer to that salvation, Roumage continued to make himself useful to Huygens. He brought the minister a handful of gems from the Brooklyn cache, which he claimed to have discovered in a third party's possession. It's likely Roumage had an ulterior motive. The stones he offered would have been difficult to sell without attracting attention, as they included a $12,000 sapphire Emperor Alexander I had bought for Anna in Paris. Roumage also turned over a brilliant, two large pear-shaped pearls, a square emerald, and a large diamond with a scar caused by prying it out of its setting.[27] He didn't tell Susanne about this goodwill gesture since he'd promised they would return everything to Anna. Roumage believed their freedom was worth the lie. It was the only time, he said, he ever broke a promise to Susanne.[28]

Three days after his arrest, the authorities transferred Polari from the Watch House to the penitentiary at Bellevue. Holding prisoners was perhaps the least well-known function of the Bellevue complex. In 1795, New York City's Common Council had leased the then-vacant property on the East River to use as overflow for victims of the yellow fever epidemic. During a second outbreak in 1798, the Common Council purchased Bellevue outright.[29] Later, its expanded complex included not just a pesthouse, but a morgue, orphanage, penitentiary, asylum, almshouse, and infirmary, all set behind a 10-foot stone wall high above the river. The penitentiary was a grim two-story stone building next to the Alms House, directly behind the main hospital. As of May 1, 1831, the penitentiary housed 245 men and 182 women.[30]

Polari was given a room upstairs, generally larger than those downstairs. He had a table and chair, plentiful food, and an iron-barred window that allowed him to look outside. Minister Huygens commissioned Collet, the wine merchant who owned Polari's former boarding house, to supply Polari with essentials, which he paid for with cash fronted by Seely. Polari appreciated Collet accepting the commission and looked forward to his friend's weekly visits, for supplies as well as conversation. He later described Collet as 'brave' and 'generous,' noting that 'without this help, I might not have been able to bear such a fate...'[31] Collet kept the other residents of his boarding house informed about Polari's case. Some of them also considered Polari a friend, and wanted to help.

On Polari's second day in Bellevue, he and his lawyers attended a formal inquiry, as did Huygens and Seely. They watched a single witness spend an exhausting three hours under interrogation: Constantia Huygens, the Dutch minister's wife, a 'very clever woman' according to James A. Hamilton.[32] Her husband had given reluctant permission for her to participate since she was the only person on the American continent who had firsthand knowledge of Anna's jewels.

Looking at the seized items, Constantia confirmed as Anna's the large sapphire described as 'saphir d'une couleur parfaite.' She recognized another sapphire (the 'carbochon' formerly set with brilliants), an emerald, a buckle set with pearls and diamonds, a gold box set with turquoise, and more. The loose stones were harder to identify. She could only confirm there were similarities between them and the ones that belonged to Anna. A piece of lapis lazuli, she noted, looked like it had come from one of Anna's bracelets.[33]

When she finished examining the jewels, Polari's lawyer asked to cross-examine her. Judge Hopson refused to allow it. The Dutch had won the first skirmish in what was to become a protracted legal battle over Polari and the jewels.

Chapter 13

A Reputation Rehabilitated

No one in the Netherlands knew about Polari's arrest yet. The news would have been welcome, but the royal family had more pressing problems. The country was at war, attempting to assuage King Willem I's wounded pride and forcefully retain Belgium as part of the kingdom. On August 2, a Dutch force of 37,000 men invaded Belgium.[1] The king had appointed Willem Supreme Commander of the Dutch army and given him a very clear mission: regain our lost territory. The soldier's rush of adrenaline and mad bursts of courage – dormant since Waterloo – stirred once more in Willem's veins. This campaign offered him a path to redemption. If all went well, it would only take four marches for his army to reach Brussels.[2]

When Willem left at the head of the Dutch army, Anna sent him off with a portrait of herself. This time, she wore no tiara – just a simple traveling costume: high-necked blue dress, gloves, hat, and veil, with a cashmere shawl over her arm. In the upper-left corner, painter Cornelis Kruseman added a small orange shield with a special message from Anna: '*Plutôt une cabane avec mon Guillaume que de souscrire au déshonneur*' ('Better a cabin with my Willem than subject to dishonor'). Rolled up, the painting was easy for Willem to transport as he progressed. She hoped her gesture would contradict all the slanderers who had tarnished his reputation: now, they would see how much she still loved him. Willem wrote back, 'I was deeply moved by it and thank you with all my heart.[3] Her obligation to Willem satisfied, she turned to that of her adopted country. In preparation for war, Anna established the Willemshospitaal in The Hague, paid for with her own money. Once the wounded began to arrive, she would visit all 70 of them and make sure their needs were met.[4]

What became known as the Ten Days' Campaign began on August 2, 1831, Polari's first day in Bellevue. Leopold got word of the Dutch invasion as he was touring his new country. He dashed off messages to London and Paris, asking for help. As he waited for a response, he put himself at the head of a hastily assembled and poorly supplied Belgian force. The Dutch brushed them aside in a few skirmishes. 'See what I get by way of welcome,' Leopold said.[5]

On August 3, the Dutch invaders reached the Belgian town of Ravels. Willem led his soldiers on foot as they stormed the town, forcing Belgians out of their homes. He sent Belgian sabers home to his sons, and a Belgian soldier's shako to his daughter. Next, he marched at the head of two divisions to Hasselt on August 8. The Belgian army of the Meuse, led by General Daine, threw down its guns and fled. A delegation eager to avoid destruction presented him with keys to the city on a silver platter. Onward he marched to Leuven and Boutersem, where a chaotic battle took place on August 12. In the sixteen years since Waterloo, Willem had lost none of his bravado. When a cannonball struck and fatally wounded his horse, he said, 'It is nothing, gentlemen, there are more horses.' Fearless for himself, he only worried about retrieving his saddle and gear, gifts from Wellington.[6]

King Leopold arrived to lead his forces, hoping his presence would inspire them. It didn't work. Leopold was almost captured near Leuven and fled to Mechelin, with a cavalry division for protection. Countess Nesselrode, firmly on the Dutch side, wrote, 'How I regret that he was not taken prisoner.'[7] In Britain, Wellington blamed King Willem I for the entire situation. He remembered the days before Waterloo, when he had called the king 'the most difficult person to deal with I have ever met.'[8] Little, it seemed, had changed.

But Dutch luck didn't hold. At the moment Willem was about to take Leuven, he learned that an army larger than his was only twenty kilometers away, racing to Leopold's rescue. The King of the French, Louis Philippe, had answered his future son-in-law's call for help and dispatched an army under Marshal Gérard. The news forced King Willem I to reconsider his plans. Taking on the weak, disorganized Belgian army was one thing. Confronting the French army, one of the strongest in the world, was quite another.

The Ten Days' Campaign ended when Willem was allowed a symbolic entrance to Leuven, after which he returned to Dutch soil to avoid war with France. Both parties now agreed to an armistice. In front of the whole world, the Dutch had proved themselves a fiercely independent power and humiliated Leopold. When Willem and his brother Frederik returned to The Hague, church bells rang, government buildings flew the Orange standard, and city residents draped garlands of flowers from windows and balconies. Overwhelmed with emotion, grateful onlookers unhooked the princes' carriage and pulled it to the palace themselves, where the king and the rest of the royal family greeted them.[9]

The victorious campaign bolstered Willem's image among the Dutch people. News of the Customs seizure in New York further vindicated him in European eyes. After all, if he had arranged the theft, the diamonds would be in Machado's hands, not across the Atlantic. 'Everything contributed to raise the Prince of Orange in public opinion, even the discovery of the diamonds,' Countess Nesselrode wrote to her husband.[10] Anna reveled in her husband's new-found glory. When an officer asked if she regretted losing her palace in Brussels, she shocked him by saying she did not. 'Not everything is material,' she replied. Besides, Brussels had lost any claim to her loyalty because 'they do not appreciate what I hold most dear,' a clear reference to the way its citizens had turned on Willem in the wake of the jewel theft and in 1830.[11]

Representatives of the Great Powers set to writing, crafting a second set of divorce papers for the Netherlands and Belgium. Because of Willem's success during the Ten Days' Campaign, they awarded additional territory to the Netherlands. This gesture enraged the Belgians, who felt they were the wronged party. Once again, the combatants' representatives bickered over the details. Countess Nesselrode shook her head in disbelief. 'Humanity,' she wrote, 'has degenerated.'[12] It degenerated still further when King Willem I refused to sign the treaty. Buoyed by his son's success, he refused to acknowledge Belgium as an independent country. Instead, he paid for mobilized troops to patrol the Belgian border, as if he might try again to force the rebels to his will. The powerful Austrian chancellor, Klemens Metternich, wrote, 'This king is…one of those men who forget and learn nothing, and with this fault we lose thrones.'[13] Why, the world wondered, had he backed down in the face of the French army if he wasn't willing to accept a treaty? Belgium had only belonged to him because the Great Powers had allowed it in the first place. If they now agreed the situation should change, what right did he have to argue?

By mid-October of 1831, the Great Powers declared the updated treaty, the Twenty-Four Articles, final. No one was happy with it – not Leopold, who refused to give up additional territory in Limburg and Luxembourg, and not King Willem, who refused to give up two captured forts in Antwerp. But despite both rulers' complaints, the rest of the world wanted them to move on. The Belgian Chambers authorized Leopold to sign the treaty, which he did, albeit begrudgingly. Austria and Prussia then accepted Belgium as an independent nation, leaving Russia as the sole holdout.[14]

Although Belgium had now been recognized by most of the Great Powers, the situation remained unsettled. Even France, the first nation to come to Belgium's aid, was less than optimistic about the country's success. According to Charles-Maurice de Talleyrand-Périgord, the French ambassador in London, Belgium was doomed. It was 'not a nation, two hundred protocols will never make it a nation; this Belgium will never be a country, it cannot hold.'[15] Willem agreed, predicting that Belgium would either become part of France or return to the Netherlands.[16] In the meantime, he made Tilburg his new permanent headquarters, overseeing the troops guarding the southern border. The decision meant frequently living apart from Anna and his children. But even had they presented a united front, it wouldn't have been enough to pry Anna's jewels and the accused thief from the clutches of the American legal system.

Chapter 14

The Third Betrayal

As Prince Willem of Orange regained his popularity by thrashing the Belgian army, another famous soldier, President Andrew Jackson, tried to avoid doing battle. When Secretary of State Edward Livingston received Minister Huygens's request to extradite Polari, he realized the issue was bigger than the State Department. He asked Jackson and Attorney General Roger B. Taney for help. Taney advised both men to keep out of it and let the courts decide the fate of Polari and the seized jewels. Jackson's feelings mirrored Taney's. The president told Livingston he didn't think the Constitution allowed him to grant the extradition personally, nor remove the jewels from Customs' libel. In his personal notebook, he summarized Polari's situation: 'No power in the President unless under an article of treaty, and act of congress pointing out the mode by which he is to be identified, & surrendered.'[1] Since there was no extradition treaty with the Netherlands, Jackson considered himself excused.

With no presidential intervention on the horizon, Huygens and Seely prepared for a protracted legal battle. Seely decided to focus on the state of New York rather than the federal government. Under New York's Revised Statutes 8–10, the governor had the power to authorize extradition for someone charged with a theft that had no jurisdiction in the United States. Huygens and Seely asked New York's governor, Enos T. Throop, for permission to extradite. Just three weeks later, on August 20, Governor Throop granted a provisional mandate to deliver Polari into Huygens's custody.[2] The Dutch had scored yet another victory, albeit one that would prove Pyrrhic.

Soon after Polari's arrest, Jean Roumage began to wonder: what if the US government rebuffed the Dutch extradition request and set Polari free? Polari would eventually figure out who had provided the tip that led to his arrest and Roumage wanted to be far away when that happened. He realized there was one way he could avoid Polari and still make himself useful to the Dutch: he and Susanne could retrieve the jewels buried outside Brussels, bringing the case to a triumphant close. This would give Susanne 'the honor of presenting these immense restitutions to the Princess herself, reserving for myself the glory of having discovered everything, of having directed everything…'[3] To that end, Roumage asked Huygens for official permission to retrieve the Brussels cache. Huygens agreed, but with one stipulation: he and Susanne must travel with a guard or agent, under the direction of the Dutch government. For Roumage, this was impossible. How, under government surveillance, would they be able to add the Brooklyn cache to the Brussels cache? Combining them was the only way to return everything to the royal family, as Susanne had asked, without further implicating them both.[4] Perhaps intentionally, Roumage overlooked the easiest answer: re-bury the Brooklyn cache and notify Huygens, leaving only the Brussels cache to retrieve. Instead, Roumage clung to the jewels already in his possession.

He convinced Susanne it was too risky to travel with a Dutch official who could have them arrested at any time. They must retrieve the jewels in Brussels alone and present them to the royal family as a *fait accompli*. Susanne accepted his logic, and offered to leave Rosine in New York 'as a proof of my good faith.'[5] She believed this gesture would convince Dutch officials she didn't intend to steal the jewels and disappear. She arranged for Rosine to stay at a French boarding school in New York, and Roumage paid for three months' board.[6]

Their next step was figuring out how to smuggle the Brooklyn cache across the Atlantic. For this, Roumage needed an ally. He turned to his brother Frédéric, who lived in Philadelphia. On August 12, Roumage sealed the jewels in a box and gave it to a business associate of Frédéric's named Horstman. Roumage asked Horstman to store the box but *not* to ship it, as he would retrieve it soon.[7] During these preparations, Frédéric visited New York. Roumage had likely realized it was best not to commit the details of his plan to paper and summoned his brother for a quick conference. Back in Philadelphia, with his brother's instructions in hand, Frédéric purchased two tickets from Philadelphia to Liverpool on a packet ship. He selected the

Monongahela, sailing under Captain Charles Dixey, and paid $133.33 for each fare.[8] Next, he made a hollow crutch lined in red leather for Roumage to take on board the ship.

As August waned, so did any remaining goodwill between Susanne and Polari. A Bellevue jailer, George W. Taylor, later testified that Polari 'behaved very strangely towards this woman, telling her that he would kill her if she was still in his presence.'[9] Her last visit took place on August 19, 1831. Sensitive to his need for money, she brought him a wallet that contained about $200, likely provided by his agent, Bergonzio. When she tossed it onto his bed, Polari screamed at her. He accused her of having betrayed him, of wanting to abandon him. He threatened to have her chased down by an American ship and prosecuted if she dared to leave the country with Rosine. The argument turned into a brawl, witnessed by the undercover police marshal, George Raymond. Polari chased Susanne away, saying, 'Go away, I don't want to see you again.'[10]

Susanne took him at his word. Before that day, she had intended to seek a pardon for him in Europe. When this fight brought back memories of Polari's abuse, Susanne abandoned the idea. She 'no longer had any desire to be useful to a man who had treated her so horribly.'[11] Upon leaving Bellevue, she told Roumage, 'Let's go, please; if this man gets out, I am lost.'[12] The couple dropped Rosine off at boarding school and made their final preparations to leave. Each now had a reason to keep their departure as quiet as possible: Susanne, for fear of Polari's wrath, and Roumage, for fear of the Dutch minister's discovery and retribution.

To retrieve their precious parcel, Roumage went to see his brother's business acquaintance, Horstman. But Horstman told him it was too late — the crate had already been shipped to Philadelphia. When he returned empty-handed to Susanne, he had no choice but to tell her the truth. With all the charm he could muster, he pretended he had meant to do it, that his brother would deliver the jewels to them before they left for Liverpool.

Roumage and Susanne left New York on August 20, 1831, crossing the North River to New Jersey by steamer. There, Roumage dropped into a barbershop to have his sideburns shaved in an attempt at disguise. He also reverted to his alias, traveling as 'Mr. Robert.'[13] At 4 p.m., the pair boarded the mail stagecoach, a common form of public transportation. It likely took the

Old York Road south, passing through Scotch Plains and Somerville on the way to Philadelphia. Not trusting his clean-shaven disguise, Roumage held a handkerchief to his face the entire time.

Nearly twelve hours later, at around 6 a.m., the stagecoach rumbled into Philadelphia.[14] Roumage's brother Frédéric met them, disguised in shabby clothing, walking with a limp and a crutch. Frédéric guided them to an inn near the port for breakfast, where he delivered a devastating piece of news: Horstman's package hadn't arrived yet. A nervous Roumage told Susanne that if it didn't arrive before noon, she would have to board the ship alone and he would follow on the next one. Susanne immediately suspected a ruse, devised by Roumage to send her away and keep the jewels. She refused to be separated from him, and no amount of charm or cajoling could persuade her otherwise. Roumage left the dining room with his brother. The two men had an intense and quiet conversation, after which Roumage returned alone.[15]

Thirty minutes later, Frédéric arrived with the sought-after package. According to Susanne, it bore no marks of having been sent by post or mail stage. Frédéric said only that the courier had taken it to the wrong address and he'd had to search for it. He then bid them goodbye and headed for the docks. Before following, Roumage and Susanne rented a room in the inn to divide the jewels. They filled Polari's hollow umbrella shaft with 'twenty-two beautiful stones, which were wrapped in small pieces of paper.'[16] They placed the rest in Susanne's trunk.

With all the jewels accounted for, the couple made their way to the wharf. Frédéric was already there, but as part of their plan, he and Roumage pretended not to recognize each other. Frédéric, still holding the crutch, limped his way on board. He wordlessly passed the crutch to Roumage before departing the ship.

The *Monongahela* left Philadelphia on schedule. Like the *François I*, men and women slept in cabins in segregated areas. With only one other female passenger on board, Susanne had the women's room largely to herself. She and Roumage took advantage of the privacy (and a ten-day lull) to recount and repackage the gems. But as Susanne pulled diamonds from the hollow umbrella shaft, she began to worry. There were supposed to be 22, but she counted only eleven. When she pointed this out to Roumage, he pulled eleven more from deep in the cane using a stuffing jack he'd bought in New York.[17]

If his attempt to get her to board the ship alone had alarmed her, this moment would not have eased those suspicions. Was he hoping she'd forgotten how many diamonds there were?

As they catalogued the jewels, Roumage added a small handful of diamonds. They were the ones she'd stolen from Polari in Pearl Street and given to him for safekeeping before the Customs raid. Once again, Susanne felt her suspicion grow. Why had he kept these stones separate until now? The inventory also forced Roumage to confess that, before leaving New York, he had given several stones to Minister Huygens, including a large nicked diamond, a sapphire, an emerald, and a pair of drop pearls.[18] Susanne reproached him, but whether for keeping secrets from her or for separating the stones she planned to return to Anna, she didn't specify. They separated the stones into two packets, one for the umbrella shaft and one for the hollow crutch.

Now that the jewels were properly catalogued and hidden, Roumage and Susanne discussed how to proceed when they landed at Liverpool. Initially, the plan had been to proceed to Brussels and retrieve the buried jewels. Roumage now suggested they write to Prince Willem from Liverpool, explain the situation, and wait for his orders. If they received no reply, they would proceed to Willem's camp at Tilburg. Roumage had a friend there, Monsieur van Diepen, who could present him to the prince.[19] Susanne didn't want to wait in London. She preferred to dig up the jewels first and carry them all to Anna, throwing herself on the princess's mercy. As the voyage wore on, Roumage presented a third plan: he now wanted *her* to stay in London while *he* retrieved the jewels. Susanne tried to hold back her irritation. Each time he pressed her for the jewels' exact location in Brussels, she grew more confident in her decision to keep the information to herself.[20]

The morning after Susanne and Roumage left New York, Seely and Minister Huygens discovered they were gone. Ever since Polari's arrest, Seely had paid George Raymond, his French-speaking police marshal, to follow them both. It was likely Raymond who first realized their targets had vanished. Huygens, in particular, felt betrayed. What had happened to the diamonds Roumage showed him the day of the Customs seizure? At the time, Roumage had claimed he needed to return them to Susanne to keep her trust. Since he hadn't turned them in, Huygens could only assume Roumage had kept them for himself – a theft within a theft.

Seely hurried into the streets of New York, checking passenger lists and way-bill books for all methods of transportation in the area. He compared signatures to a handwriting sample from Roumage's 1829 arson case. The moment he saw 'Mr. Robert and lady' in the way-bill book for the mail stage, he knew he'd found them.[21]

There was no time to lose. Seely sent George Raymond by express coach to Philadelphia to track them down. There, Raymond discovered Roumage and Susanne had already left for Liverpool on the *Monongahela*. A man fitting Roumage's description had been seen walking with a crutch, 'pretending to be afflicted with the gout.' When Raymond asked how far the ship could have gone, he learned it would have just cleared the capes of the Delaware River. He hurried back to New York to strategize with Seely. By now, it was August 24; Susanne and Roumage had a head start of three to four days. But thanks to Huygens's information about the handful of diamonds Roumage had kept, Seely and Raymond had enough evidence to arrest the couple when they landed – if they could catch them. Huygens hurriedly wrote Raymond a letter of introduction for the Dutch consul in Liverpool, Daniel Willink, who could help arrange the arrest with the British police.

Seely found a packet ship leaving New York for Liverpool that very day. He dropped Raymond off at the *Sylvanus Jenkins* and spoke to Captain Francis P. Allen. He offered the captain a reward if he could reach Liverpool before the *Monongahela*. The *Sylvanus Jenkins* was four days behind the *Monongahela* on a one-month voyage. Captain Allen accepted, and launched his ship in pursuit.

As Raymond and Captain Allen sped full sail into the blue horizon, Seely and Huygens pursued the case's loose ends. Seely questioned Roumage's brothers, Frédéric and Constant, and both provided information about Roumage's past but no information about his plans once he landed in Liverpool. One day in late August, Huygens visited Polari in Bellevue. After ensuring Polari was being treated well, Huygens reached into his pocket and pulled out six gemstones, including a damaged diamond and a large sapphire: the stones Roumage had turned over before he fled. Huygens asked Polari if he recognized them. Polari did, of course. He knew they had been buried in Brooklyn, a location known only to Susanne. He had repeatedly asked her to surrender them to win his freedom – had she finally done so? Fearing a trap, he said only that he had buried all the jewels Customs didn't seize. This was new information for Huygens. The surprised minister rewarded Polari with information of his own: these stones had come from Jean Roumage. For Polari, the conclusion was inescapable. Susanne had betrayed him. While the accused man was in a vulnerable state, Huygens repeated his offer of a pardon if he went to The Hague and made a full confession.[22] Polari refused.

With little else to think about, Susanne's betrayal gripped Polari's mind. Days later, when Seely, Huygens, and Huygens's son Roger visited Bellevue, Polari refused to answer their questions. Susanne, he said, knew all his secrets. They ought to ask her anything they wanted to know. In his desperation, he railed against his lover's ingratitude. 'I rescued her from the most abject condition,' he said. 'I cured her of the most horrible diseases. I myself looked for remedies and I saved her reputation.' And now, she had proved to be 'more scheming than any other woman he had ever known.'[23]

It was now useless, Polari decided, to keep the Brooklyn burial site a secret. On September 4, 1831, he wrote to Samuel Swartwout and said he wanted to tell him where the rest of the jewels were buried – a million francs' worth, he claimed. He asked Swartwout to come immediately, bringing Eugene Bergonzio as an interpreter. The next day, Swartwout took Polari out of prison with an escort that included Huygens, his son Roger, Seely, and three police officers. Polari directed them to the outskirts of Brooklyn and led the small party 'a distance of nearly three miles by a shaded and solitary road…there they had left the causeway to enter a thick wood, situated about a hundred feet from the road…' In an overgrown thicket, Polari showed them marks he'd made on nearby trees to remember the spot. He retrieved the spade hidden in the brush, the one stolen from Du Flon's garden, and began to dig. The jewels, as he expected, were gone. As the onlookers stared at the empty depression in the earth, Polari told Seely about the hollow umbrella shaft and cane he'd used to smuggle the jewels into the country. Men from the police escort immediately went to retrieve them from Polari's room in Du Flon's hotel. They found only the cane, as Susanne and Roumage had taken the umbrella.[24]

Although the Brooklyn burial site was empty, it hadn't been a wasted trip for Samuel Swartwout. By design or accident, he overheard Huygens and Seely discussing the handful of jewels Roumage had given Huygens before leaving the city. Swartwout insisted Huygens turn them over to Customs. They had been smuggled, too, and were as subject to libel and forfeiture as the rest.

The request upset Huygens, whose goal was to recover the jewels for Anna – not give more of them to Customs. 'These articles were of the utmost importance to me,' he wrote, 'as furnishing proofs of the identity of the whole with those which had been stolen. I had…used them for that purpose in my transactions with the district attorney.'[25] He asked Secretary of State Livingston for help, and Livingston duly intervened, fending off Swartwout and US Customs by asking District Attorney James A. Hamilton to take possession instead.

It wasn't an ideal solution, but Huygens trusted Hamilton more than Swartwout and agreed to surrender the six stones to him. Swartwout immediately complained to Andrew Jackson. The president, ever ready to help his loyal supporters, took Swartwout's side. Jackson passed word through the State Department that Huygens must turn the stones over to Swartwout instead.[26] Was Jackson remembering the winter of 1830, when Huygens and his wife had found themselves enmeshed in the biggest scandal of Jackson's first term? Was he secretly pleased to thwart Huygens now? There was nothing Huygens could do but obey. Customs placed a libel on the surrendered stones, and its officers waited expectantly for the moment the jewels were declared forfeit and could be sold for a profit.

The hundred-mile-long St. George's Channel separates the east coast of Ireland from the west coast of Wales. The *Sylvanus Jenkins* and the *Monongahela* entered it at the same time. Since leaving Philadelphia, Captain Allen of the *Sylvanus Jenkins* had demolished the other ship's multi-day head start.[27] At the latitude of Dublin and Liverpool, the channel widened and both ships steered for the British port city on the right bank of the River Mersey.

The *Sylvanus Jenkins* got there first. When the ship reached Prince's Dock, police marshal George Raymond hurried to find the Dutch consul, Daniel Willink. Raymond explained why he had come and provided his letter of introduction from Minister Huygens. Quickly grasping the situation, Willink contacted the Liverpool police and procured an arrest warrant for Susanne Blanche and Jean Roumage.[28]

As Raymond worked with local authorities, Roumage and Susanne debarked as if they were casual tourists. To clear customs, the ship's staff took passengers' luggage directly to the Customs House for a clerk to examine. Meanwhile, passengers proceeded to their lodgings with their overnight bags, expecting to collect their luggage the following morning. Instead of using the cane and crutch to carry the jewels off the ship, Roumage and Susanne had bundled them into two packets, now slipped into Roumage's boots. He walked them straight to a nearby inn where he and Susanne checked in as a couple. Once inside, Roumage hid the packets on top of his bed canopy.[29]

According to Susanne, Roumage wanted to leave alone for London that very night, where he would acquire passports for Mr. & Mrs. Robert and daughter. Susanne asked how that was possible when the wife and daughter weren't with him, but Roumage insisted he knew what he was doing. Susanne held firm, however, and neither left the hotel that night. The next morning, they had to retrieve their luggage from the Customs House. They left the jewels in their room, as far from prying eyes as possible. But when they returned to the bustling Liverpool harbor and made their way to Prince's Dock, the police – with George Raymond and Consul Willink in tow – were there to arrest them.[30]

Liverpool police separated Susanne and Roumage immediately, suspecting Roumage would try to influence Susanne during questioning. If he spun a story and she stuck with it, they might never learn the location of the Brussels cache. George Raymond, who had eavesdropped on Susanne and Polari in Bellevue, knew she was the more emotionally vulnerable of the pair. Likely on his recommendation, Consul Willink focused on Susanne rather than Roumage. He reassured her that no one would press charges against her if she cooperated. He asked her to travel to The Hague, where Dutch investigators would pursue the matter further. If she did, she would be a free woman afterward. In front of Raymond, Willink, and the Liverpool Superintendant of Police, Susanne agreed to cooperate in full.

If Susanne felt betrayed when she recognized Raymond – clearly not just a Bellevue jailer – she didn't show it. She may even have been relieved to see a familiar face. It was to Raymond alone that she confessed the location of the jewels in the inn. The three men immediately escorted her back for a search. Susanne watched Raymond place a chair on a table to reach high enough to retrieve the jewels from the bed canopy. Although the men searched the rest of the room, no one found Roumage's hollow crutch, likely abandoned on the *Monongahela*. They left Susanne in possession of the hollow cane. Later that day, before the Mayor of Liverpool, Susanne affirmed that the jewels in Willink's possession had come from Polari, and she knew where more were buried in Brussels. Officer Raymond then took Susanne to London, where the Dutch ambassador, Anton Reinhard Falck, would arrange for them to be escorted to Amsterdam.[31]

Roumage wasn't questioned until the following day, September 23. He told Consul Willink he had come with Minister Huygens's full knowledge and approval. That wasn't true, but he believed it would take Willink a month to receive any word to the contrary. He didn't know that Raymond had already briefed Willink, telling him Roumage was *not* traveling with Dutch approval. Two Liverpool police officers carted Roumage to London for Ambassador Falck to deal with.[32]

With the fugitives gone, Consul Willink turned his attention to the jewels. Over the next two weeks, he created a new inventory, weighing each stone and wrapping it in cotton. He sorted the diamonds and pearls into twelve small packets, each stamped with the consulate's seal. According to Willink, package nine contained 46 large pearls, 'badly damaged from the rough way they were packed when they were delivered to me.' He placed the value of the diamonds at £15,700 and that of the pearls at £16,615. He gave the first nine bundles, holding the most valuable jewels, to his son and asked him to carry them personally to The Hague. The remaining bundles, with jewels of lesser value, went by messenger to Ambassador Falck in London.[33]

The younger Willink departed on a mail steamer on October 10. By then, both Susanne and Roumage had arrived in The Hague, where Dutch authorities eagerly awaited any information the pair could provide about the theft. Finally, it seemed, the royal family and the public would have the answers they sought. Dutch politician Jacob van Zuylen van Nijevelt wrote to a colleague, 'It is extremely fortunate that the truth will finally be known in a conspiracy that, like the necklace of the Queen Marie Antoinette, I believe aimed at discrediting an illustrious character. The Orange sun shines brightly.'[34] The complete rehabilitation of Willem's reputation seemed near at hand.

When Susanne Blanche arrived in The Hague, officers of the Minister of Justice escorted her to the Groot-Keizershof Hotel in Buitenhof Square, near government offices. British tourists visiting The Hague were told the hotel was 'much frequented by the members of the States-General, distinguished families, or single gentlemen, for whom it is peculiarly well adapted by its large or small apartments.'[35] Susanne was likely given one of those small apartments, at government expense.

When Roumage arrived, no one made him the offer of eventual freedom in return for his cooperation. Dutch officials locked him in the house of civil and military detention in The Hague, where his first interrogation took place on October 8. During the trip from Liverpool, Roumage had decided on a defense strategy: blame Susanne. He claimed any jewels found in Liverpool had been carried there by Susanne and Susanne alone. The hollow umbrella had been hers, he said, and he knew nothing about what may have been stored in her trunk.[36]

Roumage did not, however, plead ignorance when it came to Polari. He knew the Dutch desperately wanted to prove Polari's guilt and he promptly told investigators how he could help. Polari, he said, must have had help executing the theft. 'I am sure,' he wrote, 'it would be easy for me to get to know his accomplices.'[37] The Dutch did not take him up on his offer.

When the authorities failed to see him as the injured party, he emphasized his role as an informant, accusing Consul Zimmerman and Minister Huygens of everything from incompetence to corruption. If the situation had been mismanaged, it was their fault. He insisted he had not only discovered the jewels, but arrested Polari. Roumage performed his one-man-act of mock offense so well that the authorities began to reconsider what might have happened. From his cell, Roumage wove a tapestry of words that he hoped would secure not only his release, but the reward he felt he was owed. A glittering future was still within his grasp – if he kept his wits about him.

Chapter 15

Law and Disorder

Minister Huygens now found himself in a difficult position. As the senior representative of the Netherlands in America, all official communication regarding Polari's case had to go through him. He had become part lawyer, part prosecutor, and part public relations specialist in his effort to do the one thing his country had asked of him: get Polari and the jewels back. He did this knowing he and his wife were at the heart of a scandal that had inflamed American politics – and Andrew Jackson's temper. Luckily, his friend Martin Van Buren had remained an advisor to Jackson after his resignation as Secretary of State, putting in a good word for Huygens when he could. But even Van Buren couldn't persuade Jackson to turn over Polari or the jewels. Jackson wrote, 'Mr. Hyggens [sic] has no right to make reclamation for Belgium…the court must decide the facts…'[1] But which court?

In the fall of 1831, Polari's lawyers requested a hearing before the Recorder of the State of New York, Richard Riker. As judge of the Courts of General and Special Sessions, the Recorder had the authority to rule on the legality of Polari's imprisonment and Governor Throop's extradition mandate. Polari's lawyers hoped to prove he was being held illegally and, at the same time, could not be extradited. If they succeeded, the New York authorities would have no choice but to set Polari free.

But Richard Riker had his own history with one of the case's famous names. Almost thirty years earlier, Riker, a supporter of Alexander Hamilton, had fought a duel with Samuel Swartwout's brother, a supporter of Aaron Burr. Swartwout's brother shot Riker in the leg, leaving him with a permanent limp.[2] Riker could not have been unaware that his former enemy's brother was the driving force behind Customs' attempt to steer Polari's case.

Perhaps the poorly mended tissues of Riker's leg pulsed with a distant ache that day. Or maybe he truly believed New York's governor had the power to do what the president did not. Riker ruled that Throop's extradition mandate was legal. Neither the president nor the Constitution held such power so it must, by default, lie with the states.[3] It was exactly what Huygens wanted to hear, even if Riker couldn't negate the Customs case against Polari for smuggling. Encouraged, Huygens forwarded Riker's opinion to Secretary of State Livingston. He asked again for Jackson to intervene and return Anna's jewels to their rightful owner.

But letting go of the jewels was the one thing Samuel Swartwout refused to do. He earned nothing by returning them, as opposed to the profit he would make if the jewels were condemned as forfeit and sold. He launched a two-pronged attack designed to prevent anyone else from influencing Polari's case. First, he recruited an ally: his new boss, Secretary of the Treasury Louis McLane, promoted from the diplomatic corps after the great Cabinet shake-up. Swartwout and McLane were close, professionally and personally, and Swartwout submitted a report that, according to Huygens, was based on 'inexact, if not false' information on the legality of extradition. Just as Swartwout hoped, McLane took his side.[4]

Swartwout then set his sights on District Attorney James A. Hamilton. He prodded Hamilton to declare the seized jewels as forfeit, clearing the way for their sale. But Hamilton believed the jewels were Anna's, as Constantia Huygens had testified. An angry Swartwout gave Hamilton 'an emphatic denial.'[5] Meanwhile, one of Swartwout's employees, Customs Surveyor Mordecai M. Noah, published an article attacking Hamilton. When more character attacks surfaced in public and private, all launched by Customs officers, Hamilton realized Swartwout had declared a public relations war against him. He warned Treasury Secretary McLane that 'the honor of the country would be stained' if the jewels were appropriated and sold for personal profit.[6]

But McLane remained firmly on Swartwout's side. As a delaying tactic, he created an extra layer of bureaucratic red tape for Hamilton. If Hamilton wanted the jewels returned to the Dutch, he must 'appear for the Prince of Orange as owner and claimant.' Hamilton duly prepared a claim on Willem's behalf and forwarded it to Andrew Jackson. The jewels, he argued, would have been forfeit if they had belonged to Polari, but they didn't, so the US had no claim to them. The evidence proved 'these jewels were those which had belonged to the Princess of Orange, and that they ought to be restored to her.'[7] Any further delay risked the country's reputation.

Now pressed by both Hamilton and Secretary of State Livingston, Andrew Jackson took the matter to his Cabinet Council on November 9. Was it time, he asked, to intervene? But Secretary of the Treasury McLane had come prepared. He argued that an act of Congress passed on March 3, 1797 gave the Secretary of the Treasury – and *only* the Secretary of the Treasury – the power to 'mitigate or remit' any 'fine, forfeiture or penalty' in Customs cases.[8] No one was willing to argue against an act of Congress and McLane's argument carried the day. The president, his Cabinet informed him, was powerless.

Susanne Blanche's first interrogation in the Netherlands took place four days after she and Roumage were arrested in Liverpool. On September 27, Minister of Justice van Maanen sent a senior secretary, C. Asser, to perform the first in a long series of interviews. In her room at the Keizershof, Asser asked Susanne 36 pre-written questions in French and transcribed her answers. When he asked about the whereabouts of the jewels buried outside Brussels, she told him they were locked in a box in a location known only to her and Polari. She believed there were cameos and portraits of Anna's family inside. Asser also asked if she owned any diamonds or precious stones. She showed him her diamond ring and a buckle with diamonds on the clasp, both gifts from Polari. Asser confiscated them. When she had answered all 36 questions, he asked her to review and sign the transcript.[9]

Susanne and Asser repeated this process every few days, with lists of two to 48 questions per visit. Over the course of sixteen interrogations between September 27, 1831 and May 28, 1832, Susanne Blanche answered 424 questions. Isolated, in a country where she knew no one, she realized her best hope for the future was to ingratiate herself with the Dutch. She turned over the brown silk umbrella with a hollow shaft as evidence. By the seventh interrogation, perhaps realizing the process would take longer than expected, Dutch officials moved her to the Imperial Crown Inn. There, she destroyed her letters from Polari, severing one of her last connections to him.[10]

About three hundred meters north of Susanne's hotel lay Kneuterdijk Palace, nestled in the curve of a street that bore its name. Willem and Anna's home had a modest two-story ornamented brick façade in classic French style, with seventeen arched windows overlooking the street. Inside, it held a neoclassical ballroom with white columns, white salons with ornate chandeliers, Willem's red study with its dark coffered ceiling, and of course, Anna's Russian chapel. In the early days of their marriage, Willem had doubted the palace could hold all of Anna's enormous trousseau. But on October 15, 1831, Anna was only concerned with the contents of two canvas bags in the hands of Willem Willink, son of the Dutch consul in Liverpool.

At 11 a.m., a small group gathered inside the palace to see what those bags held, including Willem Willink, Minister of Justice van Maanen, Attorney General Philipse, Anna, her secretary Schultz, her chambermaid Natalia, her grand mistress Baroness van Nagell, and her chamberlain Baron van Nagell. Willink set the canvas bags on a table and turned the procedure over to Van Maanen. One by one, the Minister of Justice removed nine sealed packages from the bags, broke their seals, and revealed the contents. It was the first time Anna had seen any of her stolen jewels since they vanished.

Sparkling brilliants. Creamy pearls. Handfuls of smaller stones, pried from their settings in earrings, necklaces, bracelets, brooches, and tiaras. If touching the battered remnants of her jewels disturbed Anna, she didn't show it. She and her ladies sifted through them to identify square-, pear-, and oval-shaped diamonds from Anna's 'grand diademe en brillans,' depicted in her portrait by Van der Hulst. Of the 59 large pearls, Anna recognized about thirty of them from a necklace Willem had given her. Seven pear-shaped pearls had come from a comb, eleven were from a Sévigné brooch, and one very large pearl from the clasp of a diamond and turquoise bracelet. Many of the smaller pearls had once encrusted two jeweled fleurs-de-lis. The women also found blue-hued pearls, once mounted with diamonds, that Anna had inherited from her mother.

Van Maanen authorized Anna to keep the jewels, but asked her to leave them in their current state. If they were able to put Polari on trial, the jewels might be needed as evidence.[11] To Anna, they were a different kind of evidence – that of a past life, before her brother and mother had died, before her husband was blamed for the theft, before a revolution drove them from their home. Perhaps leaving them alone was not such a hard decision to make.

Her father-in-law, King Willem I, had not come to Kneuterdijk Palace that day. The older man remained at his desk, doing the paperwork required to keep the Dutch army mobilized at the southern border. He still refused to back down in the face of pressure from the Great Powers. Of the five, Russia was the only one that hadn't recognized Leopold as King of the Belgians. As long as there was a holdout among the Great Powers, the Dutch king had something to cling to. But even that last sliver of support was soon to vanish. In February of 1832, Nicholas I sent an emissary to The Hague to persuade King Willem to accept the Twenty-Four Articles. The Russian emperor had decided to recognize Leopold, and he now urged his sister's father-in-law to do the same.[12]

Back in America, Minister Huygens had received permission from King Willem I to return home for a leave of absence. His son, 26-year-old Roger, would stay in America as interim chargé d'affaires. Huygens didn't want his son to inherit Polari as a problem, but there seemed to be no way to extricate Polari or the jewels before he went home.

To try and create a break in the case, Huygens sent Roger to offer Polari another pardon. As before, it required him to come to The Hague for a public confession, after which he would be pardoned for any 'crime of larceny' having to do with Willem and Anna's property.[13] But as he read the text, Polari suspected a trap. According to him, newspapers had said the theft was committed by breaking and entering, not larceny. Was the language of the pardon meant to trick him? He told his lawyers he would only accept the pardon if he were allowed to make revisions. But when the updated version didn't include his changes, he refused to sign, preferring to shiver in Bellevue rather than trust anything proffered by Huygens.

On January 5, 1832, Minister Huygens took his son Roger to Washington to present him to President Andrew Jackson as his interim successor.[14] This handover officially made Roger the top-ranking Dutch diplomat in the United States. His father would remain in America for another month as he finalized his travel plans, but Roger was the new face of the Dutch fight to extradite Polari and claim the jewels. In the end, he would resort to measures as illegal as the theft itself to achieve his ends.

❖

With no heating, the cells in Bellevue were brutally cold during the long winter of 1831-2. Although Polari had a room to himself and food and wine provided by Joseph Collet, confinement took its inevitable toll. His incredible strength diminished and his stocky frame began to shrink. His mind, however, remained active. Later, he would claim he had learned how to open his cell, sliding his arm out the food delivery slot and using a spoon handle to open the lock. One night, he said, a jailer saw him walking up and down the corridor. Polari hurried back to his cell, and when questioned, insisted the jailer must be joking. He was more careful after that.[15]

Perhaps inevitably, Polari began thinking of escape. In January of 1832, he and two prisoners condemned to death for murder decided to give it a try. One of the men, a clockmaker, asked Polari to bring him a clock or a watch. Polari requested one from Collet, and gave it to his partner in crime. The clockmaker opened the watch, removed the spring, and used it to create a tiny saw. The three men passed it between them, slowly filing through the iron bars over their windows. They were not the first to have attempted such an escape. Other prisoners likely remembered that, in 1830, ten men had escaped from the southeast room of the second story by sawing off the same iron bars, creating an opening ten inches wide, and descending twenty feet to the ground with blankets tied together.[16]

That January, Polari filed through one bar after another. The work was tedious: file, brush away the filings, remove successive bars to test the width available for an escape, and replace the bars quickly when footsteps sounded in the corridor. He succeeded in sawing through three bars, with his jailers none the wiser. The space was almost wide enough for his shoulders to pass through – just one more bar would likely do it. Then, one night, when he was about to pull the fourth bar free, he knocked at least one of the other bars into the yard below. The echoing clang roused the night watchman. Seconds later, all of Bellevue was on high alert. Guards made a new head count and searched every room.[17]

When the guards realized what Polari had done, they transferred him downstairs, into a small cell that was eight feet long and six feet wide.[18] This cell had no table or chair. Christiaan and Roger Huygens offered to bring him replacements, but Polari refused. He still had food and wine, faithfully supplied by Joseph Collet, one of his few approved visitors. Collet remained his lifeline, connecting him to New York's immigrant community, which had begun to take an interest in his case. After all, if Polari could be held indefinitely while the state and federal government bickered over his fate, couldn't the same thing happen to them?

As the day of Minister Huygens's departure neared, Polari and the jewels remained mired in a bureaucratic hellscape. However, Secretary of State Livingston believed he'd finally found a way to release the jewels. Working with Attorney General Taney, he proposed Jackson issue a *nolle prosequi* – a legal notice of intent not to prosecute – for the smuggling charge against Polari. That would free the jewels from libel so they could be returned to the Dutch.[19] By the end of December, they had Jackson's approval, but on January 1, Treasury Secretary McLane argued (again) that Jackson had no power to intervene. Frustrated with McLane and Swartwout's delaying tactics, the trio of Livingston, Taney, and James A. Hamilton united to convince Jackson to act. It was unthinkable that the American government would seize and sell gems stolen from the ruling family of a friendly nation.

Finally, Jackson agreed. He decided to offer Roger Huygens two options. 'I will grant a pardon,' he wrote, 'and leave both its effect & the ultimate disposition of the property seized to the judgment of the court; or I will direct the atto. for the District, to enter a *nolle prosequi*, without further order…'[20] Since either option freed the jewels from forfeit, Roger chose the *nolle prosequi*, likely not wanting his quarry to have a pardon from another country. James A. Hamilton completed the paperwork and ordered the jewels delivered to Roger's father before his departure. Secretary of State Livingston included a note of apology:

The President desires me to assure you that he regrets the delay that has taken place, which has arisen from a necessary caution not to interfere in the decision of a judiciary, and he hopes that in the determination to which he has now come, you will see a new evidence of the desire he has always felt to show his respect for the King your Sovereign...[21]

Almost six months after their seizure, the jewels were released from Mechanics' Bank. On January 21, 1832, Marshal William Coventry Waddell delivered them to Seely, Huygens's attorney. Waddell opened the box in Seely's presence, with clerks and jewelers on hand to inventory the contents. Once the jewels were appraised and bonded, the clerks re-sealed the box, bound it with orange ribbon, and applied four stamps for delivery to the departing Dutch minister.[22] Huygens took possession of the jewels on January 31, his last full day in New York. He offered his 'sincere thanks' to Hamilton for his help. Hamilton, glad to be rid of the jewels, called the whole affair a 'most laborious and vexatious business.'[23]

That night, Huygens met with Seely for the last time. The two had never discussed payment, but now, Huygens thanked Seely for his dedication and suggested the Dutch government's reward go to him. Seely replied that he wanted no reward, but would accept the same amount offered as a fee for services. He submitted a list of expenses, which Huygens agreed to pay. Both agreed that the issue of 'fees and remunerations' should wait until the 'promised reward should be decided.'[24]

On February 1, 1832, Christiaan Bangeman Huygens signed a deputation making his son the rightful wielder of the power conferred on him by Governor Throop's extradition mandate. He also agreed on the sum to be paid to Seely. Finally, all loose ends tied, Christiaan, Constantia, and his three unmarried daughters set sail in the packet ship *Columbia* for London. Huygens departed knowing that his unintentional participation in the Eaton Affair hadn't damaged his country's standing with Jackson, and he could hold his head high when he knelt before Anna and presented her with the recovered gems.

Chapter 16

A Hero, a Spy, and a Scoundrel

After escorting Susanne Blanche to The Hague, New York police marshal George B. Raymond found himself face-to-face with the Netherlands' Minister of Justice, Cornelis Felix van Maanen. The powerful Dutch minister had a new job for him: retrieving the last cache of buried jewels from Belgium. If all went well, the job would be relatively simple. He would pose as a tourist, dig up the jewels without being seen, and smuggle them across the border into the Netherlands. If a Dutch officer attempted the task and got caught, he would be arrested as a spy or executed outright. An American stood a better chance of being treated fairly if something went wrong.

Raymond took the job on one condition: the Dutch must help provide for his wife and children during his absence. Van Maanen obliged, and Roger Huygens paid a monthly stipend to Raymond's family while he was gone.[1] The Dutch gave Raymond everything he needed to plan the mission, including a letter of credit at Rothschild & Co. and letters of introduction with safe conduct passes for 'the first houses of Holland, France, Germany, and England…'[2] Should the mission go awry, Raymond would be able to get help in nearby countries.

Raymond's path lay between two hostile armies, the Dutch at Groot-Zundert and the Belgians at Wuustwezel. He would have to slip past them both. On January 4, 1832, the Dutch States General had voted to keep the army in a state of readiness for the entire year. The Belgians had little choice but to do the same. Citizens and soldiers of both countries remained on edge. Travelers crossing the border described their carriages being 'constantly stopped by some official or other' with requirements to show a passport. When the daughter of a British diplomat crossed from Belgium into the Netherlands, 'three soldiers were drawn up on the side of the road with muskets pointed at us.'[3] Just a few years later, in 1836, a Dutch traveler crossing the border jumped when he heard 'the discharge of artillery on the city walls,' imagining

Right: Anna Pavlovna, Princess of Orange painted by Jean Baptiste van der Hulst in 1829, the year of the jewel theft. (Public domain via Wikimedia Commons)

Below left: Emperor Alexander I, Anna's oldest brother. He suggested Anna as a bride for Prince Willem of Orange. (Unknown artist. Courtesy of the Digital National Museum in Warsaw)

Below right: King Willem I of the United Kingdom of the Netherlands in 1819, four years after his inauguration. (Painting by Joseph Paelinck. Courtesy Rijksmuseum, Amsterdam)

Above left: Prince Willem of Orange, later King Willem II. Brussels gossip targeted him as a suspect in the jewel theft. (Anonymous print after painting by Cornelis Kruseman, c. 1831. Courtesy Rijksmuseum, Amsterdam)

Above right: Emperor Nicholas I, Anna's brother and fellow Triopathy member. (Unknown artist. Courtesy of the Digital National Museum in Warsaw)

Willem, Anna and their four children, from left to right: Willem (the future Willem III), Alexander, Willem (the future Willem II), Anna, Sophie, and Hendrik. (After a painting by Jean Baptiste van der Hulst. Courtesy Rijksmuseum, Amsterdam)

Above: 'The Battle of Waterloo' by J.W. Pieneman (1824). Wellington is in the center, receiving news that the Prussians are on the way. Prince Willem of Orange is in the left foreground, already wounded and about to be transported off the field. (Courtesy Rijksmuseum, Amsterdam)

Below: Drawing of Anna's palace that accompanied a 2-volume publication of case documents. This drawing illustrates the earthen terrace connecting the palace to the side street by which the thief approached and departed. (Unknown artist. Published in *Procès de Constant Polari, Deuxième Partie*; see bibliography for full details)

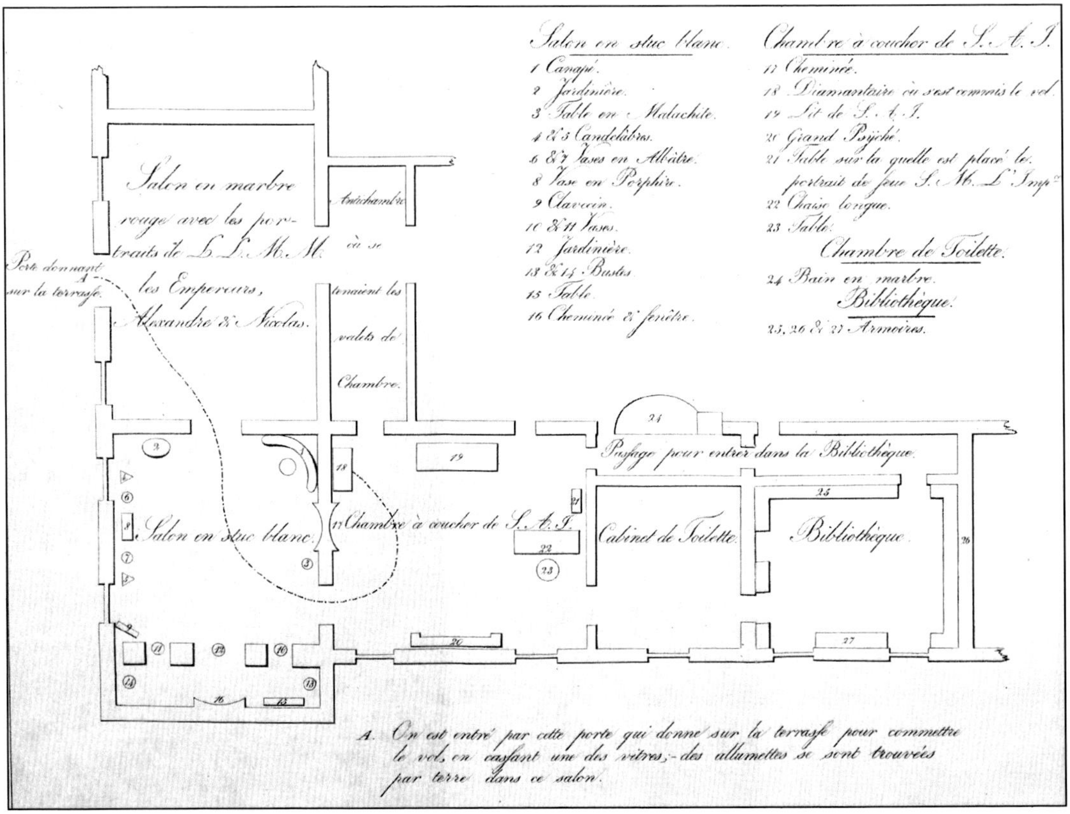

Drawing of the thief's route inside the palace that accompanied a 2-volume publication of case documents. This drawing shows the thief's entry through the Red Marble Room and passage through a white salon into Anna's bedroom. (Unknown artist. Published in *Procès de Constant Polari, Deuxième Partie*; see bibliography for full details)

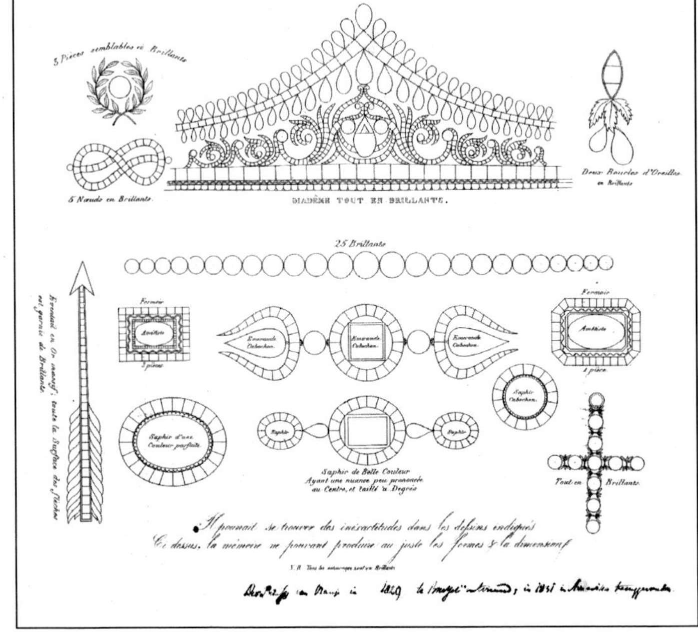

Drawing of some of Anna's missing jewels, including the 'grand diademe en brillans' she wore in an 1829 portrait by Jean Baptiste van der Hulst. By the time she received the finished portrait, the tiara was gone. (Unidentified print maker, possibly Johannes Paulus Houtman. Courtesy Rijksmuseum, Amsterdam)

Above left: Drawing of Constant Polari dated to 1835, after he was convicted for the jewel theft. (Print by Jean Zacherie Mazel. Courtesy Rijksmuseum, Amsterdam)

Above right: Cornelis Felix van Maanen, King Willem I's feared Minister of Justice. (Anonymous print. Courtesy Rijksmuseum, Amsterdam)

Right: President Andrew Jackson. The Eaton Affair, jewel theft, and extradition of Polari took place during his first term. He served two terms total, from 1829–1837. (Painting by Thomas Sully (1845). Courtesy National Gallery of Art, Washington, DC)

John Eaton, Jackson's friend and first Secretary of War. When his wife was ostracized by Washington's society leaders, Jackson defended her fiercely, triggering a Cabinet crisis. (Drawn and engraved by J.B. Longacre. Courtesy The New York Public Library)

Above left: Martin Van Buren, Jackson's friend and first Secretary of State. Proud of his Dutch ancestry, he befriended Minister Huygens and his family and enjoyed speaking Dutch with them. (Engraving by John Sartain. Courtesy The New York Public Library)

Above right: Edward Livingston, Jackson's second Secretary of State. His prior work on the Louisiana criminal code earned praise from King Willem I and Emperor Nicholas I. (Engraving by E. Wellmore from a drawing by J.B. Longacre. Courtesy The New York Public Library)

Above: Du Flon's Military Garden, a Brooklyn landmark later remembered by Walt Whitman. (Unsigned print c. 1843. Courtesy The New York Public Library)

Right: Anna commissioned this painting for Willem to take with him during the Ten Days' Campaign. The inscription at top left reads: 'Better a cabin with my Willem than subject to dishonor.' (Painting by Cornelis Kruseman c. 1831, public domain, courtesy RKD Research)

Two of Anna's gold-and-turquoise bracelets, bearing the names 'Anne' and 'Guillaume,' c. 1822. From a thief's point of view, customized jewelry like this (often containing initials, portraits, and human hair) was less desirable than tiaras, necklaces, and brooches with large stones that could easily be removed for quick sale. (Photo by Jane023, public domain via Wikimedia Commons)

Willem and Anna's palace today, now called Palace of the Academies. It houses Belgium's Royal Academy of Science and Arts and the Royal Academy of Medicine. (Photo by Romaine, public domain via Wikimedia Commons)

the long-anticipated attack had begun.[4] It was ceremonial fire, announcing the birth of Prince Frederik's son, but his reaction proved the threat of an attack was constant and real.

If Raymond made it across the border, he needed to know exactly where to go. For this, he turned to Susanne Blanche. She helped him map out a route to the corner of the Saint-Josse-ten-Noode cemetery in the Brussels suburb of Schaerbeek. With safe conduct passes in hand and the location pinpointed, Raymond waited for the go-ahead from Van Maanen. The timing had to be right, since armies were drilling, training, and moving in the border area. Finally, the Dutch sent him off in mid-January with the names of two secret agents in Belgium who would help him. Raymond traveled 110 miles from The Hague to Brussels, where he made contact with Van Maanen's 'trusted persons.'[5]

On January 17, 1832, the trio made their way to the walled cemetery of Saint-Josse-ten-Noode. Inside, stone pathways led visitors past graves and monuments, sheltered between hedgerows and stands of cypress and yew trees. Using Susanne's directions, Raymond located the section of the cemetery wall Polari had chosen in 1831. He must have been confident in his agents' abilities to turn away curious bystanders. They started digging at 8 a.m., without waiting for the cover of darkness.

The first few hours yielded nothing. The men dug deeper and further, likely wondering if Susanne had been mistaken or had lied to them. It took six full hours for their effort to be rewarded. At 2 p.m., one of their shovels struck something hard. Scrabbling with their hands to find the object's edges, they uncovered a square object two feet beneath the foundation of the cemetery wall, a total of six feet below the surface. Just as Susanne had described, it was a box made of sheet metal or beaten iron. Though a thick layer of clay clung to the metal, Raymond saw the glimmer of gold through a gash in the metal. He removed the box carefully as the other men dug, still searching for other boxes. When nothing new turned up at a depth of eight feet, they knew there was nothing left to find.[6]

There was no time to examine the box's contents. The three men simply tried to protect the exposed objects, which turned out to be cameos covered in mud. Reaching through the gash in the metal, Raymond folded cotton cloth around the visible cameos, then stuffed the box with more cotton to seal the gap. One man produced a large white handkerchief, which they tied around the box. All three men stamped wax seals, imprinted with their initials, onto the handkerchief.

Raymond left for The Hague that evening. He later described this return trip as difficult and dangerous. According to the *Poughkeepsie Journal*, in crossing the frontier between Holland and Belgium, he was severely wounded by a horseman who slashed at his head with a saber, supposing him to be a spy.[7] Injuries notwithstanding, Raymond arrived in The Hague on January 21 at 9 p.m. and reported straight to Van Maanen. When the much-feared Minister of Justice complimented his work, Raymond responded with a stroke of diplomacy worthy of Chevalier Huygens. He credited his success to the confidence the royal family and government officers had bestowed on him.[8]

Four days later, Raymond delivered his handkerchief-wrapped box to Anna personally. He accompanied Van Maanen and Attorney General Philipse to Kneuterdijk Palace, where Anna had assembled the same group of staff and courtiers to inspect what was left of her jewels. Once Raymond turned over the box, Anna verified the seals were intact and gave Van Maanen permission to break them.

Van Maanen untied the white handkerchief and lifted the lid of the box, flaking bits of dried Belgian mud onto the table and floor. Beneath the carefully folded cotton lay 31 loose cameos representing members of the Russian imperial family, one small damaged opal, and three larger cameos with portraits of Catherine the Great and Paul I. Together, Anna and her courtiers identified the 31 cameos as belonging to a parure that had once contained a tiara, a chain, a necklace, two clasps, and earrings. The single opal had once been part of a parure as well. After carefully removing these items, Van Maanen revealed a tangled mass of intact settings, broken settings, broken bits of jewels, and a few pieces that had managed to survive. The rest of the items in the box required careful washing and sorting to identify.

Natalia Petrovna Chernysheva took the lead in pairing items from the wreckage to the list of missing jewels. She identified a bracelet with portraits and the hair of Anna's parents, the tip of a diamond and turquoise arrow, a gold bracelet with Nicholas I's portrait engraved on amethyst, and two bracelets with the initials and hair of King Willem I and Queen Wilhelmina and their children. She also identified fragments of Anna's large tiara, and the remnants of two golden fans. Some of the settings were so damaged it was impossible to guess what they had once held. Nineteen surrounds, however, were in good condition, including one for the sapphire of 'parfait couleur.' After an exhaustive comparison, Anna and her ladies identified the remnants of thirty items. Fragments of her bejeweled floral bouquet lay gouged and broken. A handful of tiny diamonds, rubies, and emeralds clung to their settings, overlooked by the thief's prying knives.[9]

At that moment, no one in the Netherlands knew that Christiaan Bangeman Huygens was about to take possession of the jewels seized by US Customs. Thinking she might still have to prove they belonged to her, Anna gave Van Maanen permission to send the nineteen recognizable settings to America with Raymond. If American authorities needed further proof the jewels were hers, all they had to do was re-insert the stones into their settings.[10] Like Cinderella's glass slipper, a perfect fit indicated ownership. Anna also agreed to leave the rest of the day's findings in their current state as evidence.

To thank George Raymond for his help, Anna and Willem wrote him a personal letter, enclosed with a pin for himself and diamond ring for his wife.[11] He left the Netherlands in February, a hero to everyone except one man. Still imprisoned in The Hague, Jean Roumage fumed against Raymond for his influence on Susanne. It was Raymond who had convinced Susanne to cooperate with the authorities, he decided. On February 13, he wrote to Attorney General Philipse and retracted his statement in Liverpool, where he had blamed Susanne for the whole caper. All he wanted, he said, was to help a weak woman escape a terrifying man. If he had pursued the reward from Huygens, he had done so to start a new life with Susanne and Rosine. 'Everything would have happened like this,' he wrote, 'without the intervention of Mr. Raymond, who sullied this unfortunate woman with his perfidious advice. This is what I had to confess, what weighed on my heart...'[12] Like Polari, Roumage held himself blameless in his version of events.

George Raymond arrived in New York near the end of March 1832, on board the *York*. He told his colleagues about his adventures and showed them the rewards he'd received. A bitter Samuel Swartwout described him as the 'bosom friend of the King of Holland.'[13] Swartwout claimed Raymond had said the Dutch government authorized him to pay any claims against the jewels and given him $30,000. Swartwout couldn't believe that a mere police marshal would have been given such authority. He wrote to a Treasury official in Washington and asked him to find out the truth. Raymond was 'causing the whole affair to be blown & the honest Prince & Princess to get their own again. Go this thing, heavy, powerful, *strong*!' Jackson, he finished, had always intended '*we* should be paid.'[14]

Raymond had indeed come home with more than a letter, pin, and ring – but not with the authority to pay claims. If he did bring funds from the Netherlands, that money would have been turned over to the Dutch legation, which, as would soon be made clear, was the only authorized source for reimbursing claims. What Raymond *did* have was the offer of a royal pardon for Polari. Excited, Polari said he would accept as long as he could read it and ensure it was signed by Roger Huygens. But when Raymond brought the pardon to Roger, the diplomat refused to sign. He believed the pardon his father had offered on the day of Polari's arrest was still valid.[15]

Neither Polari nor Raymond gave up on the idea of a pardon. When Polari said he would accept the edited draft he'd provided in November, Raymond promised to do what he could. He went so far as to gather the Recorder and a Supreme Court judge at City Hall, where Polari appeared with two witnesses. But, in the Recorder's office, Polari once again found problems with the document. It contained 'articles and reservations that made it null and void, and that pardon had a particular seal, and not the seal of the [Dutch] legation…I did not want to accept it.'[16] Instead, Polari begged Raymond to take a letter from him to Willem and Anna, a letter in which he begged for forgiveness. He claimed he felt a duty to them and wanted to be done with America. As he wrote, 'despite all the fine laws of the Americans, their freedom and their independence, I was detained worse than in the inquisition in Spain, without examination and without trial.'[17] What more did Polari think Willem and Anna could do when they had already sent a royal pardon? He blamed America when the police escorted him back to Bellevue and his jailer closed and locked his cell once more.

❖

The pardon had failed, by fumble or design, but Roger Huygens was still determined to extradite Polari. He suspected someone close to Polari was feeding him information about legal strategy: language to watch out for, seals on documents, and the like. But who? In late February or early March, Roger decided to hire a spy to gather information from Polari's friends in Joseph Collet's boarding house.

He found the right man for the job in Jacob de Brauw. A Dutch immigrant left unemployed by the Belgian revolution, De Brauw had sailed from Helvotsluys the previous fall. When the *Hercules* docked in New York, De Brauw had debarked into a city full of snow, mud, and ankle-deep mire, frozen hard in the sub-zero temperature. With a letter of recommendation from a relative of Constantia Huygens, De Brauw had made contact with both Consul Zimmerman and Minister Huygens. Since then, he'd had no luck finding a suitable and profitable job. But when Roger offered him the job of informant, De Brauw hesitated. He was there to find honest work, not act as a spy. But, out of loyalty to the Netherlands and the House of Orange, he accepted. In mid-March, he moved into Joseph Collet's boarding house.

The residents at the time made an interesting group. They included a former governor of Mexico with his family, a colonel from Guatemala, a former Cabinet secretary of Napoleon, a Sardinian native who became a member of the Italian carbonari, and a handful of immigrants from Great Britain and other American states.[18] It wasn't long before the boarding house's occupants took a fellow European into their confidence. When De Brauw mentioned Polari, many residents remembered him – and the fact that he had beaten Susanne. But they were skeptical about a new rumor that he'd murdered the accomplice who helped him steal the jewels so he could abscond with them. When Collet told Polari about the rumor, Polari responded with a written denial that a boarding house friend translated into English and sent to a newspaper for publication.

In reporting back to Roger Huygens, De Brauw named Collet as Polari's most active defender. Collet had free access to Polari in the penitentiary, a ready channel to carry messages from the outside world. That April, however, Collet complained Bellevue staff repeatedly denied him access to Polari. He even published a transcript of one such attempt with Taylor, the deputy keeper at the penitentiary.[19] New York's immigrant community, it seemed, had learned the power of the press.

The last thing Roger Huygens wanted was for Polari's case to receive more attention. He turned to Seely for help. At Seely's request, Bellevue warden George B. Thorp published a notice that Polari's 'friends have always had free access to him – he has lived well – daily having his wine – and has been permitted to have every indulgence consistent with his safe custody. – Since his attempt to escape, greater restraint has been deemed necessary – but he suffers for nothing.'[20] If Collet had been turned away, the article noted, it was at Polari's request. This response helped dim the public's interest in Polari. Between his multiple refusals of a valid pardon, his violence toward Susanne, and his frequent outbursts toward visitors like Seely and Roger Huygens, Jacob de Brauw realized the man would likely turn on even his closest supporters. Polari's personality was full of 'unbridled passion' which was too far 'beyond reason' to control.[21] In other words, he was – and would always be – his own worst enemy.

On March 18, 1832, Polari's former conspirator, Roudez, wrote a letter to Prince Willem of Orange. He said he remembered the jewel theft from the newspapers and had kept it in mind during his subsequent travels. Now, nearly three years later, he had vital information to share. Three thieves had stolen the jewels, he wrote, but one was dead, which left only two to track down. The jewels, he wrote, have been 'for the most part buried; they must be unearthed before the men. If not, these objects will be buried forever.' With 'secrecy, patience and money,' he offered to continue his investigation.[22] To keep his family uninvolved, he requested a reply via *poste restante* in Lyon. He signed himself as Roudez, jewelry merchant. He said nothing about his past association with Polari.

The letter was ignored.

Chevalier Christiaan Bangeman Huygens finally set foot on Dutch soil on April 4, after completing the quarantine required due to cholera's recent spread. He immediately set out for The Hague with Anna's jewels.[23] This third and final unboxing took place on April 9 on 10 a.m. at Kneuterdijk Palace, with the same cast in attendance and the same procedures followed. This time, the recovered jewels included a 64-carat sapphire (the one Roumage had given Huygens before sailing to Liverpool), a 162-carat sapphire, 18 topazes, 118 emeralds, 221 turquoises, 63 amethysts, and two tin boxes of pearls, many of which Anna identified on sight thanks to their bluish color. She also recognized sixteen peridots from her mother, a carnelian from a talisman bracelet, a brooch that had been a gift from her sons, and a gold buckle with pearls and diamonds that had been a gift from her mother in 1825. Still missing was one of two very large pear-shaped pearl earrings.[24]

After delivering the jewels, Huygens was finally able to speak to Van Maanen and other government officials in person. For the first time, he heard the lies Roumage had told about working with Huygens and Zimmerman to find the jewels and capture Polari. Huygens set them straight. Not only had Roumage lied, but Huygens believed he should be prosecuted for the handful of Anna's diamonds he'd had in his possession *before* the Customs seizure. The problem, Huygens learned, was that he himself had allowed Roumage to retain possession of those diamonds. Even though he'd done it hoping that Roumage would lead him to more of the jewels, his actions presented a problem for the prosecution. In the end, Roumage was too slippery to trap and Dutch authorities released him for lack of evidence. Instead of having the good sense to vanish, Roumage petitioned for the reward money until Dutch authorities tossed him out of the country.[25]

Although torturous at times, the jewel recovery process didn't affect the diplomatic relationship between the United States and the Netherlands. In May, shortly after the last of the jewels had been returned, Martin Van Buren visited the Netherlands for several weeks. He traveled to Amsterdam with his old friend Chevalier Huygens and America's diplomatic representative in the country, Major Auguste Davizac. King Willem I greeted Van Buren warmly. He regaled Van Buren with the story of a historic Dutch Minister of Foreign Affairs of the same name, suggesting the two must be related. Because one of the king's own titles was 'Count Buren,' derived from a former earldom near Utrecht, King Willem hinted that the Van Burens and the Orange family might be related, too. The patriotic Van Buren felt 'no temptation' to 'claim family relationship' with the royal family or the Counts Buren.[26]

Chapter 17

Cholera

Avid readers of American newspapers knew a deadly outbreak of cholera had appeared in eastern Europe in the fall of 1830. Isolated cases of *cholera morbus* were nothing new, but this was something different. Reports from Russia warned the disease was 'prevailing to a most lamentable extent' in St. Petersburg. Less than a year later, in June of 1831, it killed Anna's brother Constantine in present-day Belarus. European countries took quarantine precautions, but the so-called 'Asiatic' or 'foreign' cholera proceeded westward at a steady pace.[1]

Doctors diagnosed the first case in the Netherlands in June of 1832.[2] As the disease spread, Anna summoned her courage, telling her brother Nicholas that 'there is not one of us who would not give his life for this upright country.'[3] Her life was not the one required, however. Cholera killed several people who worked in Anna and Willem's palace, but left their family unscathed. As she did with every disaster, Anna sent funds from her personal fortune to governors of afflicted provinces. Over 10,000 people died of cholera in the Netherlands, most of them in the densely populated cities of Leiden and Amsterdam.[4]

American newspapers reported the spread with a combination of dread and forlorn hope that the Atlantic Ocean would act as a barrier. When New York's Board of Health publicized a special meeting to investigate the disease, doctors who had treated cholera wrote long letters of advice and opinion. From Philadelphia, Dr. M. Burroughs wrote that, based on his experience as a ship's doctor in India, he believed it to be not contagious but epidemic, and like other epidemic diseases, it followed the course 'of the prevalent winds.'[5] But winds or not, as long as people moved west, so did the disease.

On June 6, 1832, the health commissioner of Québec visited Grosse Isle, the quarantine point for all immigrant ships. There, a ship from Ireland contained passengers 'under undoubted suspicion of the cholera morbus.' After his inspection, the health commissioner noted the cases were similar to cholera, except for the accompanying fever. Québec's Board of Health jumped at the opportunity to declare their city cholera-free. They allowed one ship, the *Voyageur*, to continue to Montréal. Six days later, 94 cases had been reported there. The disease then followed the local waterways, from the St. Lawrence River to Lake Champlain and then the Hudson.[6]

Cholera had come for New York.

The city wasn't entirely unprepared. It required a minimum ten-day quarantine for ships coming from Russia and the Baltic even with no evidence of cholera on board, with an indefinite quarantine for ships with known cholera victims.[7] They later extended this requirement to all arrivals from Europe and Asia. However, New York's Board of Health – composed of the port's health officer, the city's resident physician, and the city inspector – usually only took action when an epidemic had already been identified, at which point treatment rather than prevention became the mandate. Like Dr. Burroughs, few recognized cholera as a contagious disease. Instead, most people believed cholera spread via 'filth of the streets and houses; miasmatic effluvia from sewers, docks and wharves, in the vicinity of the contaminated atmosphere elicited by the breath, and transpiration of a multitude of persons living together.'[8] Even worse, most believed cholera only attacked people who were dirty or had weakened their bodies with too much food or drink: in other words, it killed the poor, the drunk, and the gluttons. Those who led a clean, godly life would be safe. That wasn't always possible in New York City, however, where pigs still roamed the streets, scavenging to remove filth and garbage but adding excrement to the mix. Scheduled street cleanings frequently failed to occur, and the city had no municipal water supply.[9]

On Friday, June 15, reports from Albany reached New York City, telling of the deaths in Montréal. That weekend, the mayor instituted a severe quarantine, keeping ships 300 yards from the city and vehicles a mile and a half from City Hall.[10] Newspapers printed advice from doctors, including one who had treated cholera in Constantinople. He suggested people seek medical attention as soon as symptoms presented. Laudanum, bleeding, and doses of oil of peppermint in hot whiskey or gin worked as treatment. 'Cholera is not contagious,' he wrote.[11]

About ten days later, on June 26, the first reported case surfaced in New York City. Decades later, it was discovered that the city's quarantine records for April, May, and June were missing, perhaps removed to cover up the city's slow preparation and sloppy quarantine practices.[12] Jacob de Brauw reported that, initially, 'the number of the sick was small, being only fifteen to twenty people a day, of which half perished...but it was not long before the disease spread through the whole city.'[13] The most terrifying aspect of cholera was its speed, taking victims from life to death in as little as three hours. The bacteria responsible made the stomach wall more water-permeable. As the body tried to rid itself of excess water, victims suffered from diarrhea, severe stomach cramps, and vomiting, which led to dehydration and, sometimes, cyanosis – when skin turns blue due to lack of oxygen in the blood.[14] Eventually, dehydration led to systemic organ failure.

One New York doctor, Edward H. Dixon, spoke with a healthy man shortly after 5 p.m., when he detected 'something about his face that...told me that the fiend was at work within him.' The man shook off Dixon's concerns, but about an hour later, his wife sent for Dixon: her husband had collapsed. Before midnight, he was dead. His wife buried him the following morning and died that night.[15] Another man reported feeling fine until the moment he fell down in the street 'as if knocked down with an axe.'[16] Tens of thousands fled to the countryside for cleaner air and water. Between the fled, the sick, and the dead, New York City came to a standstill.

Roger Huygens and John Zimmerman had an additional worry. What happened if Polari died in Bellevue? What if he died so suddenly there was no time for a deathbed confession to clear Prince Willem's name? To avoid such a catastrophe, Roger Huygens asked Seely to have doctors keep an eye on Polari.

The same fear of cholera struck Polari, who asked Seely and George Raymond to visit him. On June 19, in their presence, he wrote a letter to Willem and Anna. He described himself as 'penetrated with remorse' and declared himself ready to repair their 'noble reputation' at the cost of his life. Polari volunteered to go to The Hague, and during a 'judgment in open audience,' tell Willem and Anna everything about the theft. He didn't trust Roger Huygens, so he wrote that he was sending this letter in the hands of George Raymond.[17] Polari made no mention of the fact that he had been offered this deal multiple times, complete with a pardon, and balked every time.

A copy of this letter made its way into Roger Huygens's hands, probably through Seely. Seizing the opportunity, Roger forwarded it to Secretary of

State Livingston and asked him to speak to President Jackson. Now that Polari himself had said he was willing to go to the Netherlands, Roger hoped Jackson would waive the Customs penalty Polari still owed – the last barrier to extradition after the *nolle prosequi*. But, as before, nothing happened.

Nine days after writing to Willem and Anna, Polari wrote a rambling, vitriolic note to Roumage. He blamed Roumage and Susanne for any fate that might befall Rosine, since they had condemned her innocent father to prison. 'Recognize, infamous traitors, greedy of human blood, the vengeful hand of the Supreme Engine…it will never cease to pursue you as long as this unhappy infant breathes,' he wrote. He hoped Roumage would be sent back to France to complete the prison sentence he'd escaped. As for Susanne, he predicted she would die alone and miserable, abandoned by everyone including Rosine. Then, at the end of the letter, perfectly calm, he wrote, 'Forgive me, scoundrel, if I mock you for a moment. It comforts me a little in my misfortune…Your intimate for life. CONSTANT POLARI.'[18] It's unlikely Roumage ever received the letter.

Outside Bellevue, a stricken city held its breath. Officials canceled all public gatherings for fireworks on the Fourth of July. Buildings and ships quietly flew the American flag instead. *The Evening Post* blamed an uptick in cholera cases on 'a degree of intemperance in eating and drinking' over the holiday.[19] But excess wasn't to blame when cholera struck the Bellevue Alms House. It soon became one of the city's five cholera hospitals. Next door, in the penitentiary, the Court of Sessions ordered all prisoners awaiting trial for minor offenses to be released on their own recognizance. The court would only try those accused of serious offenses to avoid further spread of the disease.[20]

The city needed more than just hospitals to cope. By early July, there weren't enough coffins for all the victims. Dead bodies lay in the city's gutters. Ash fell like snow from piles of burning bedding and clothing, as families attempted to rid their homes of the disease. People looted empty houses, which caused the Board of Health to authorize funds for additional night watchmen.[21] Still, misinformation about the disease flourished. When 45 people died on July 10, the city's Special Medical Council announced that they were 'the imprudent, the intemperate, and…those who injured themselves by taking improper medicines.'[22] However, when the respected

Deputy Keeper of Bridewell came down with cholera, the newspapers were forced to admit that 'several cases…were persons of good habits.'[23] No one, it appeared, was safe.

Roger Huygens grew increasingly anxious as the disease spread through the city's hospitals and jails. On July 13, he wrote again to Secretary of State Livingston, requesting Polari be extradited quickly due to the cholera emergency. When nothing happened, he recruited a family friend to help. On July 15, Martin Van Buren wrote to James A. Hamilton, 'I have only time to say a word to you in behalf of my old friend the Chevalier. Do not let the cholera kill his man of jewels…'[24] Roger Huygens's fear was not unreasonable. The city was already scrambling to find a way to disperse inmates from its jails. On July 17, the mayor authorized moving prisoners from multiple holding facilities to any of the city's islands until it was safe to return them. Ten days later, Hamilton had released ten prisoners at Bellevue on their own recognizance. Polari was not among them. His case was sufficiently interesting to the general public for *The Evening Post* to note, 'there seems to be some question amongst the authorities, as to whether he is to be considered a prisoner in the charge of the State of New York, or in the charge of the United States.'[25] No one, it seemed, was willing or able to take responsibility for him.

Then, at the height of the outbreak, it happened: Polari showed signs of cholera. Seely asked Mr. Tella, the penitentiary caretaker, to find a qualified French-speaking doctor. Tella moved Polari to the Bellevue cholera hospital and put him under Dr. Thomas Devan's care. The fight against cholera required every ounce of Polari's renowned strength. As Dr. Edward Dixon noted, cholera killed the weak quickly, but strong men 'struggled fearfully against the terrible and unknown enemy…'[26] Devan visited Polari at least twice a day, often at night, and more frequently if needed. Under Devan's care, Polari survived. He later wrote, 'This brave and knowledgeable citizen… lavished on me all the care imaginable' as he fought a disease that had brought him 'to the gates of the tomb.'[27] But not everyone was so lucky.

Marshal George Raymond was about to depart for the Netherlands to return the jewel settings he'd dug up outside Brussels. As they had crossed in transit with the stones held by US Customs, there was no need for them to remain in America. But Raymond fell ill before he could depart. He left New York for a friend's home in New Jersey, hoping the fresh, clean air would help. It did not. Raymond died of cholera on July 6, 1831. His loss was painful.

Everyone from Polari to Susanne to Seely had trusted him. He left behind a widow, Susan, and nine children.[28]

When Raymond died, Seely planned to leave the city temporarily. Roger Huygens begged him to reconsider. He felt the Polari case was at a turning point, and Seely was the only one who could keep abreast of any government plans for the prisoner. Seely reluctantly agreed, but the decision cost him dearly. He came down with cholera and 'narrowly escaped with his life, in the services of his clients; while recovering, a relapse occurred, from which he was saved with the aid of three physicians.'[29] Like Polari, he survived – but the disease had taken its toll.

During the epidemic, Bellevue's hospital admitted more than 2,000 cholera patients, 600 of whom died. Throughout the city, the disease killed 3,513 of the city's more than 202,000 inhabitants.[30] By the end of the summer, however, the worst of the crisis had passed. It wasn't until 1854 that an obstetrician named John Snow proved that contaminated water caused cholera, allowing authorities to help limit future outbreaks.

Like Roger Huygens, Polari sensed his case was at a turning point. His near-death experience made him bolder, and on August 16, he wrote directly to President Andrew Jackson. He asked to be released from prison since he couldn't pay the Customs penalty of $43,000 and was afraid to die of cholera.[31] Confident he would be released, Polari rescinded his deathbed agreement to go to the Netherlands and wrote an open letter to American citizens, referencing his soon-to-be-gained freedom. He thanked Americans for refusing to bend to the will of foreign powers, complimenting 'the energy of your republican character and the greatness of your generous souls...'[32] But Roger Huygens intercepted the letter, likely through Seely, and suppressed it. The American public never received Polari's premature thanks.

Polari's petition landed on Jackson's desk alongside an announcement from Louis Philippe, King of the French. As was customary for heads of state, the king notified the president of important family news. His daughter, Princess Louise, had just married King Leopold I of the Belgians.[33] The marriage cemented the alliance between Belgium and France – the same alliance that had driven the Dutch out of Belgium and ended the Ten Days' Campaign. The marriage was based on necessity, not love. In the drawing room of her new home, Louise would find a full-length portrait of Leopold's first wife, Charlotte – the only woman he would ever love.[34]

Chapter 18

Extradition

Roger Huygens had come to a decision: it was better to beg forgiveness than ask for permission. Since neither the state nor the federal government would help him, he decided to extradite Polari himself using a combination of bribes and audacity. But when Roger brought the idea to Seely in mid-to-late August, the lawyer told him it was impossible. After all, Polari still owed US Customs its smuggling penalty. Roger set out to negate that penalty by offering Samuel Swartwout a bill of exchange for $10,000, to be paid by King Willem I.[1] It was less than Polari owed, but enough to buy Swartwout's silence. The Collector split the money with the colleagues who stood to collect if the jewels had been declared forfeit: surveyor M.M. Noah and naval officer John Ferguson.[2]

With the federal obstacle removed, Roger approached the state government and requested Governor Throop's 1831 mandate be honored. Lieutenant Governor Edward P. Livingston, the Secretary of State's cousin, was tasked with finalizing Polari's transfer into Dutch custody. Two Americans were assigned to escort Polari to the Netherlands and ensure he didn't escape: 24-year-old George W. Taylor, a deputy jailer, and 34-year-old Benjamin Hays, son of High Constable Jacob Hays.[3] To recruit extra ground support, Roger told the prison warden and marshal of the district about his plan. He also contacted his one-time spy, Jacob de Brauw. It was the right moment to approach the homesick Dutchman, still upset by his inability to find work. De Brauw accepted the offer of a free ride home in return for his service as interpreter. Polari didn't speak English, but since De Brauw spoke English and French, he could communicate with Polari and the American police escorts. De Brauw would also be responsible for collecting Rosine from boarding school before the extradition. With Susanne detained in the Netherlands for interrogation, Rosine couldn't be left alone in America without a parent. She would have to accompany her father.

To carry Polari across the Atlantic, Roger hired a schooner, the *Gazette*. The ship's owner had never sailed beyond sight of the shore, so Roger also hired an experienced captain and crew. He rented a steamer, the *Hercules*, as a shuttle and towboat. It would pick up De Brauw at Whitehall, the southernmost point of the Battery, and tow the *Gazette* to Bellevue. Once Polari was on board, it would tow the *Gazette* out to sea, past the bay of New York.[4]

Although Roger had deliberately left Seely out of the loop, he wasn't ignorant for long. The prison warden consulted a lawyer about his potential liability in Roger's plan, and through professional courtesy or industry gossip, Seely heard about it. He confronted the younger man and attempted to explain the plan's legal pitfalls. Without Polari's consent, he warned, this would be a kidnapping, not an extradition. Seely asked to accompany Roger when he set his plan in motion so he could offer Polari the Dutch pardon one last time. Roger agreed, faced with little choice if he wanted Seely's cooperation.

On the morning of August 23, 1832, Jacob de Brauw collected five-year-old Rosine from boarding school and proceeded to the dock where the *Hercules* waited. Roger Huygens had ordered him to keep the girl out of sight, in case one of Polari's friends recognized her and guessed what was about to happen. De Brauw took Rosine below deck and waited for the lieutenant governor. Two hours later, Edward P. Livingston arrived and approved Polari's transfer.[5]

The *Hercules* headed for its rendezvous point with the *Gazette*. But as soon as De Brauw saw the waiting schooner, his heart sank. The *Gazette* was a small, two-masted pilot ship, primarily used to guide larger boats safely through the bay. The low-profile vessel had been built for speed, not to crest the towering waves of the open ocean. One vicious summer storm and they could all be swept into a watery grave. De Brauw had given his word, however, and it was too late to turn back now. The *Hercules* took the *Gazette* in tow and chugged up the coast to Bellevue. There, the *Gazette* dropped anchor while the *Hercules* continued to the prison's private dock.

Meanwhile, Roger and Seely had gone to collect Polari from Bellevue. Roger's plan hinged on catching Polari unaware, so they pretended it was a routine visit. Polari agreed to see them, and prison deputies escorted him into the yard in handcuffs. There, Roger asked Polari if he still refused to go to the Netherlands. Polari said he did. That was the agreed-upon signal for Roger's hired help, Hays and Taylor, to close in and seize him.

The moment Seely feared most had now arrived. He jumped in and asked the deputies to stand down. Approaching Polari calmly, he urged the prisoner to accept the Dutch pardon. If he agreed to go to the Netherlands willingly, he would be set free after the investigation to start a new life with Rosine.[6]

When Polari refused, he gave Roger Huygens another opening. If Polari would not come willingly, he said, they would transfer him by force. At Roger's signal, the two officers reached out to grab him. Suffused with panic and rage, Polari fought. Just as on the day of his arrest, Polari's uncanny physical strength was more than any of them expected. Roger's two paid escorts couldn't contain Polari, let alone subdue him. Polari's cries drew more prison staff to the yard.

From the *Hercules*, Jacob de Brauw watched in horror as fourteen men carried Polari out of Bellevue, pallbearers for a live man.[7] His clothes had been mostly torn off in the struggle. Almost naked, he screamed in French for help. 'Scoundrels, thugs, murderers; Americans, your laws are being violated!' The men deposited a still-struggling Polari beside the steamer. Taylor and Hays dragged him on board as he screamed to no one and everyone at once. 'He foamed at the mouth,' De Brauw later wrote. 'He was so overcome with rage that he had fallen into utter senselessness.'[8] The Dutchman worried that people who lived nearby would hear the commotion and raise an alarm. But no one intervened and Polari disappeared from America's sight. Seely summarized the morning with wounded hauteur: '…the prisoner was taken from the penitentiary in which he was confined, and sent to Holland – with what warrant, for what considerations, and under what agencies, being unknown…'[9] He viewed the extradition as a kidnapping and wished no further part in it.

Once on board, Roger Huygens asked Taylor and Hays to carry Polari below deck. De Brauw tried to hurry Rosine into the second cabin, not wanting her to see her father in such a state, but he wasn't fast enough. Polari caught a glimpse of her and cried, 'My God, my child!'[10] He demanded to see Rosine and raged when told he could not. At Roger's request, De Brauw cracked the door to the second cabin so Polari could see his daughter curled up on a couch, unharmed. Roger's hunch paid off. With Polari momentarily calm, Roger ordered the steamer to depart.

The *Hercules* took the *Gazette* in tow and led it out of the bay, past the quarantine hospital at Staten Island and the Sandy Hook lighthouse. When it was time to transfer to the *Gazette*, Polari didn't protest. Like De Brauw, however, he was surprised at the smallness of the boat. 'So much the better, that the sea swallows us all,' he said.[11] His resignation didn't last. A few minutes after the passengers had boarded the *Gazette*, Polari's rage emerged again. 'Take these irons away from me!' he yelled at Roger, downstairs in the lower cabin. When no one answered, he hurled himself down the stairs toward Roger. Taylor, Hays, and some of the ship's crew grabbed Polari and attempted to restrain him. This time, while they had him down, they shackled his ankles and fastened the shackle to the floor. If he erupted again, they warned, they would tighten his restraints to keep him from moving at all.

Once Polari had calmed down, Roger Huygens attempted to question him about the theft. Perhaps unsurprisingly, the prisoner refused to speak. Roger continued for nearly 24 hours before giving up. There was nothing left to do but speed Polari on his journey to a public trial. Roger said farewell to De Brauw and returned to the steamer. He would never see Polari again, but the case would haunt him for years to come.

That night, the little schooner sailed past the lighthouse at Sandy Hook. Behind them, the New Jersey coastline and the heights of Staten Island faded into nothingness. Farther from shore, their captain steered them past the buoys that indicated shallow water. They were at last on open sea. A few days later, on August 30, they sailed into a storm that whipped the sea into white-capped waves. Water pounded the deck and streamed through the opening to the cabin below, where Polari lay on a mattress on the floor. The crew moved several chests together and lashed his mattress to the top, keeping him out of the water.

Each day on the uncomfortably small ship felt longer than the last. The two policemen rewarded the prisoner's good behavior by removing his handcuffs, although his feet remained shackled to the floor. They allowed him to shave and use a knife to cut toys for Rosine, but Polari wasn't interested solely in his daughter's entertainment. He also tried to turn her against Susanne. He claimed Susanne had abused Rosine and begged De Brauw to keep his child away from her mother. He told his daughter repeatedly, 'You have to tell her; I no longer want to recognize you as my mother; it is you who are the cause that my father is in irons; you made me poor.'[12] He forbid Rosine to talk about Susanne, forcing the little girl to seek out De Brauw as her confidante. She whispered to him that she loved her mother more than her father, a confession that didn't surprise the Dutchman. Polari frequently scolded Rosine 'in a gruff tone, his temper always excelling, and his expressions then were quite coarse…'[13] A father with children of his own, De Brauw concluded that, when it came to providing 'a delicate and moral education for a girl,' the prisoner 'was certainly not the man who had any aptitude for this.' He did not share this opinion with Polari, if only to keep the peace.

Susanne wasn't Polari's only target. He was also angry at the Americans who had detained him illegally for thirteen months and handed him over to the Dutch. De Brauw pointed out that Polari was the one who'd asked for trouble, showing stolen jewels to strangers. Polari replied, 'I thought I was so safe in the United States, that if even the Prince of Orange had come there, I could have safely said "behold, there are your jewels" and it could not have caused me the slightest difficulty.'[14] He claimed he had studied American laws beforehand, but hadn't expected Americans to be so pliable in the face of bribery. De Brauw agreed, his time in America having convinced him that its citizens 'rape their own laws for money.'

On September 10, 1832 – seventeen days after leaving American shores – the ship's crew spotted Lands' End and, on the next day, Plymouth. Briefly, sailors from a British pilot ship came aboard to negotiate a price for guidance through the channel. The door to the cabin below remained firmly shut, which upset Polari. De Brauw, suspecting Polari had a publicity stunt in mind, warned him to control his temper. They continued through the English Channel, reaching the heights of Ostend on September 18. At noon, a pilot ship guided them into the new canal at Helvoetsluys.[15] The speedy little schooner had done exactly what Roger Huygens hired it to do, arriving in Rotterdam in 25 days.

News of the incident at Bellevue appeared in American newspapers the next day, and for several weeks afterward. The *Commercial Advertiser* explained that Polari had been 'delivered up to the agent of the Dutch Government,' an event that 'has given rise to much speculation, and been supposed to be connected with some mysterious maneuvers.'[16] The *New York Journal*'s contribution only enhanced speculation about Polari's removal. 'The treatment adopted towards him in this city is certainly without precedent, and unless it can be defended by some very strong arguments, having a reference to the laws of the country, is as unjust as it is novel.'[17] No one, it seemed, could explain what had happened or why – only that Polari was gone.

Roger Huygens worked quickly to dampen public interest in the case. He paid $350 to an unnamed editor on August 30.[18] That editor was probably M.M. Noah, editor of the *Morning Courier and New-York Enquirer*. Noah was also the US Customs Surveyor, a Swartwout employee who had received a share of Roger's $10,000 bribe. Both Noah and Swartwout would have been anxious to suppress questions about the extradition's legality. On September 1, Noah published an article with Roger Huygens's desired slant.

> …Polari was surrendered up on the mandate of the Governor…Of the legality therefore, of this proceeding, there can be no doubt…no censure whatever, has been or can attach to the Representative of the Government of Holland in this transaction…in as much as our laws have not been violated in his surrender, we are pleased at the departure of one, who by his recent confessions…is an old and hardened villain…[19]

For Roger, this was money well spent. No defense or rebuttal appeared from any of Polari's former friends and supporters.

In Rotterdam, the police arrived at the dock before Polari had even stepped off the *Gazette*. Hays and Taylor transferred Polari to their custody, successfully completing their assignment. The police then transported Polari to The Hague's city prison. De Brauw followed them there, where he reported on the extradition and voyage to the Ministers of Justice and Foreign Affairs. Once he'd given his report, he was released from duty and sent home to his wife and children. Hays and Taylor also gave brief depositions to the Attorney General in The Hague. They would remain in the Netherlands while the Dutch completed their investigation, not returning home until early January of 1833.[20]

On September 21, three days after Polari's arrival, Attorney General Philipse visited the prison to interview him. In two lengthy sessions, Polari told the story of his bleach factory, his visits to Mr. Rey, and the morning he'd spotted three hunters burying something in the forest. He told Philipse about taking the jewels, selling diamonds with Roudez, and making plans to smuggle the rest to America. Then, from his prison cell, Polari wrote two additional notices which he asked to be appended to the interrogation transcripts. In the first, he apologized for the harm he had done to Prince Willem's reputation. He lambasted Susanne Blanche, describing her as a greedy, weak-minded woman who succumbed 'to the will of a perverse man…to the point of making her deny her infant, her blood itself.'[21] He asked his captors not to return Rosine to Susanne. If they did, he feared 'her honor would be sacrificed to the greed of her mother at an adolescent age…' He feared, in other words, that Susanne would turn their daughter into a child sex worker.

In the undated second letter, Polari attempted a sort of defense. On the night of the theft, he said, he ate dinner with a visiting tanner, Xavier Gregoire, at the Auberge du Cerf on the Rue de Boucher. They stayed out past midnight and Polari returned home, feeling ill. He remained at home in bed, 'attacked by a nervous disease that I am often subject to.'[22] His servant, Victoire Desaye, could testify that he was 'in no condition to commit this theft….' Even if he had been in perfect health, he argued, he had never set foot in the palace and knew no one inside. How could he have avoided being seen by the sentries or servants inside? And what if Her Highness had been in the apartment? What if she'd gone to retrieve her jewels at that very moment? He would have had to be 'a sorcerer to find where the jewels were to go steal them' without getting caught. As to the question of an accomplice, Polari denied it. If he had an accomplice, wouldn't he have been caught with fewer stones? And if he had made off with an accomplice's share, why would he have come back to Brussels – the scene of the crime – from early February until the end of April 1831? Would he really have applied for a passport *in his own name*, which would have told his accomplice(s) where he was going next?

Having presented his alibi, he reminded his interrogators that the stakes were high. As he would throughout the trial, he referred to his status as a father to evoke sympathy. 'It is on you, gentlemen, that the fate and future of a miserable 5-year-old orphan also depends,' he wrote.[23] His life, in other words, only held meaning because of his daughter. But would the Dutch judges believe him when he had first largely ignored and then endangered Rosine's life by his actions?

Chapter 19

The Brink of War

When Polari arrived in the Netherlands, the royal family had no time to spare for him. To her brother, Anna wrote only that the suspect in the theft had finally been extradited.[1] She was increasingly occupied with the king, supporting him in his insistence on a full restoration of the United Kingdom of the Netherlands. Both were blind to the reality that, short of war, it was impossible. King Willem let his pride dictate his policy, however, and still refused to sign the treaty acknowledging Belgium as independent.

Britain and France, exasperated by his recalcitrance, decided to teach the king a lesson. In November of 1832, they sent a joint naval force to blockade the Dutch coast. King Louis Philippe also sent a French army to recapture the Belgian city of Antwerp, held by 4,000 Dutch soldiers ever since the Ten Days' Campaign.[2] The French bragged that they were on a '15-day stroll,' anticipating a quick victory.[3] When they marched past the battlefield of Waterloo, they took offense at the sight of the 200-foot-tall mound topped by a bronze lion, raised by King Willem on the spot where his son had been shot. Soldiers lopped off part of the lion's tail. Only the intervention of the French leader, Marshal Gérard, kept them from doing further damage.[4]

As the French advanced, the Dutch army's 70,000 – 80,000 troops, a full 10% of the country's men of working age, patrolled in a semicircle along the Belgian border.[5] Although several of the king's ministers supported a fight if necessary, Minister of Justice van Maanen wasn't one of them. He had had enough of Belgium, where the rebels had looted his home and would have killed him if he'd fallen into their hands.[6] Van Maanen preferred to focus on The Hague, where he was overseeing Polari's prosecution.

As the state gathered evidence against Polari, the defendant and relevant witnesses appeared before the examining magistrate, Arend-Jacob-Adrien Drabbe. On October 29, 1832, Drabbe summoned former Director of Police

Pierre Michel-Charles de Knyff de Gontrœul. De Knyff de Gontrœul reiterated his opinion that, based on the footprints leading from the palace to the wall, the thief or thieves had *not* climbed the exterior wall to enter the garden and then the palace.[7] They had, he believed, come from inside the palace.

Next, Drabbe interrogated Polari himself. He asked why Polari had a birth certificate for Charles Dominique Carara in his possession. Polari said he'd met Carara in Lyon, where he learned they'd both been in the British army during the Napoleonic Wars. When Carara left suddenly, without his birth certificate, Polari kept it. Next, Drabbe attempted to elicit a confession. According to articles 59 and 62 of the penal code, a man concealing objects he knew to be stolen automatically became an accomplice to the theft and subject to the same penalties. Since, by this definition, Polari was already an accomplice, why not confess? But Polari refused, insisting he wasn't the thief. Drabbe sent him back to prison until further notice.[8]

The magistrate's next interrogations left the case clear as mud. He questioned Susanne Blanche on November 9, but many of her answers contradicted what Polari had written in his alibi letter from prison. For example, when asked how Polari had come into possession of the jewels, Susanne relayed his found-in-the-forest story. Polari, she said, had told her this happened on the night of the theft. When confronted with Susanne's testimony, Polari said he had never told her the timing of his discovery and it had most certainly *not* happened on the night of the theft.[9] Who could Drabbe believe?

Next, Drabbe asked Susanne if Polari had showed her how the thief or thieves entered the palace. Yes, she replied. Polari had taken her to an alley next to the palace. There, he showed her the part of the garden wall where the ladder had been found. But the ladder *hadn't* been found at the garden wall – it had been found outside the city wall. Drabbe pounced on the discrepancy and asked why she hadn't mentioned this before. Susanne couldn't explain why, but affirmed it was the truth. According to her, Polari had said, 'Here is the place of the climbing and where the next day they found the ladder.'[10] If Polari had committed the theft, he should have known where he left the ladder. Was this evidence to prove his innocence? Or did Susanne mis-remember what he said? Drabbe brought Polari into the courtroom and asked Susanne the same questions. None of her answers changed in his presence.

The new inquiry left multiple questions unanswered. Investigators couldn't find Polari's rented Brussels house, near the Namur gate, despite his detailed description of its location and owner. Case documents make no mention of any attempt to find Polari's former housekeeper to confirm his story about being home sick the night of the theft. Drabbe blamed the difficulties on the Belgian revolution, which made it nearly impossible to investigate matters in the city where the theft had taken place. 'I find myself lacking,' he wrote, 'all the basic documents of the investigation and unable to obtain information about the location due to the political circumstances of the two countries.'[11] Drabbe decided to seek out other witnesses and sources of information.

He chose Polari's former residence, Lyon, as his starting point. On December 2, he wrote to Monsieur Favre, the city's examining magistrate, and explained the situation. Drabbe said he didn't believe Polari's story about discovering the jewels in the forest. The tale was 'so implausible' that he believed Polari 'was the thief or one of them, and that he had accomplices among the Prince's servants, or at least among people known in the palace.'[12] He had also heard that, while in Lyon, Polari had committed fraud and possibly even forgery. Drabbe asked for any information the Lyonnais magistrate could send him, including the possibility of locating Roudez. Having sent the letter, there was nothing for Drabbe to do but wait.

Meanwhile, a letter from King Willem I of the Netherlands arrived on Andrew Jackson's desk. Dated September 6, 1832, it announced the recall of Chevalier Christiaan Bangeman Huygens. The letter asked Jackson to forgive the fact that Huygens had not taken final leave of him before returning home for his visit; Huygens hadn't known of the king's plan to recall him when he left. Roger Huygens, the interim chargé d'affaires, would remain the senior Dutch official until a permanent replacement could be sent.[13]

At that moment, Roger Huygens was anything but capable of shouldering his father's responsibilities. He had fallen dangerously ill after Polari's extradition. The illness, which may have been cholera, left him bedridden for two months.[14] Only in early November was he able to pack up the damaged jewel settings Raymond had brought back from Brussels. He sent them to

Consul Willink in Liverpool aboard an American steamer, the *Napoleon*. Willink would take possession of the trunk in Liverpool and transport it to The Hague.[15] Once it arrived, every known scrap of Anna's stolen jewels that hadn't been sold would have been returned.

A French army of 70,000 men under Marshal Gérard reached the Belgian city of Antwerp on November 15, 1832. They began digging trenches in the rain-soaked earth outside Fort St. Laurent, a fortress in the pentagon-shaped citadel guarding the city.[16] The 4,000-strong Dutch garrison, under the command of Waterloo veteran General Chassé, unleashed a cannonade on the soldiers digging beneath the fort. Despite being wildly outnumbered, Chassé declared himself ready to defend his fortress to his last breath.[17] The French worked quickly, and their breaching batteries were soon near enough to fire on the fort, inflicting considerable damage. A British visitor, Charles Stuart Wortley, paid eighteen pence to go up to the garret of the Antwerp theater for a panoramic view of the siege. The theater owners had poked holes in the wall 'expressly for the use of the many anxious spectators who came there.'[18] At night, he wrote, the shells flew overhead like shooting stars.

Throughout the month of December, the French crept ever closer to the citadel, preparing to breach and storm its walls. Their constant cannonfire almost completely destroyed it. Full of holes, walls and ceilings wobbled and threatened to crumble into the ditches below. Six years later, a Dutch visitor was astounded by the amount of damage still visible. 'Old shoes, soles, pieces of leather, shattered tin kettles and a number of other objects were mingled with the rubble of the vaults, which had collapsed in several places,' he wrote.[19] Finally, after an all-night bombardment on December 22–23, 1832, General Chassé surrendered. The only consolation for the Dutch was in having fended off a vastly superior force for 24 days. Upon touring the citadel after their victory, a French general told Charles Stuart Wortley 'how gallantly the [Dutch] troops had behaved, what hardships they had endured, and that, if their master the King of Holland had required it, they would have stood the assault, and defended the breach to the last man.'[20] But despite his men's courage, King Willem I had lost. The United Kingdom of the Netherlands was gone forever, and the history he had tried so desperately to revise turned out to be written in stone.

Despite their clash in Antwerp, France and the Netherlands had no animosity when it came to judicial cooperation. Early in 1833, Monsieur Favre, the examining magistrate in Lyon, sent Drabbe what little information he'd uncovered. Although he tracked down Roudez, Polari's one-time accomplice refused to share what he knew. He would only do so in Brussels, he said, at the Prince of Orange's expense.[21] Through the Lyon police commissioner, Favre had also confirmed that Carara was not the suspect's real name. In 1830, he had applied for a passport from the Swiss consul under the name Constant Polari.

When Drabbe replied, he asked Favre to question Roudez in Lyon. Favre obliged, but when the police went to see Roudez a second time, he was gone. They learned he had moved to Toulouse, but when they passed Drabbe's request to the authorities there, the police couldn't find him. No one by that name lived there or had checked into a hotel or boarding house. Roudez, it seemed, had vanished.

With no further avenues of inquiry open, Drabbe concluded his investigation. On September 25, 1833, he presented the evidence against Polari to The Hague's First Court of Instance. The court charged Polari not only with theft, but with having 'concealed and removed from investigation jewels that the defendant knew to come from the theft…'[22] The public prosector was tasked with continuing the case.

Meanwhile, in New York, William Austin Seely had finished his list of expenses incurred during the Polari case. Based on his last conversation with Christiaan Bangeman Huygens, Seely expected as his fee the 50,000 guilders (about $20,000) offered by the Dutch authorities. But in the months since Polari's extradition, he had heard nothing from them. After putting his business on hold for almost two years to help catch and extradite Polari, Seely wanted to collect his payment and move on.

He wrote a flurry of letters to Roger Huygens in the spring of 1833, but there was little Roger could do. By a royal decree of March 26, 1833, Roger had been honorably recalled as interim chargé d'affaires. His replacement was on the way and Roger was ordered home to provide an account of the Polari affair and settle his expenses.[23] While waiting for his replacement, Roger found time to reply to Seely from Philadelphia that May. He asked Seely to stop pestering him about payment because he had no further information to provide. If they weren't on such good terms, he said, he would have been 'extremely offended' by the 'want of confidence and reliance on my word.'[24] He said he would try to help once he returned to New York in a few days. But Seely heard nothing more from him that spring.

On July 11, Roger took his replacement, Adrien Martini, to Washington and presented him to President Andrew Jackson.[25] As of that moment, Roger was no longer an active diplomat and could do nothing to help Seely, at least officially. Martini, previously the chargé d'affaires in Brazil, was now the highest conduit for Dutch diplomacy in the United States.

The staffing change prompted Seely to reach out to Christiaan Bangeman Huygens, the Dutch contact he knew and liked best. The elder Huygens, who had been reassigned to Denmark, replied from Copenhagen that July. He told Seely a few hard truths, including the surprising news that his son had already dispensed the reward money to the US Customs officers – the price of their approval for the extradition. Even though they had behaved with 'a revolting obstinacy' during the case, Huygens pointed out that they were the first to find the jewels, to remove at least part of them from Polari's possession, and 'by their assenting no longer to oppose the extradition of the man, of putting him within the power of our judicial jurisdiction.' As a result, Seely's rights to any Dutch funds were 'problematical, at least diminished and considerably reduced…'[26] All future requests for information, Huygens said, must go to the Dutch legation in the United States. To placate Seely, he said that he, too, had spent thousands on the case, but 'preferred the loss to appearing selfish under circumstances so delicate.'[27] Huygens's implied advice was to absorb the financial loss and move on.

The news shocked Seely. The reward money had gone to the same agents who had blocked every effort to extract the jewels and Polari? And in the eleven months since the extradition, no one had thought to communicate any of this to him, or provide instructions for reimbursement? He replied to Huygens, noting how awkward it would be to prepare an invoice for the royal family for services like manipulating the press, having his reputation attacked by said press, incurring physical damage during Polari's arrest, and facing death during the cholera epidemic at the request of Dutch officials. The case had been 'beset with every intricacy; requiring results unheard of in international policy' and had pitted him against 'the most abandoned, desperate, and hardy felon of the age...'[28] How was he supposed to put a price tag on those things? To avoid that, Seely asked Huygens to use his discretion and obtain what he felt was a fair payment for him. Seely failed to grasp the main point Huygens had made in his previous letter: all official communication, including a request for payment, must now go through Martini, the current chargé d'affairs.

Instead, Seely continued writing to Christiaan and Roger Huygens. Roger had not obeyed the Dutch king's order to return home, so Seely was able to get in periodic written contact with him during the summer of 1833. Since Christiaan's last letter had indicated Roger was still compiling his expenses, Seely hoped his fee would be included. But neither Seely nor Christiaan Huygens knew what was taking so long. With little communication from his son, Christiaan Huygens suspected he was in some sort of trouble. The elder Huygens asked James A. Hamilton to write a letter of reference for Roger, explaining what a good job he'd done in wrapping up the Polari case. If Hamilton obliged, it was likely with a twinge of displeasure. For his own 'great labor and important services' on the Polari case, he had received only $69.32 from the US government.[29]

Finally, by the late summer of 1833, Seely had managed to make an arrangement with Roger. They would meet in New York, sail overseas, and settle their accounts in The Hague together. Seely had no illusion the trip would be a quick one, and asked his wife to join him. He applied for a passport on October 15, 1833 and booked tickets for the packet ship *Napoleon*, which he and Roger had agreed on. Roger booked, too, and appeared on the list of passengers as 'Messr. Huggins' of New York.[30] But when Seely and Hannah arrived to board on November 18, Roger was nowhere to be found.

Why didn't Roger appear? At first, his father believed he may have been on board the *New England*, a steamboat traveling from New York to Hartford, Connecticut. The boat's two boilers exploded on the stormy night of October

8, 1833, killing fourteen people.[31] 'I do not know whether he was on board… his fate truly disquiets me,' the elder Huygens wrote to Seely.[32] It's possible that Roger had given his father outdated or misleading information about his whereabouts. But no matter Roger's reason, Seely was determined to see the matter through. He and Hannah boarded the ship without Roger, sailing for a country on the brink of war.

Chapter 20

A Dubious Confession

While William Austin Seely made his way to the Netherlands, Constant Polari did something drastic to change the course of his case. Over the past year, the Dutch authorities had completed their investigation, agreed on the final charges, and forwarded the paperwork to the prosecutor. The scene was set for the public trial they wanted so badly. And then, on November 15, 1833, Polari asked Minister of Justice van Maanen to send a magistrate to him: he wanted to confess.[1]

Three days later, Attorney General Philipse arrived to take Polari's statement. Polari said he had only concealed the truth to protect his daughter's honor. But now, if he wasn't found guilty, the Prince of Orange's enemies could still spread lies about his involvement in the theft. Polari believed it was his duty to stop this from happening. As for the consequences, he told Philipse he trusted in the mercy of God, the king, and the king's children.

He had committed the theft alone, he said, with no help and no informants, having never been to the palace before. On that fateful night, he arrived between 10 and 11 p.m. After using a ladder to climb the garden wall, he approached the terrace door, applied clay to a glass pane, and broke it. He had brought a *lanterne sourde* with closable shades, which he lit with matches once inside. He went into Anna's bedroom, saw the diamantaire, and broke the glass. He took a cashmere shawl and three boxes filled with jewels, then left as quickly as possible. Outside the city wall, he tossed away the shawl because he didn't think it was worth anything. He carried the jewels to the forest of Soignies and hid them under grass and dry leaves. He returned the next night with proper tools and buried the boxes in the nearby woods.

Such was the entirety of his confession.

Prior to that moment, Polari had written tens of thousands of words from prison on the theft's aftermath: his attempts to convince Mr. Rey to use his bleach, his conversation with the Spaniard in the park, his attempts to find a blind man to return the jewels, fleeing from the merchant in Frankfurt, his diamond-selling trip with Roudez, their Algiers backstory, and Susanne's treachery in New York. Now, that same man had a scant few hundred words to say about the theft itself. He said so little that Attorney General Philipse postponed the rest of the interview until he could return with a list of questions. Two days later, Polari's answers to those 55 questions proved spectacularly unhelpful. He insisted that 'no particular thing' had prompted the theft.[2] He didn't remember the weather that night, where he had stolen the ladder, or how many rooms he had to pass through to find the diamantaire. It was only 'by chance that he found diamonds' in the palace.[3] In the end, he provided nothing that hadn't already appeared in newspaper reports.

Polari's confession meant the investigation had to be re-opened. On December 18, 1833, Christiaan Jacobus Scholten van oud Haarlem, a member of the indictment division of the Superior Court of Justice, re-interviewed Polari. This time, Polari tried to add a few details to his story. The idea for the theft, he said, had come from one simple thought: surely the palace contained jewels. This contradicted his claim to Philipse that he had only by chance found diamonds there. When asked about the ladder, he said that seeing it in the courtyard of a house that day had solidified the plan in his mind. As for the clay smeared over the glass pane, it had come from his bleach factory, but he 'cannot remember precisely how' he applied it.[4] There was much he couldn't remember, including whether he cut himself on the glass door pane or carried a knife. He remembered nothing about the palace rooms or any precious objects found there. As for the diamantaire, he only remembered breaking the glass with his hand. Polari blamed the 'time that has since elapsed, his long detention, and his state of illness' for being unable to recall more details.[5]

Two days later, Scholten van oud Haarlem returned and asked a familiar question: what had given him the idea for the theft? On this, the third time he'd been asked the same question, Polari said he was inspired by something visible from outside the palace, but would only reveal what it was during the trial. Scholten van oud Haarlem asked if the object was 'a vermeil service or *dejuner* placed in front of a window in the second room and which was visible outside.'[6] Polari said no – but the question was oddly specific, if not downright suspicious.

To the rest of the questions, Polari replied that he didn't remember. He didn't remember where in the diamantaire the caskets had been or how he knew they would contain something valuable. He didn't remember how he had scaled the garden wall while carrying three large, heavy caskets. He didn't remember the shoes he wore that night. His foot – when compared to the sketch of the well-shod footprint – proved to be 'somewhat wider and longer.'[7]

Despite Polari's inability to recall any specific details, on December 23, the Superior Court's Indictment Division determined there was enough evidence to charge him with 'the theft of a considerable quantity of pearls, diamonds and precious objects, by means of climbing, as well as exterior and interior burglary…'[8] The Dutch authorities were about to get what they had always wanted: a trial backed by a full confession.

By December 16, the *Napoleon* had arrived in Liverpool.[9] Seely and his wife Hannah continued to London, where they waited for Roger. Since he had missed the *Napoleon*, Seely expected Roger to take the next packet ship and catch up with them there. But once again, Roger failed to appear…because he had never left New York. On December 6, while Seely and Hannah were at sea, Roger attended the annual banquet held by the St. Nicholas Benevolent Society of Albany, in a hall owned by two of Herman Melville's uncles, both of Dutch ancestry.[10] Confused by Roger's absence, Seely wrote to Roger's father to ask what might have happened to him. Then, having done all he could, he and Hannah proceeded to The Hague.

In January, Seely received a kind response from Christiaan Bangeman Huygens, who confessed he didn't know where to find his son. The only information he could pass along was that Roger hadn't submitted his expenses yet – which had caused the Dutch government to balk at some of the bills they received on Roger's behalf. All he knew was that Roger should have sailed on a packet ship from New York on January 10, but since his son's health was 'entirely broken down,' he believed Roger may have been too ill to travel.[11]

This did not reassure Seely. He decided not to wait for Roger, but to present his case to Dutch officials directly. Huygens had suggested he contact Minister of Justice van Maanen for help, so Seely submitted a petition for payment with supporting documentation to the minister's office. When nothing happened, he complained to Christiaan twice more about his government's lack of response. Huygens replied from Copenhagen on February 25, reminding Seely he must submit his requirements to the Dutch legation in New York. He had only suggested Seely approach Van Maanen in an advisory capacity – not to demand payment. Now, Seely had likely annoyed the powerful Minister of Justice. 'My functions are entirely at an end in this whole affair,' he wrote. 'It is by the legation that you have been employed, and it is properly by it that you should be paid.'[12] Although Huygens was too polite to say it, he implied that Seely was destined for disappointment in Europe.

On January 10, 1834, a new indictment was issued against Polari, charging him with 'theft committed at night, with the aid of climbing, as well as of exterior and interior burglary in an inhabited house.'[13] The exterior burglary was for breaking into the palace, while the interior burglary was for breaking into the diamantaire. Inevitably, more questioning followed. On January 23, Polari spoke to the President of the Court of Assizes, David Westenberg. He confirmed his age as 54, which meant he had celebrated a birthday in jail since his last interrogation. When Westenberg asked the all-important question – what had given him the idea to commit the robbery – Polari had a new answer. This time, he said it was 'the golden objects, which you could see from the outside windows.'[14] Had he taken this information from Scholten van oud Haarlem's oddly specific question back in December?

Then, in a leading question of his own, Westenberg asked 'if he did not also find in the upper part of the diamantaire the keys of the caskets, in which the diamonds were.' Polari replied that he only remembered finding the key to the lower section.[15] This was his first mention of keys in all the published trial documentation. When Scholten van oud Haarlem had asked about the lower section's key back in December, Polari said he didn't remember. Now, it appeared, he *did* remember. Was Polari feeding Westenberg tidbits that Scholten van oud Haarlem had provided? Or was this a shred of proof that he'd seen the diamantaire for himself?

Westenberg appointed Jan de Bas as Polari's defense lawyer. He told Polari the law gave him five days to file a request to have the judgment against him annulled.[16] When Polari met with De Bas, the lawyer urged him to argue that the court had no jurisdiction to try him. Polari refused. 'I have been guilty of a crime,' he said, 'and I wish to be tried as soon as possible, asking you to very humbly point out to Monsieurs the members of the court the length of time that I have been detained.'[17] Polari clearly hoped for a reduced sentence based on time served. After two and a half years of imprisonment, he had realized that the only way out was to give the Dutch what they wanted: a public trial based on a full confession.

Chapter 21

The Trial

On the morning of March 7, 1834, a clamoring crowd flooded The Hague's Court of Assizes, anxious to catch a glimpse of Polari. It wasn't every day that a man who had robbed a princess was called to account for the crime. In the courtroom, a cadre of observers from the government and diplomatic corps sat on benches usually reserved for the Bar, including the Dutch Minister of Finance, members of the States-General, the Prussian minister, and the French chargé d'affaires.[1]

Unlike America, the Dutch trial process did not involve a jury of one's peers. A board of judges, usually trained lawyers and jurists, decided a defendant's fate. In the High Court, this was known as the Court Council. Polari's was headed by President H. van der Burgh (replacing the ill Westenberg), with four additional counselors and a registrar.[2] Attorney General J.W. Junius van Hemert represented the state as prosecutor, with Polari represented by his court-appointed lawyer, Jan de Bas.

The proceedings began at 10 a.m., when the court clerk read the long indictment in Dutch, after which a translator repeated it in French for Polari. The document included the prosecution's desired penalty: public display on a scaffold wearing a statement of the crime, imprisonment for 15 years, and a bill for the cost of the trial.[3]

After the reading and translation, court officials temporarily dismissed the crowd. Only those in the box reserved for members of the Bar – diplomats and court officials – were allowed to see what happened next.[4] Before the abbreviated audience, the Attorney General began to call his witnesses, from a list that had been provided to Polari in advance. It contained only three names: Pierre Michel-Charles de Knyff de Gontrœul, former chief of police in Brussels; Karl Ivanovich Schultz, Anna's faithful secretary; and Natalia Petrovna Chernysheva, Anna's now-retired chambermaid, who had been asked to come all the way from St. Petersburg to testify.

The first witness, De Knyff de Gontrœul, restated the results of his investigation. When he finished, the President allowed Polari a response. Polari noted that, although De Knyff de Gontrœul's testimony regarding multiple sets of footprints pointed to more than one thief, he was the sole culprit.[5] At this point, the President reminded Polari that he had promised to reveal his motivation for the theft during the trial. That moment, the President said, had come.

Polari began by reaffirming his guilt. 'I am guilty, my judges, of a grave crime…committed against a person exalted in rank and famous for his bravery. My awakened conscience feels an urgent need to make a frank confession before you, especially since terrible slander has attributed the crime, of which I am the only perpetrator, to others.'[6] After doing his best to verbally exonerate Prince Willem, he claimed he had decided to carry out the theft a few days beforehand, having walked past the palace and seen some valuables through a window. President van der Burgh pursued the issue. He asked why Polari hadn't left the palace when he couldn't find those valuables, and why he hadn't noticed other valuables in the first room he passed through. 'A thief,' Polari replied, 'does not look at everything closely enough to be able to give a correct description of it afterward.'[7] Instead, he had lit his lantern and made his way to Anna's bedroom. There, he saw the diamantaire – and a key lying beneath the glass. He broke the glass to get the key, tried using it to open the lower part of the cupboard, and was rewarded. He took the three boxes inside, wrapped them with the shawl, and left the palace the way he had come, climbing over the wall.

Here, Van der Burgh attempted to stitch Polari's story to the facts related by De Knyff de Gontrœul. He mentioned the sharp scratch marks on the lower part of the diamantaire, and asked Polari to explain how they had appeared if he had not carried a knife. Polari could not. 'I certainly don't remember anything about that,' he replied, 'but this must also be attributed to my rushed position. Meanwhile – I think I had a large knife with me.'[8] Was Polari simply taking facts from the question itself and embedding them into his answer? Or was this the truth?

With Polari's motivation now on record, the proceedings continued with the testimony of the second and third witnesses. Court staff brought the recovered jewels, stones, and settings forward as exhibits. Schultz testified that he recognized some of the jewels. Natalia, who had arrived the previous night at 10:15 p.m. and been driven to court in one of Anna's own carriages, recognized all the jewels present as Anna's.[9] When court staff showed Polari further exhibits, including the hollow cane and umbrella, he acknowledged they were his. He also identified the two items seized from Susanne during her first interrogation, and the iron pot he had buried in the Saint-Josse-ten-Noode cemetery.[10]

By now, it was 2 p.m. and the court adjourned for a thirty-minute break. Afterward, the session was declared public once more and the waiting crowd let back into the court. According to one onlooker, this process took fifteen minutes. During that time, Polari 'appeared much collected.'[11]

Now, with a full room of spectators, Attorney General van Hemert presented his argument. Its text of about 3,500 words includes prose more appropriate for a novel, with its description of crime as a 'dark march' that was 'favored by the shadows of the night.'[12] Polari, he said, was clearly the culprit because all three jewel caches – from Brussels, Liverpool, and New York – had been in his possession. And thanks to Anna's staff members, everything recovered had been identified as hers. Even if Polari hadn't confessed, possessing those jewels marked him as guilty. He then rushed to the conclusion he wished the Court Council to make: regarding this case, 'its judgment cannot be considered subject to the smallest difficulty, neither in terms of proof of the crime, nor as to the guilt of the accused.'[13] Van Hemert sat down, believing he had sealed Polari's fate.

Next, Polari's lawyer took the floor. Jan de Bas was in a strange position, and he began by telling the court how strange it was. He wanted to argue that a Dutch court had no jurisdiction to try Polari for a crime that had been committed in Belgium, but his client had directed otherwise. 'I thus find myself,' he said, 'in the singular position of having to speak before a court which, in my opinion, is not competent to hear the case.'[14] Since he was duty-bound to attempt a defense, he attacked the validity of Polari's confession.

A confession, De Bas argued, could only be used to convict someone if it was sincere and accurate, with no reason to believe the accused had an ulterior motive. That was not the case here. At this, Polari shook his head, as if to dissent.[15] Despite his client's chagrin, De Bas continued. Who could say whether Polari's confession was accurate? No one had seen him commit the theft. None of the witnesses had ever seen him with the jewels. Yes, the trial documents contained information about the Customs seizure, but many of them were unsigned, copies of copies of documents drawn up in America. Was that enough to decide a man's guilt?

De Bas also pointed out that the confession contained no new information. He connected its bare-bones details to two articles published in the *Haarlemsche Courant* in October of 1829.[16] He strengthened his point by referencing the transcipts of Polari's interrogations, explaining how Polari had inserted details from the questions straight into his answers. Polari had only mentioned the precious objects seen through the palace window, for example, after being asked about them.

There were also too many inconsistencies in Polari's interrogations and confession to be believed. Why hadn't he taken any valuables between the Red Marble Room (his entry point) and Anna's bedroom? Why didn't Polari's exit route, from the terrace to the garden wall, match the route of footprints found in the garden? Why didn't that exit route place Polari where the pearl-encrusted watch had been found? How had Polari carried three full caskets out of the palace and over the wall without help, or leaving more traces of his path? The story, De Bas argued, made no sense – yet it was believed without question.

As for why Polari might confess in the first place, De Bas asked the court to consider the length and trauma of his imprisonment. He had been jailed more than a year in America, forcibly transported to the Netherlands, and held a month before a warrant was issued to bring him before the examining magistrate, violating Article 168 of the Dutch Constitution.[17] Then, after the warrant was issued, he was held for more than a year before he confessed. De Bas compared this series of imprisonments to something medieval in nature: '…I ask you after all that precedes, if this confession is voluntary, if it cannot be compared to that which our ancestors obtained from torture.'[18] When he concluded his speech, a courtroom spectator said it 'appeared to make a great impression' on the audience.[19]

With each side having presented its argument, the President asked the interpreter to remind Polari what sentence the prosecution had chosen to pursue. Polari, who likely needed no reminder, pulled out a piece of paper and handed it to the President. It was a petition for mercy addressed to the king. He didn't want to be acquitted, he said, but asked for 'a mitigation of punishment for the unfortunate fate of his child.'[20]

Next, it was the Attorney General's turn to respond to De Bas's argument. The court was fully qualified to try Polari, he said, since the crime had been committed in the Kingdom of the Netherlands, albeit a version with an altered composition. As for the lack of proof that Polari had been in possession of the jewels, Van Hemert argued that it wasn't necessary to re-prove what US Customs agents had already proven. The jewels had a documented chain of custody as they passed from US Customs to Chevalier Huygens, who brought them to the palace, where the two witnesses present had testified regarding their origin.

As to the confession's lack of detail, Van Hemert explained it away as typical behavior for a criminal. 'A thief who breaks into a house at night and commits theft…takes little pains to acquire an exact knowledge of localities and other particulars, which are important in the eyes of justice,' he said.[21] It had been five years since the events of that night. It was only natural that Polari wouldn't remember everything. But the facts Polari *did* remember all lined up with the truth: the stolen ladder, the smashed pane of glass, the matches, the lantern, three jewel caskets, and the shawl. Plus, he said, there were things Polari mentioned that proved he had been at the scene of the crime. Upon leaving the palace, for example, Polari said he had crossed some brush at the foot of the garden wall. The brush, Van Hemert claimed, was not something mentioned in press coverage. That meant Polari had firsthand knowledge of the location of the theft. He also claimed Polari had described the exact shape of the diamantaire when this had never been in print. 'If such a body of evidence is not enough, it will be necessary to absolve all criminals, and frankly abolish all criminal justice.'[22] It was simply not possible, he said, to provide more proof.

In his rebuttal, De Bas reminded the Council that the prosecution had failed to produce any direct proof that Polari ever possessed the jewels. The confession contained nothing that hadn't been made public in the newspapers, down to the specific dimensions of the jewel caskets published in the *Haarlemsche Courant*. Contrary to Van Hemert's assertion, Polari had *not* given an exact description of the diamantaire. He had only said it was covered with glass, a fact everyone knew from the press coverage. And as for the brush alongside the garden wall, De Bas dismissed it as inconclusive. 'I must point out that it was probably known in Brussels,' he said. 'There remains nothing left by which a judge could obtain a conviction.'[23] Given the fact that there were still more questions than answers about this crime, he concluded, Polari's confession was hardly credible.

De Bas had managed to build momentum and sympathy for Polari, but would it have an effect on the judges? At 5 p.m., the President adjourned the session and declared the verdict would be given at noon the next day.

That Friday night, citizens of The Hague snatched up their evening newspapers to read the latest on the trial. Many papers printed the full text of the indictment and summarized the arguments. The country waited anxiously, wondering what justice would mean in a case with this much intrigue and glamour.

It didn't take long to find out. On Saturday morning, just before noon, the Court Council reassembled along with the court clerk, the translator, Polari, and De Bas. There were no spectators, witnesses, testimonies, arguments, or rebuttals. The session had only one purpose: to end the case. It began with the judgment. The court recorder read the original document in Dutch, then the interpreter repeated it in French for Polari.

> The Court of Assizes in the province of Holland (southern part), having regard to the indictment drawn up by the Attorney-General in accordance with the judgment of the Superior Court of Justice at The Hague, Indictment Division, dated December 23, 1833 against Constant Polari…[24]

The long preamble must have taxed De Bas's nerves. Had he succeeded in casting enough doubt on Polari's confession? Though he had accused the prosecution of failing to procure witnesses to prove Polari's guilt, he had been unable to produce any to prove his client's innocence. If Polari had let him, could he have tracked down Victoire Desaye to confirm Polari's alibi?

>...also named Carara, 53 years old, merchant and manufacturer by profession, born in Wicq, canton of Ticino in Switzerland, having last lived in New York, referred by the aforementioned judgment to this Assize Court to be judged by it...[25]

It's unclear how much Polari would have understood of the Dutch-language reading. He would have recognized his name, his alias, the town and canton of his birth, and the city of New York. He had heard them all in previous court proceedings in English.

>...all the formalities prescribed by law, insofar as they are still in force, having been observed: Declares the accused Constant POLARI, having also named himself CARARA, guilty of theft committed during the night with the aid of climbing and exterior and interior break-in in an inhabited house.[26]

Guilty.

Would he have been able to intuit the result after it was read in Dutch simply by watching De Bas's face? Or would he have had to wait until the verdict was read in French? No accounts of the trial describe his behavior at the crucial moment.

After declaring him guilty, the court sentenced Polari to half-an-hour's exposure tied to a post, wearing a sign that stated his crime. He would then be taken to prison for a term of twelve years, and charged for the trial's cost. They ordered the verdict to be printed and displayed in The Hague and in Brussels.[27] Journalists reported wryly on the second half of that order. The Dutch courts, they noted – following the example of their king – did not acknowledge Belgium as an independent nation.[28] That part of the order would never, could never, be carried out.

As far as the press was concerned, the story of the jewel theft had come to an end. But had the trial succeeded in its goal - was Prince Willem's reputation restored? Not according to a private correspondent from Rotterdam, whose letter was published in London's *Evening Mail*. According to him, Polari had protested Willem's innocence too much, making the confession suspicious.

De Bas had done too good a job to believe Polari was the culprit. The mysterious correspondent, who signed himself 'O.', said that even Willem's friends whispered behind closed doors that he had been more involved than anyone suspected.[29]

Polari's petition for mercy made its way to King Willem I's desk. He ignored it. With no royal intervention, Polari's sentence was carried out as ordered. At 12 p.m. on April 2, 1834, Dutch authorities brought Constant Polari to the Grote Markt in The Hague, where a scaffold had been erected for the sole purpose of displaying Polari and two other convicted criminals. A crowd had gathered to watch, eager to catch a glimpse of the man who had stolen Anna's jewels.[30]

Dressed in a hat, glasses, and olive-green overcoat, Polari held a handkerchief to his face on the way to the scaffold. Although he walked up the platform of his own accord, the so-called 'executioners' had to pull him to the post. They removed his hat and glasses and tied his arms behind the post. One of them slipped a sign over his neck. It hung over his chest, listing his crimes in a language he couldn't read. Somehow, he found a way to slip one arm through the rope, reach into his pocket, and bring his handkerchief to his face once more. The executioners forced his arm down and bound him tightly, making further movement impossible.[31]

Polari let his head sink to his chest. His uncut hair hung over his face, covering all but his thickly bearded chin. One observer thought he had intentionally avoided shaving since the day of his sentencing in anticipation of this very moment. For half an hour, he remained tied to the post, looking away from the crowd.

When his thirty minutes were up, the executioners untied him. He immediately reached for his handkerchief and hid his face as they led him back to prison. The Chief Registrar of the Superior Court of Justice, J.H. Spierman, watched the proceedings from an apartment overlooking the square. He produced the official minutes for court files to prove justice had been done.[32]

William Austin Seely was in The Hague during Polari's trial. It's likely he attended – or tried to. But his first order of business was making headway with the Dutch government in terms of payment. In early March, Seely wrote a letter to the king. He attached a 'detailed epitome' of his services and claims, including Huygens's letters. He explained the particular type of help he had provided 'through great peril and difficulties.'[33] Now, he asked the king to resolve the matter.

In April, he received a reply from Minister of Justice van Maanen and Interim Minister of Foreign Affairs Jacob van Zuylen van Nijevelt. The king had read his letter, they said, and asked for a report on the matter. But since the people who should be consulted were absent – presumably Christiaan Huygens, Roger Huygens, and Adrien Martini – the matter could not be solved yet. It would 'not be in the interest of Mr. Seely to await the result in this country.'[34] They were asking, in other words, for him to leave.

Seely refused. He was still in the Netherlands two months later – and still waiting for Roger Huygens. When Seely finally managed to book a meeting with Van Zuylen van Nijevelt, the minister told him that the king and the royal family regretted how far the situation had gone, but until Roger could provide the necessary paperwork, nothing could be done.

After his public display, Constant Polari was transported to Woerden, a castle that had been converted into a prison in 1830. He became one of 350 prisoners held there. Like the rest of the men, the wardens put him to work. Perhaps because of his prior experience working with bleach and fabric, he worked in the weaving mill.[35]

With Polari behind bars, the Dutch authorities informed Susanne Blanche she was free to leave The Hague. For almost two years, since September of 1832, Van Maanen's secret police had controlled and watched her every move. It was no surprise that, when told she could go, she did. She requested permission to leave the country with Rosine, which was granted. In May of 1834, she was paid 4,000 guilders from an account belonging to the secret police and sent on her way.[36] After that payment, she and Rosine disappeared from the case's paper trail.

Jean Roumage also disappeared from the record after being tossed out of the Netherlands. Did he return to France under a new name? Or did he go back to America, where his brothers Frédéric and Victor lived? One small clue may point to Roumage's whereabouts. In November of 1834, a group of New York City's French and Italian immigrants met to discuss the upcoming presidential election. They favored Andrew Jackson and pledged to support his fight against the Bank of the United States, which they considered a despotic monopoly. The men formed a vigilance committee tasked with helping their fellow countrymen procure their naturalization papers in order to vote. Members of the committee included Polari's former translator, Eugene Bergonzio; jeweler Joseph Deguerre, who had bought diamonds from Polari; and one Jean Robert, the alias Roumage had once used in Europe before fleeing to America.[37]

Seely and Hannah waited out the long, hot summer in the Netherlands. Roger never appeared. In August, Seely wrote to the king again, proposing arbitration – a hearing to settle the question of payment, based on any paperwork the government already had. He received no answer. The government hadn't heard from Roger, either, and was unwilling to commit to a solution until it had.

As it turned out, Roger Huygens was still in New York City, being sued by a servant for back wages. When the case went to court that spring, a judge found in favor of Roger's servant.[38] That June, Martin Van Buren's son spoke with Roger at the races in New York and learned he had been 'discharged from arrest…on motion.'[39] It's unclear whether Roger knew how much trouble he was in back home, or how desperately Seely wanted his help.

Finally, in early December of 1834, the Dutch government made a formal response to Seely's many requests: Van Maanen offered him a single payment of six thousand florins (about $2,400). That was less than Seely had already spent on living expenses in the Netherlands while pursuing payment.[40] Compared to what he'd spent and what he'd given up, the amount offered was an insult.

Seely declined the offer and made plans to leave the Netherlands. He hired a Dutch lawyer, D. Donker Curtius, and authorized him to try to get clarification and reparations from the royal family in his absence. Having done what he could, he and Hannah left for France. In Havre-de-Grâce, they boarded the packet ship *François Depaw*, and arrived in New York on March 9, 1835.[41] They had been gone a year and four months with nothing to show for it.

Meanwhile, Donker Curtius did his best to help. He wrote to the king to suggest arbitration, but as usual, heard nothing in reply. When Donker Curtius updated Seely, he said he knew Prince Willem had been told about the situation. 'He treated it very lightly, and showed no desire of speaking of it to the king his father,' he wrote.[42] To someone who had worked tirelessly on his behalf, Willem showed little gratitude. One month later, King Willem I refused the request for arbitration.

Back home, Seely calculated the amount of money he had lost while working for the Dutch. As of March 1835, he had spent three years and eight months involved in Polari's case and its aftermath. Had he turned the Dutch away when Huygens offered him the job, he would have made at least $10,000 per year. To his $38,000 of lost earnings, he added $4,000 in expenses during his sojourn at The Hague. In total, he had lost approximately $42,000 on the Polari case – the rough equivalent of $1,504,000 today.[43] Seely resumed his work as an attorney and attempted to make up for lost earnings, but his resentment never faded.

Chapter 22

A Walking Stick in America

With the trial concluded, Anna no longer had to leave her jewels in their damaged condition. Bent, broken, and decayed settings could be discarded. Damaged stones could be recut and repolished. Half-intact pieces of brooches and necklaces could be recast or repaired. Any bad memories from the frightening period after the theft could be safely interred and laid to rest. It was a chapter closed.

Or was it? Although Pereira and Machado had gone, Willem's need for men like them had not. 'What terrible things I hear about the behavior of the Prince of Orange in Tilburg,' wrote journalist Henri Box. 'I dare not commit it to paper…If what they say is true, I tremble for the future.'[1] Several more blackmail incidents proved Willem's judge of character had not improved. One of them, dating to the 1840s, cost Willem at least 115,000 guilders.[2]

When Willem's mother died in 1836, his father isolated himself, further losing touch with his subjects. The king could not – or would not – see that the country suffered from his policies of high taxation and widespread surveillance by the secret police. He had depleted the treasury for years, paying for troops to stand in readiness at the Belgian border.[3] It wasn't until April 19, 1839 that he finally signed the Great Powers' protocol, acknowledging Belgium as an independent nation.[4] For the aging king, the treaty was a permanent emblem of his failure. Tired and disillusioned, he longed for quieter days with a loving wife at his side. He chose Henriette d'Oultrement, his dead wife's lady-in-waiting and a Belgian Catholic. After all he had done to repress both Belgians and Catholics, to mold them into model Dutch citizens, King Willem chose to spend the rest of his days with a woman who embodied everything he had fought against since 1815.

Willem, who adored his mother, felt his father had betrayed both her memory and the nation as a whole. He leaked his father's engagement to the press, provoking confusion, anger, and outrage. Willem's press campaign created such a hostile atmosphere that his father abdicated on October 7, 1840. The former king moved to Berlin, where he married Henriette. He would die there of a stroke on December 12, 1842, still convinced the loss of Belgium was everyone's fault but his own.[5]

Willem and Anna did their best to banish memories of the old king's bourgeois court. They patronized the arts, bringing craftsmen, jewelers, architects, poets, playwrights, and painters to The Hague to display their skills. Theirs was a court of pageantry and elegance, of balls and exhibits and plays and concerts. In 1845, Anna sat for another portrait by Jean Baptiste van der Hulst, wearing a tiara, cross, and earrings of gold and turquoise. The cross, engraved with the motto 'don't forget me,' had been stolen in 1829 and was one of the few jewels returned intact.[6] It had appeared on the list of missing items as number 62, *'une croix ne m'oubliez pas, turquoise et or.'*[7] That same year, Anna wore her incredible sapphires – returned without their settings and diamond surrounds – for another portrait, depicting her in Russian court dress. The deep blue stones gleamed in dress ornaments, a brooch, and a spectacular diamond tasseled belt.[8] But this time, Anna had learned her lesson. She no longer kept her jewels in the palace. Every morning, a jeweler brought her the pieces she wished to wear that day.[9]

In 1837, three years into his sentence, Constant Polari made a request to his jailers at Woerden: would they give him permission to write his story? The request was troublesome. At the time, King Willem I was still on the throne and had not yet signed the treaty recognizing Belgium's independence. Polari's memoir might bring back memories of a time many in the Netherlands would rather forget. People who sympathized with Polari might even blame the Dutch for what had happened to him. On the other hand, if Polari's writing reinforced his guilt rather than Willem's, it could act as a counterweight to the bad press the prince's behavior was still generating. The king agreed to let Polari write, with the understanding that his book would have to pass inspection before publication.[10] No memoir by Polari ever appeared, however. It's unclear if he completed or even started it.

Almost five years later, in early 1842, Polari fell ill with 'a glandular disease.'[11] His phenomenal strength long since diminished by disease and imprisonment, he knew he wouldn't survive. He petitioned the king for compassionate release to see Rosine one last time, but he had waited too long. Constant Polari died on the morning of February 21, 1842.[12] He was 62 years old and had served eight years of a twelve-year sentence. An announcement appeared in the newspapers the next day with a literal grace note. Upon his deathbed, the notice claimed, Polari spoke to the prison's pastor, Mr. Van den Burgh, who converted him to Catholicism. 'Having belonged to the so-called freethinkers and deniers of Christianity throughout his life,' Polari now wanted to die with the hope of salvation. Before he died, he 'confirmed that no one but he was guilty or complicit in the theft.'[13] This description of his last moments ties up the story neatly, with Polari repeating his confession and receiving absolution, leaving no loose ends for further speculation. Its believability is suspect.

But even though Polari was gone, his story lived on. Eilert Meeter, a journalist disgusted by King Willem II's profligacy and sexuality, left a strange rumor about Polari in his book, *Holland: Its Institutions; Its Press, Kings, and Prisons*, published in 1857. Polari, Meeter wrote, had not died in Woerden. Instead,

> he was put on board a vessel, with some thousands of guilders in his possession, to be taken, with his own free consent, to America, on which passage, however, (during a dark night, he being alone with a well-known secret police character, whose public hotel in Brussels, now more than ten years since, suddenly sprang up into magnificence), he accidentally fell overboard and was drowned, the mystery of the famous robbery going with him.[14]

This alternate ending, more poetic than the truth, put a tragi-comic gloss on the story. Another alternate ending surfaced in New York City, claiming Polari and Susanne had arrived in the city not with their daughter but with their son. According to legend, that boy remained in the care of a friend and, upon Susanne's death, inherited a fortune from the proceeds of the stolen jewels. 'Polari's grandchildren,' the report claimed, 'live in one of the finest mansions on Fifth Avenue.'[15] It was an irresistible American story – the grandchildren of a Napoleonic deserter, perhaps the most famous thief of his day, were now among the city's richest residents. But not a word of it was true.

Back in America, it was business as usual for Samuel Swartwout, who kept his job for the rest of Andrew Jackson's second term. Jackson's successor, Martin Van Buren, promptly removed him in 1837, after which Swartwout moved to London. But when Van Buren's replacements reviewed the previous administration's finances, they found a significant amount of money missing.

An investigation by the House of Representatives found that Swartwout had stolen at least $1,225,705.69 of public funds during his tenure as Collector.[16] After interviewing numerous witnesses, the committee characterized Swartwout as unfit for office: 'He was wholly irresponsible in pecuniary reputation, notoriously prone to hazardous speculations, deeply embarrassed from them, and always in want of funds.'[17] Swartwout's disastrous personal finances had led him astray. This was exactly what Van Buren and Hamilton had warned Jackson about years ago. Swartwout himself didn't return to the US until 1841, when the government assured him it wouldn't prosecute.[18] He died in New York on November 21, 1856 at the age of 73. In announcing his death, the *New-York Daily Tribune* reminded readers that the term 'Swartwouting' had been coined to refer to debtors and defaulters who fled their responsibilities.[19]

Unlike Swartwout, James A. Hamilton was happy to leave his job behind. He resigned as District Attorney for the Southern District of New York after Jackson's first term, spending his time traveling instead. While passing through Denmark, he visited Chevalier Christiaan Bangeman Huygens, his wife, and daughter, all of whom remembered him from New York.[20]

In Russia, Hamilton met Anna's brother, Emperor Nicholas I, and – surprisingly – Roger Huygens. The diplomat's son had found a way out of his legal troubles in the United States and, as of 1838, resurfaced as his father's legation secretary in Copenhagen. Now, in St. Petersburg, it seems Roger was still prey to questionable decision-making. In Hamilton's room, Roger complained about the emperor and the government. Hamilton jumped up to shut the door, aware that anyone outside could easily listen in on their conversation. The action spooked Roger, who fled. Two days later, the chief of the secret police pulled Hamilton aside at a ball and politely asked him not to allow his guests to disparage the government. Any other foreigner, he said, would have been escorted 'to the frontier of the empire.' Hamilton thanked the man for not evicting him. 'I must say,' Hamilton wrote afterward, 'that I found the Russians the most civil and obliging people I ever met with.'[21]

The case was now closed for everyone except William Austin Seely. In late 1845, he applied to the US State Department for help forcing the Dutch government to pay what it owed him. The State Department obliged, asking the American chargé d'affaires at The Hague to make an informal inquiry. The Dutch government did not respond.[22]

In 1847, over a year later, Seely tried again. He wrote to Secretary of State James Buchanan to explain how he'd lost at least $42,000 pursuing the Polari case. Considering all Seely had done for the Dutch, Buchanan wrote, 'I am astonished that his claims have been so long disregarded.' He felt the Dutch owed more than just the money, however: they owed America an explanation since the country had 'interfered in their behalf, in a manner we had never done before, and have never done since.'[23] This time, he asked the chargé to make a formal inquiry and elicit a response from the Dutch before the next Congressional meeting. But when almost a year had gone by with no response, Buchanan had no recourse. 'No such want of courtesy…has ever been manifested by any foreign government,' he complained.[24] Seeing they'd get nowhere with another inquiry, Buchanan advised Seely to apply to Congress for help.

Seely duly submitted a petition to Congress on January 2, 1850. In it, he proposed a unique solution. The United States owed money to Holland through a debt incurred by the city of Washington, DC. Why not divert a number of payments to him until his expenses had been reimbursed? Seely even provided legal precedent for such a solution.[25]

Eight days later, Senator Henry Clay of Kentucky presented Seely's petition to Congress. However, that session soon devolved into an argument about whether abolitionist literature encouraged slaves to rebel. Jefferson Davis, then a senator from Mississippi, labeled such literature 'aggression upon the rights of the south' and warned that if anyone present 'were here to bring about a civil war, here then let the first battle be fought.'[26] The country clearly had more pressing issues than a lawyer's request for payment. Seely's petition landed in the hands of the Senate Committee on Finance, where it languished. But interest in the Polari case reignited when reporters covering the Congressional session summarized the petition and the decades-old case it referenced. In reviewing the role Customs had played in the case, the editor of the *New York Daily Herald*, James Gordon Bennett, took Seely's side. He accused Customs Surveyor M.M. Noah of having 'pocketed nearly three thousand dollars of the reward – we call it blackmail – offered by the Dutch government' that should by rights have gone to Seely.[27] According to his biographer, Noah had done exactly that, but he now sued Bennett for libel. Noah also published an article in his own paper, *Sunday Times and Noah's Weekly Messenger*, where he attempted to clear up Bennett's misunderstandings about the case. However, Noah's article also contains a number of inaccuracies and obfuscations about Polari's arrest, the role Customs had played, and the $10,000 Roger Huygens had paid to extradite Polari.[28] Noah was gathering more information on the jewel theft when he died of a stroke in 1851.[29]

The story of Polari's extradition angered a new generation of journalists and editors, keen to protect American liberties. A summary of the case in Bennett's *New York Daily Herald* asked, 'Of what worth are our constitutional provisions as to personal liberty – of what value is the boasted writ of *habeas corpus*, if these things can be done with impunity?' As for Polari's extradition, it had been carried out 'by violence and in defiance of our laws, and was an outrage for which the Dutch government should atone.'[30] But just as with Seely's petition, the temporary burst of press coverage produced no effect. The petition was printed and bound as part of Senate Document No. 127, an obscure file doomed to gather dust on a shelf and disappear from public memory.

William Austin Seely died on December 30, 1862 at age 75. Everything he owned – three horses, two wagons, farm equipment, six oil paintings, a pair of bronze candlesticks, and a gold watch – was valued at a total of $1,281.75. The furniture and law books held in his New York City office were valued at

$671.66.[31] The Board of Aldermen in New York, responsible for reporting its members' yearly receipts and expenditures, forgot to report on Seely's final year. They accounted for his last year of income and expenses as a lawyer in 1866, almost four years after his death.[32]

After King Willem II's death of a heart attack in 1849, Anna never wore diamonds again. She gave them all away to her daughter, sister-in-law, and niece.[33] With her brother Nicholas's approval, Anna used her dowry money to buy the palace of Soestdijk, a place that held many happy memories of Willem and the children. There, she curated her memorabilia of him as a war hero. She delighted in showing guests her collection, telling and retelling the story of Willem's spirited defense of Quatre Bras and his shoulder wound at Waterloo. Around her wrist she wore a gold bracelet with his portrait and the names of his historic battles.[34] Anna became the keeper of his legend, reminding people of the handsome soldier prince who had won his country's heart – and hers – before the darker days of scandal and revolution.

In the fall of 1855, Anna made her last trip to Russia to attend her nephew's coronation the following spring. She considered staying permanently, but the new emperor and his family had little enthusiasm for the idea. To them, she was a relic of days gone by, difficult to relate to and problematic in terms of court precedence. When her nephew had been crowned, Anna duly returned to the Netherlands, where she lived for almost ten more years.[35]

On March 1, 1865, Anna fell gravely ill at her home in The Hague. As she lay dying, her son, King Willem III, kept Archpriest Sudakov from getting close enough to recite the proper prayers because he disliked her Orthodox priests.[36] Anna, it seemed, no longer fit in anywhere. She had outlived her many brothers and sisters, and, perhaps, her purpose. Her body was laid out in the Russian Orthodox chapel at Rustenburg, the coffin flanked by two silver-plated candlesticks that had come from Russia in her trousseau.[37] She was buried next to Willem in the royal family's vault in Delft.

In her will, Anna left her oldest son, King Willem III, one-quarter of her jewels. Half went to her only daughter, Sophie. The last quarter went to her son Hendrik, who left them to Sophie when he died childless. She had requested a few special sapphires be returned to the Dutch monarch; they appear in a tiara Queen Máxima of the Netherlands wore during her husband's inauguration in 2013.[38] Few of Anna's jewels remain in their original state today. Most of the stones have been dispersed in inheritances, re-cut and re-used as styles changed.[39]

Although her collection soon dispersed, Anna's jewels lived on in the memories of people who had seen her in them. German jurist Robert Von Mohl wrote, 'I only saw her once, in a solemn audience at eleven o'clock in the night, in which the old woman was heavily made up and wearing magnificent jewels, but especially with a pearl necklace, famous for its pricelessness...'[40] But those pearls were famous for more than their monetary worth. Snatched from the diamantaire, cut loose from their string, buried beneath the soil of Belgium and Brooklyn, stuffed in boxes and bags, carried by cane and crutch, counted by candlelight, and confirmed in a courtroom: those pearls had not come through their journey unscathed. In fact, their visible damage, so carefully noted by Consul Willink in Liverpool, became their most memorable feature.

Many years later, on a walk along the shaded garden paths of her summer palace, Anna's daughter Sophie told a story to her companion. The story was so memorable that it made its way into her companion's memoir. Lady Walburga Paget wrote:

On one of our walks she told me the curious story of her mother's pearls, which had been those of Marie Antoinette. The Queen of Holland kept all her magnificent jewels in a glass case in her bedroom – as is, I believe, the habit in Russia – for she was one of Emperor Paul's daughters. One fine morning they were all gone, and the search for them was vain; but it was generally believed that somebody very nearly related to her had taken them to pay debts. They were never traced, excepting the pearls, which many years afterwards were found hidden in a walking-stick in America, where they had evidently been all the time, for they had become quite brown and encrusted with a kind of growth. The Grand Duchess [Sophie] herself cleaned them and wore them continually, until they became quite white again.[41]

In this retelling, no longer had the numerous sparkling diamonds, emeralds, sapphires, rubies, topaz, and turquoise all made their way back to Anna – now, there were only pearls. An emblem of purity, rescued from the dirt and the muck of the New World, lovingly restored by Anna's own daughter. The story and its truth had separated, taking a shape that suited the teller until, at last, there were no more tellers left to suit.

Acknowledgements

I owe an enormous debt of gratitude to the ones who came before – the biographers, the parsers and publishers of historical documents and records, the translators, the transcribers, the reporters, and any number of independent sleuths sharing their discoveries via blogs and social media. It is only because of their work that I could even begin to tell this story. And, because of the times we live in, I was only able to continue with the help of modern miracles like digitized newspaper and genealogy archives. For stories like this one, long forgotten a century before I was born, newspapers and immigration records were often the only evidence that certain events ever took place. By consulting passenger lists, transportation schedules, passport applications, probate documents, case summaries, and – inevitably – gossip columns and letters to the editor, I was able to trace the movements of people and things across oceans and time. I can't tell you how many times I was astounded to find just one more lead, one more fact, or a whole new story thread to chase. However, there are still plenty of unanswered questions. What happened to Susanne, Rosine, and Roumage? Do Polari's military records still exist? Does a descendant of George B. Raymond still own the pin or diamond ring Anna gave him? If you have any further information or ideas, I'd love to hear from you at girlinthetiara@gmail.com.

I want to thank my family and friends for their love and support, as well as my amazing patrons, followers, and YouTube subscribers, whose encouraging notes and comments lifted me up when I doubted anything would come of my efforts. Your belief in me as a storyteller is what brought us here, together.

Notes

The most valuable source for this case is the two-volume French-language record published by the trial's court reporter, Pieter Nicolaas Arntzenius. The first volume contains the indictment, transcripts of interrogations, and letters between the participants. Because volume one repaginates after the indictment, I have indicated precise chapter and document numbers as well as page numbers to help readers locate citations. Volume two contains no repagination, so only page numbers are indicated.

Pagination is also a problem for Seely's petition, located in the bound index of miscellaneous documents from the 30th Congress, 1st session (1850). The volume contains a number of documents, each with its own pagination. Seely's petition and supporting documents are included as document 127, near the end of the volume. All paginations given here are exclusively within document 127.

Abbreviations

BNA: BritishNewspaperArchive.com
SIRIO: Sbornik Imperatorskogo Russkago Istoricheskago Obshchestva

Chapter 1: The Robbery

1. 'The King,' *London Chronicle*, October 8, 1821, BNA.
2. Stefano Papi, *The Jewels of the Romanovs: Family & Court*, revised and expanded ed. (New York: Thames & Hudson, 2013), pp. 36-38.
3. For mother's advice: Sydney W. Jackman, ed., *Chère Annette* (Stroud, Gloucestershire, UK: Alan Sutton Publishing, Inc., 1994), pp. 132-3. For jewels: Pieter Nicolaas Arntzenius, ed., *Procès de Constant Polari*, vol. 1 (La Haye: Chez Th. Lejeune, 1835), chap. 1, doc. 2, pp. 7-11. For origin of pearls: Lady Walburga Paget, *Scenes and Memories* (New York: Charles Scribner's Sons, 1912), 42.

4. 'Portret van Anna Paulowna,' *Koninklijke Verzamelingen*, accessed August 4, 2024, https://www.koninklijkeverzamelingen.nl/collectie/portret-van-anna-paulowna-7482.

5. See Stoop and Van Maanen's reports in: Arntzenius, ed., *Procès*, vol. 1, chap. 1, docs. 3-4, pp. 18, 23-24.

6. For Parfait's Brussels address and arrival time at work: Arntzenius, ed., *Procès*, vol. 1, chap. 1, doc. 1, 1. Palace details: Francis Strauven, 'Le Palais des Académies - une résidence urbaine offerte au Prince d'Orange par les Belges,' *Revue belge de philologie et d'histoire* 94, no. 2 (2016): pp. 416-19. Artwork: C.J. Nieuwenhuys, *Description de La Collection Des Tableaux Qui Ornent Le Palais de S.A.R. Mgr. Le Prince d'Orange a Bruxelles* (Brussels: Alex. De Mat, 1837), pp. 1, 6-16, 46, 50. Tourists admitted: Jacobus Noorduyn, *Herinneringen van een uitstapje naar Brussel in Augustus 1836* (Gorinchem, Netherlands: Jacobus Noorduyn, 1836), 37.

7. Location of the chest: Pieter Nicolaas Arntzenius, ed., *Procès de Constant Polari*, vol. 2 (La Haye: Chez Th. Lejeune, 1835). The end paper contains a drawing of the layout of Anna's bedroom. Cavanillas's responsibility: Dorine Hermans and Daniela Hooghiemstra, eds., *'Voor de Troon Wordt Men Niet Ongestraft Geboren': Ooggetuigen van de Koningen van Nederland, 1813-1890* (Amsterdam: Bakker, 2008), 137. Arrival at Schultz's home: Arntzenius, ed., *Procès*, vol. 2, 496.

8. Schultz's position: Arntzenius, ed., *Procès*, vol. 2, 496. Exchange with Cavanillas: Arntzenius, ed., *Procès*, vol. 2, 496.

9. Baron Camille Buffin, *Mémoires et documents inédits sur la révolution belge et la campagne de Dix-jours (1830-1831)*, vol. 1 (Bruxelles: Librairie Kiessling et cie, 1912), pp. 36-37.

10. Library location: Arntzenius, ed., *Procès*, vol. 2, pp. 497 & endpaper. Chests: Arntzenius, ed., *Procès*, vol. 1, 'Acte d'Accusation,' pp. 5-6.

11. Key stored in the upper section: *Index of Miscellaneous Documents Printed by Order of the Senate of the United States during the First Session of the Thirty-First Congress, 1849-'50*, vol. 1 (Washington, DC: Wm. M. Belt, 1850), doc. 127, 4. For contents of the diamantaire: Arntzenius, ed., *Procès*, vol. 1, chap. 1, doc. 3, pp. 21-22; Arntzenius, ed., *Procès*, vol. 2, 493. For the condition of the lower lock: Arntzenius, ed., *Procès*, vol. 1, chap. 1, doc. 1, 2; Arntzenius, ed., *Procès*, vol. 2, 498.

12. Servants' rooms on the ground floor: *Index*, vol. 1, doc 127, 2. For Cavanillas's offer: Arntzenius, ed., *Procès*, vol. 2, 498.

13. Situation of Anna's rooms: Arntzenius, ed., *Procès*, vol. 1, 'Acte d'Accusation,' pp. 6-7. For terrace: Arntzenius, ed., *Procès*, vol. 2, 618; Hermans and Hooghiemstra, eds., *Voor de Troon*, 138.

14. Arntzenius, ed., *Procès*, vol. 1, chap. 1, doc. 1, 3.

15. Ibid.

16. Arntzenius, ed., *Procès*, vol. 1, chap. 1, doc. 1, pp. 4-5.

17. Arntzenius, ed., *Procès*, vol. 1, chap. 1, doc. 1, 5.

18. Hermans and Hooghiemstra, eds., *Voor de Troon*, 137; Jacqueline Doorn, *Rusland en Orange* (Zaltbommel: Europese Bibliotheek, 1974), 132.

19. For the 77 items: Arntzenius, ed., *Procès*, vol. 1, chap. 1, doc. 2, pp. 7-11. For carats: *Index*, vol. 1, doc. 127, pp. 31-32.

20. *Index*, vol. 1, doc. 127, 30; Arntzenius, ed., *Procès*, vol. 2, 492.

21. Sydney W. Jackman, ed., *Romanov Relations: The Private Correspondence of Tsars Alexander I, Nicholas I and the Grand Dukes Constantine and Michael with Their Sister Queen Anna Pavlovna, 1817-1855* (London: Macmillan, 1969), 217.

22. Fear of missing evidence: Hermans and Hooghiemstra, eds., *Voor de Troon*, 137. Quote to Nicholas: H.T. Colenbrander, ed., *Gedenkstukken der Algemeene Geschiedenis van Nederland van 1795 tot 1840*, vol. 9, book 1 ('s-Gravenhage: Martinus Nijhoff, 1916), 382.

23. Arntzenius, ed., *Procès*, vol. 1, ch. 1, doc. 1, 6.

24. Details of the prosecutors' visit: Arntzenius, ed., *Procès*, vol. 1, chap. 1, doc. 3, pp. 17-18.

25. Arntzenius, ed., *Procès*, vol. 1, chap. 1, doc. 3, pp. 18, 25.

26. Toon Kerkhoff et al., *A History of Dutch Corruption and Public Morality (1648-1940)* (Newcastle upon Tyne, UK: Cambridge Scholars Publishing, 2020), 167.

27. *Fury*: 'Margate, Oct 1,' *Sun* (London), October 2, 1829, BNA. *Earl of Liverpool*: 'Wednesday & Thursday's Post,' *Stamford Mercury*, October 9, 1829, BNA.

28. 'Nederlanden,' *Dagblad van 's Gravenhage*, October 2, 1829, delpher.nl.

29. 'London: Monday, October 26,' *The News* (London), October 26, 1829, BNA. 'Nederlanden | Brussel den 18 October,' *Groninger courant*, October 23, 1829, delpher.nl.

30. Reward: Arntzenius, ed., *Procès*, vol. 1, chap. 1, doc. 5, 26; *Index*, vol. 1, doc. 127, 29. Van Buren's cooperation: *Index*, vol. 1, doc. 127, 2; James A. Hamilton, *Reminiscences of James A. Hamilton* (New York: Charles Scribner & Co., 1869), pp. 223-4.

Chapter 2: Happily Never After

1. *Sbornik Imperatorskogo Russkago Istoricheskago Obshchestva (SIRIO): Pis'ma Yekateriny II k Mel'khioru Grimmu (1774-1796)*, ed. I.K. Grot, vol. 23 (St. Petersburg: Russian Imperial Academy of Science, 1878), 617.

2. 'Portret van Anna Paulowna en haar Broers,' *Koninklijke Verzamelingen*, accessed March 26, 2024, https://www.koninklijkeverzamelingen.nl/collectie/portret-van-anna-paulowna-en-haar-broers-6347.

3. S.A. Poroshin, 'Sto tri dnia iz detskoi zhizni Imperatora Pavla Petrovicha,' *Russky Arkhiv* 7, no. 1 (1869): 15.

4. Countess Varvara Golovine, *Memoirs of Countess Golovine*, tr. G.M. Fox-Davies (London: David Nutt, 1910), 237.

5. Princess Lise Troubetzkoi, ed., *Correspondance de Sa Majesté l'Impératrice Marie Féodorowna Avec Mademoiselle de Nélidoff, Sa Demoiselle d'honneur (1797-1801)* (Paris: Ernest Leroux, 1896), 128.

6. M. van Tuyll van Serooskerken, 'De Erfprins te Oxford (1801-1811) (naar het Fonds Constant te Genève),' in *Bijdragen voor de Vaderlandsche Geschiedenis en Oudheidkunde*, vol. 5 (1935), 23.

7. 'Seventh Bulletin of the Grand Army,' *Sun* (London), November 4, 1806, BNA.

8. Position as ADC: Andrew W. Field, *Wellington's Waterloo Allies* (Barnsley, South Yorkshire: Pen & Sword Military, 2022), chap. 5, Kindle. Nickname: Jeroen van Zanten, *Koning Willem II 1792-1849* (Amsterdam: Boom Uitgevers, 2014), chap. 3, 'Vriendschap en loyaliteit,' Kobo. Universally liked: F. Seymour Larpent, *The Private Journal of F. Seymour Larpent*, ed. Sir George Larpent, vol. 1 (London: Richard Bentley, 1853), 111.

9. Van Zanten, *Koning*, chap. 4, 'Charlotte'; *Autobiography of Miss Cornelia Knight, Lady Companion to the Princess Charlotte of Wales*, vol. 1 (London: W.H. Allen and Co., 1861), 267; A. Aspinall, ed., *Letters of the Princess Charlotte 1811-1817* (London: Home and Van Thal, 1949), pp. 117-118.

10. 77,000 troops: Van Zanten, *Koning*, chap. 5, 'Het lot van Europa'; rain-sodden clay: Gareth Glover, *Waterloo in 100 Objects* (Stroud, Gloucestershire: History Press, 2015), Introduction, Kindle; '…and conduct…': Arthur Wellesley, *Supplementary Despatches, Correspondence, and Memoranda of Field Marshal Arthur Duke of Wellington, K.G.*, ed. Arthur Wellesley 2nd Duke of Wellington, vol. 9 (London: John Murray, 1862), 149; 'Lion of Waterloo:' Jeroen Koch et al., *The House of Orange in Revolution and War: A European History, 1772-1890*, tr. Andy Brown (London: Reaktion Books, 2022), 107.

11. Emma Sophia, Countess of Brownlow, *Slight Reminiscences of a Septuagenarian from 1802 to 1815* (London: John Murray, 1867), pp. 130-31.

12. Broached marriage: Van Zanten, *Koning*, chap. 5, 'Parijs en Sint-Petersburg'; Doorn, *Rusland*, 67. Charlotte quote: Aspinall, ed., *Letters*, 203.

13. 'Anninka': Van Zanten, *Koning*, chap. 5, 'Anna'; '…don't know': J.P. Duyverman, *Uit de Geheime Dagboeken van Aeneas Mackay, Dienaar Des Konings 1806–1876* (Houten: De Haan, 1987), 27.

14. H.T. Colenbrander, ed., *Gedenkstukken der Algemeene Geschiedenis van Nederland van 1795 tot 1840*, vol. 8, book 2 ('s-Gravenhage: Martinus Nijhoff, 1915), 18.

15. Egon Caesar Corti, *Leopold I of Belgium: Secret Pages of European History*, tr. Joseph McCabe (London: T. Fisher Unwin Ltd., 1923), 18.

16. Empress Maria Feodorovna, 'Pis'ma Imperatritsy Marii Foedorovny K'Imperatoru Aleksandru I-Mu,' *Russkiy Arkhiv* vol. 135, no. 1 (1911): 140.

17. Cash gifts: Jackman, ed., *Annette*, pp. 7, 60; Sergei Tomsinski, 'De Romanovs en de Oranjes: tsaren en stadhouders, keizers en koningen' in Sander Paarlberg and Henk Slechte, eds., *Willem II: De Koning en De Kunst* (Dordrecht: W Books, 2014), 52. Orphanages and charity work: Archimandrite Augustine, 'Velikaya Knyaginya Anna Pavlovna (1795–1865) — Koroleva Niderlandov,' *Russkiy Tolstyy Zhurnal Kak Esteticheskiy Fenomen*, n.d. (orig. published in *Neva*, no. 1, 2013), https://magazines.gorky.media/neva/2013/1/velikaya-knyaginya-anna-pavlovna-1795-8211-1865-8212-koroleva-niderlandov.html.

18. Koch et al., *House of Orange*, 200.

19. 'The Prince of Orange,' *The News* (London), November 30, 1817, BNA.

20. For this incident: Jackman, ed., *Annette*, 67. Hatzfeldt quote: H.T. Colenbrander, ed., *Gedenkstukken*, vol. 8, book 1, pp. 362–3; Clancarty: Colenbrander, ed., *Gedenkstukken*, vol. 8, book 1, 81; Wellington: Colenbrander, ed., *Gedenkstukken*, vol. 8, book 1, 83.

21. Colenbrander, ed., *Gedenkstukken*, vol. 8, book 1, 27.

22. Colenbrander, ed., *Gedenkstukken*, vol. 8, book 1, pp. 610–11.

23. Van Zanten, *Koning*, chap. 6, 'Een som van 63 000 gulden.'

24. E. Meeter, *Holland: Its Institutions; Its Press, Kings, and Prisons* (London: J.F. Hope, 1857), pp. 235–6.

25. Hermans and Hooghiemstra, eds., *Voor de Troon*, pp. 120–1; Van Zanten, *Koning*, chap. 6, 'Een som van 63 000 gulden'; Koch et al., *House of Orange*, 193.

26. Van Zanten, *Koning*, chap. 6, 'Bezinning.'

27. Murillo: Tomsinski, 'De Romanovs,' 54. Inheritance: Doorn, *Rusland*, 129; Marie Martin, *Maria Féodorovna En Son Temps, 1759–1828: Contribution à l'histoire de La Russie et de l'Europe* (Paris: L'Harmattan, 2003), pp. 201, 397.

28. Jackman, ed., *Relations*, 182.

29. Colenbrander, ed., *Gedenkstukken*, vol. 9, book 1, 139.

Chapter 3: Meanwhile in America

1. Edwin G. Burrows and Mike Wallace, *Gotham: A History of New York City to 1898* (New York: Oxford University Press, 2000), 20.
2. Washington Irving, *The Works of Washington Irving, Vol. 1: Knickerbocker's New-York*, New Edition, Revised (New York: G.P. Putnam & Company, 1854), xiii.
3. Nell Irvin Painter, *Sojourner Truth: A Life, A Symbol* (New York: W.W. Norton, 1996), 7.
4. 'A Guide to the United States' History of Recognition, Diplomatic, and Consular Relations, by Country, since 1776: The Netherlands,' *Office of the Historian*, United States Department of State, accessed April 4, 2024, https://history.state.gov/countries/netherlands.
5. Maria Hansen, 'Twaalf kranten zijn even warm als een deken: het leven van jonkheer Roger Bangeman Huygens, Graaf van Löwendal,' *Virtus* 9, no. 1-2 (2002): 49.
6. Oath released: G.J.B. Verbeet, 'Herdenking van 1813 voor Limburg historiche vergissing,' *De nieuwe Limburger*, November 30, 1963, delpher.nl. Marriage: Hansen, 'Twaalf kranten,' 49. Wedding festivities: Arntzenius, ed., *Procès*, vol. 1, chap. 2, doc. 12, 50.
7. 'Washington City, August 27,' *Arkansas Gazette*, October 4, 1825, Newspapers.com.
8. Duke Bernhard of Saxe-Weimar-Eisenach, *Travels through North America, During the Years 1825 and 1826*, vol.1 (Philadelphia: Carey, Lea & Carey, 1828), 162.
9. Martin Van Buren, *The Autobiography of Martin Van Buren*, ed. John C. Fitzpatrick, vol. 2 (Washington, DC: Government Printing Office, 1920), 8.
10. David Rubel, *Mr. President: The Human Side of America's Chief Executives* (Alexandria, VA: Time-Life Books, 1998), 52.
11. 'Public Dinner,' *The Evening Post* (New York), August 3, 1827, Newspapers.com.
12. 'Alexandria, Tuesday Morning, July 15, 1828,' *Phenix Gazette* (*Alexandria Gazette*), July 15, 1828, Newspapers.com.

Chapter 4: The Husband Did It

1. Baron E. von Stockmar, *Memoirs of Baron Stockmar*, ed. F. Max Müller, vol. 1 (London: Longmans, Green and Co., 1872), 9.
2. Colenbrander, ed., *Gedenkstukken*, vol. 8, book 1, 420.
3. H.T. Colenbrander, ed., *Gedenkstukken der Algemeene Geschiedenis van Nederland van 1795 tot 1840*, vol. 9, book 2 ('s-Gravenhage: Martinus Nijhoff, 1917), 662.
4. Colenbrander, ed., *Gedenkstukken*, vol. 9, book 1, 381.
5. Hermans and Hooghiemstra, eds., *Voor de Troon*, 138.

6. Louis-Alexandre Berthier, *Rapports Du Maréchal Berthier à l'Empereur Pendant La Campagne de 1813*, vol. 1 (Paris: Librairie Militaire R. Chapelot, 1909), 238.

7. Machado details: *The English Reports: Volume IV, House of Lords, Containing Bligh, Volumes 1 to 4; Bligh, N.S., Volumes 1 to 3*, gen. ed. A. Wood Benton (Edinburgh: William Green & Sons, 1901), pp. 1043-6; A.A. Galiano, 'Mendizabal v. Machado,' *Morning Chronicle* (London), November 18, 1826, BNA; 'French Faith,' *Sun* (London), June 9, 1823, BNA.

8. Mendizábal details: 'Court of Chancery,' *Public Ledger and Daily Advertiser* (London), December 20, 1833, BNA; 'Court of Chancery, Lincoln's Inn – Wednesday,' *Morning Herald* (London), December 19, 1833, BNA; *English Reports*, 1046.

9. Hermans and Hooghiemstra, eds., *Voor de Troon*, 139; Colenbrander, ed., *Gedenkstukken*, vol. 9, book 1, pp. 382-3.

10. Colenbrander, ed., *Gedenkstukken*, vol. 8, book 1, 691; Hermans and Hooghiemstra, eds., *Voor de Troon*, pp. 103, 139; Colenbrander, ed., *Gedenkstukken*, vol. 9, book 1, 382.

11. For the quotes and opinions of Guryev and d'Agoult: Colenbrander, ed., *Gedenkstukken*, vol. 9, book 1, pp. 96, 284, 382-3.

12. Colenbrander, ed., *Gedenkstukken*, vol. 9, book 1, 383.

13. Colenbrander, ed., *Gedenkstukken*, vol. 9, book 1, 173.

14. Colenbrander, ed., *Gedenkstukken*, vol. 9, book 1, 173.

15. Colenbrander, ed., *Gedenkstukken*, vol. 9, book 1, pp. 381-2.

16. Colenbrander, ed., *Gedenkstukken*, vol. 9, book 1, 382; Hermans and Hooghiemstra, eds., *Voor de Troon*, 141; Doorn, *Rusland*, 133.

17. Colenbrander, ed., *Gedenkstukken*, vol. 9, book 1, 382.

Chapter 5: The Belgian Revolution

1. Colenbrander, ed., *Gedenkstukken*, vol. 9, book 1, 7.

2. Johannes Bosscha, *Het Leven van Willem Den Tweede Koning Der Nederlanden En Groothertog van Luxemburg* (Amsterdam: C.M. Van Gogh, 1865), 282; Colenbrander, ed., *Gedenkstukken*, vol. 9, book 1, 381; Van Zanten, *Koning*, chap. 7, 'Politieke crisis.'

3. 'Disturbances in Brussels,' *London Courier and Evening Gazette*, August 30, 1830, BNA.

4. Van Zanten, *Koning*, chap. 7, 'Muiterij'; Jeroen Koch, *Koning Willem I: 1771-1843* (Amsterdam: Uitgeverij Boom, 2013), chap. 7, "Koning en Prinsen in tijden vanopstand," Kobo; Theo Aronson, *The Coburgs of Belgium* (London: Lume Books, 2020), prologue, part 4, Kindle.

5. H.T. Colenbrander, ed., *Gedenkstukken der Algemeene Geschiedenis van Nederland van 1795 tot 1840*, vol. 10, book 2 ('s-Gravenhage: Martinus Nijhoff, 1919), 7.

6. Doorn, *Rusland*, 137; Colenbrander, ed., *Gedenkstukken*, vol. 10, book 2, 7; Van Zanten, *Koning*, chap. 7, 'Vive le Prince.'

7. F. de Bas, *Prins Frederik der Nederlanden en zijn tijd*, vol. 4, book 1 (Schiedam: H.A.M. Roelants, 1913), 365; Van Zanten, *Koning*, chap. 7, 'Vive le Prince'; For Willem's quote: Colenbrander, ed., *Gedenkstukken*, vol. 10, book 2, 7.

8. De Bas, *Prins Frederik*, pp. 367, 373; Van Zanten, *Koning*, chap. 7, 'Vive le Prince.'

9. Van Zanten, *Koning*, chap. 7, 'Antwerpen'; de Potter quote: 'State of Belgium,' *Sun* (London), October 4, 1830, BNA.

10. Don Juan van Halen, *Memoirs of Don Juan van Halen*, vol. 2 (London: Henry Colburn and Richard Bentley, 1830), 366; Hermans and Hooghiemstra, eds., *Voor de Troon*, 154; Van Zanten, *Koning*, chap. 7, 'Antwerpen'; Koch et al., *House of Orange*, 164; Koch, *Willem I*, chap. 7, 'Koning en prinsen in tijden van opstand.'

11. 'Foreign Intelligence,' *Weekly Times* (London), October 3, 1830, BNA.

12. Colenbrander, ed., *Gedenkstukken*, vol. 10, book 3, pp. 399-400; Van Zanten, *Koning*, chap. 7, 'Antwerpen.'

13. Doorn, *Rusland*, 148; Van Zanten, *Koning*, chap. 7, 'Antwerpen'; Koch et al., *House of Orange*, 165.

14. Van Zanten, *Koning*, chap. 7, 'Antwerpen'; Colenbrander, ed., *Gedenkstukken*, vol. 10, book 3, pp. 411-12; Koch, *Willem I*, chap. 7, 'Koning en prinsen in tijden van opstand.'

15. Hermans and Hooghiemstra, eds., *Voor de Troon*, pp. 154-5.

16. Jackman, ed., *Relations*, pp. 213-4.

17. Duyverman, *Dagboken*, 107.

18. Koch et al., *House of Orange*, 169.

19. Colenbrander, ed., *Gedenkstukken*, vol. 10, book 3, 472.

Chapter 6: An American Scandal

1. John F. Marszalek, *The Petticoat Affair: Manners, Mutiny, and Sex in Andrew Jackson's White House* (Baton Rouge: Louisiana State University Press, 1997), pp. 3-9.

2. Jon Meacham, *American Lion: Andrew Jackson in the White House* (New York: Random House, 2008), 26.

3. Robert V. Remini, *The Battle of New Orleans: Andrew Jackson and America's First Military Victory* (New York: Penguin Books, 2001), chap. 7, Kindle.

4. James Parton, *The Life and Times of Aaron Burr*, vol. 2 (New York: Mason Brothers, 1864), 282.

5. Henry Clay, *The Papers of Henry Clay*, ed. Robert Seager II, vol. 7 (Lexington: The University Press of Kentucky, 1982), pp. 120-1.

6. Marszalek, *Affair*, 20.

7. Marszalek, *Affair*, 48.

8. 'Obituary. James A. Hamilton,' *New York Times*, September 26, 1878, https://www.nytimes.com/1878/09/26/archives/james-a-hamilton.html?searchResultPosition=1.

9. James A. Hamilton, *Reminiscences of James A. Hamilton; or, Men and Events at Home and Abroad during Three Quarters of a Century* (New York: Charles Scribner & Co., 1869), 77.

10. Hamilton, *Reminiscences*, 87.

11. Van Buren, *Autobiography*, 464.

12. Hamilton, *Reminiscences*, pp. 97, 215.

13. Hamilton, *Reminiscences*, 140.

14. Hamilton, *Reminiscences*, pp. 143-4.

15. Meacham, *Lion*, 72.

16. Hamilton, *Reminiscences*, 146.

17. Marszalek, *Affair*, 66.

18. Van Buren, *Autobiography*, 351.

19. Henry Clay, *The Papers of Henry Clay*, ed. Mary W.M. Hargreaves and James F. Hopkins, vol. 6 (Lexington: The University Press of Kentucky, 1981), 343.

20. Van Buren, *Autobiography*, 352.

21. Van Buren, *Autobiography*, pp. 354-5. For differing accounts of that night: Marszalek, *Affair*, pp. 111-14; 'Louisville, Friday, August 12, 1831…The public cannot have forgotten…' *Louisville Journal*, August 17, 1831, Newspapers.com; Van Buren, *Autobiography*, 352; John Quincy Adams, '3 January 1830,' *John Quincy Adams Digital Diary*, accessed June 26, 2024, https://www.primarysourcecoop.org/publications/jqa/document/jqadiaries-v36-1830-01-p334--entry3; Margaret Bayard Smith, *The First Forty Years of Washington Society*, ed. Gaillard Hunt (New York: Charles Scribner's Sons, 1906), pp. 305-6.

22. Van Buren, *Autobiography*, 352.

23. Van Buren, *Autobiography*, pp. 353-5.

24. Van Buren, *Autobiography*, 354.

25. Van Buren, *Autobiography*, 355.

26. Smith, *Forty Years*, 310.

27. Marszalek, *Affair*, 132.

28. Hamilton, *Reminiscences*, 168.

29. 'From a valued Dutch friend at the Metropolis,' *Vermont Gazette*, January 18, 1831, Newspapers.com.

30. For a taste of the coverage: 'Correspondence of the N.Y. Courier and Enquirer,' *New Bern Sentinel*, August 17, 1831, Newspapers.com; 'As the chevalier Huygens…,' *Niles' Weekly Register* (Baltimore, MD), August 13, 1831, Newspapers.com; 'Chevalier Huygens,' *Eastern Argus* (Portland, ME), August 5, 1831, Newspapers.com; 'More from Mr. Ingham,' *Eastern Argus*, August 9, 1831, Newspapers.com; 'Nothing can exceed the distress…,' *Louisville Daily Journal*, August 12, 1831, Newspapers.com.

31. For quote: Meacham, *Lion*, 175. For Jackson's reassurance to Van Buren: Andrew Jackson, *The Papers of Andrew Jackson*, vol. 9 (1831), ed. Daniel Feller, Thomas Coens, Laura-Eve Moss, and Harold D. Moser (Knoxville, TN: University of Tennessee Press, 2007), 544.

32. 'The public cannot have forgotten…' *Louisville Journal*, August 17, 1831, Newspapers.com.

Chapter 7: A Suspect Emerges

1. For Polari's story of recovering the crate: Arntzenius, ed., *Procès*, vol. 2, 301.

2. Arntzenius, ed., *Procès*, vol. 1, 'Acte d'Accusation,' 3; Arntzenius, ed., *Procès*, vol. 1, ch. 2, doc. 16, 59.

3. 'Polari, alias Carrara,' *Phenix Gazette (Alexandria Gazette)*, November 22, 1832, Newspapers.com.

4. Charles Boothby, *A Prisoner of France: The Memoirs, Diary and Correspondence of Charles Boothby* (London: Adam and Charles Black, 1898), 234.

5. Guy C. Dempsey, Jr., *Napoleon's Mercenaries: Foreign Units in the French Army under the Consulate and Empire, 1799-1814* (Barnsley, South Yorkshire: Frontline Books, 2015), 'Overview,' Kindle.

6. Desertion: *Verslag Der Teregtzitting van Het Hof van Assises, Provincie Holland (Zuider-Kwartier), Gehouden Den 7den Maart 1834, in Zake van Constant Polari…* ('s Gravenhage: De Gebroeders van Cleef, 1834), pp. 48-49; Arntzenius, ed., *Procès*, vol. 2, 420; 'Teregtzitting van het hof van Assises in de provincie Holland, Zwider-kwartier, op Vrijdag, den 7 Maart 1834, onder voorzitting van Mr. H. van der Burgh,' *Dagblad van 's Gravenhage*, March 7, 1834, delpher.nl. Given his freedom: Arntzenius, ed., *Procès*, vol. 1, 'Acte d'Accusation,' 8.

7. 'Paris Papers,' *Instructor and Select Weekly Advertiser* (London), January 5, 1814, BNA; 'London, Tuesday, Jan. 25,' *Norfolk Chronicle*, January 29, 1814, BNA.

8. Hamilton, *Reminiscences*, 289.

9. Arntzenius, ed., *Procès*, vol. 2, 352.

10. Martin, *Maria Féodorovna*, 61.

11. Arntzenius, ed., *Procès*, vol. 2, 352.

12. Arntzenius, ed., *Procès*, vol. 1, ch. 4, doc. 33, pp. 113-4.

13. For Polari's retelling: Arntzenius, ed., *Procès*, vol. 1, 'Acte d'Accusation,' 29; Arntzenius, ed., *Procès*, vol. 2, pp. 428-9.

14. Arntzenius, ed., *Procès*, vol. 2, pp. 323, 427.

15. Arntzenius, ed., *Procès*, vol. 2, 326.

16. Arntzenius, ed., *Procès*, vol. 2, 456.

17. Arntzenius, ed., *Procès*, vol. 2, 457.

18. For Polari's retelling: Arntzenius, ed., *Procès*, vol. 2, pp. 331-2; Arntzenius, ed., *Procès*, vol. 2, 455.

19. Arntzenius, ed., *Procès*, vol. 2, pp. 459-60.

20. For Polari's retelling of the crate retrieval: Arntzenius, ed., *Procès*, vol. 2, 336.

21. Arntzenius, ed., *Procès*, vol. 2, 338.

22. For Polari's retelling of meeting the Spaniard: Arntzenius, ed., *Procès*, vol. 2, pp. 339-40.

23. Rodney Edvinsson, *Historical Currency Converter*, accessed August 11, 2024, https://www.historicalstatistics.org/Currencyconverter.html.

24. Arntzenius, ed., *Procès*, vol. 2, 341.

25. Arntzenius, ed., *Procès*, vol. 2, 343.

26. For the 'blind man' episode and dialogue: Arntzenius, ed., *Procès*, vol. 2, pp. 346-9.

Chapter 8: The Best Laid Plans

1. Arntzenius, ed., *Procès*, vol. 2, 428.

2. For the Frankfurt goldsmith story: Arntzenius, ed., *Procès*, vol. 2, 356.

3. J. de Brauw, *Herinneringen Eener Reize Naar Nieuwyork Gedaan in de Jaren 1831 en 1832* (Leiden, Netherlands: C.C. van der Hoek, 1833), 206; Arntzenius, ed., *Procès*, vol. 2, 356.

4. For Susanne's story of Polari's return: Arntzenius, ed., *Procès*, vol. 1, 'Acte d'Accusation,' pp. 14-15; Arntzenius, ed., *Procès*, vol. 1, ch. 3, doc. 27, 92. For Polari's version: Arntzenius, ed., *Procès*, vol. 2, pp. 358-59.

5. Arntzenius, ed., *Procès*, vol. 2, 359.

6. Arntzenius, ed., *Procès*, vol. 2, 360.

7. Arntzenius, ed., *Procès*, vol. 2, pp. 361, 503.

8. For Polari and Roudez's plan in this paragraph: Arntzenius, ed., *Procès*, vol. 2, 364.

9. Arntzenius, ed., *Procès*, vol. 2, 365.

10. For the specific amounts of carats and francs: Arntzenius, ed., *Procès*, vol. 2, pp. 365-6.

11. For the Algiers plan: Arntzenius, ed., *Procès*, vol. 2, pp. 367-8.

12. For the entire Bordeaux episode: Arntzenius, ed., *Procès*, vol. 2, pp. 371-375.

13. Susanne's ring is mentioned multiple times: Arntzenius, ed., *Procès*, vol. 1, 'Acte d'Accusation,' 28; Arntzenius, ed., *Procès*, vol. 2, pp. 319, 440.

14. Arntzenius, ed., *Procès*, vol. 1, ch. 4, doc. 36, 134.

15. Arntzenius, ed., *Procès*, vol. 1, ch. 4, doc. 39, 158; doc. 47, 206.

16. Arntzenius, ed., *Procès*, vol. 2, 453.

17. Arntzenius, ed., *Procès*, vol. 2, 377.

18. Arntzenius, ed., *Procès*, vol. 2, 565.

19. Arntzenius, ed., *Procès*, vol. 1, ch. 4, doc. 47, 209.

20. Arntzenius, ed., *Procès*, vol. 1, ch. 4, doc. 34, 124; Arntzenius, ed., *Procès*, vol. 2, pp. 447, 469.

21. Arntzenius, ed., *Procès*, vol. 1, 'Acte d'Accusation,' 15.

22. For Polari showing Susanne the jewels: Arntzenius, ed., *Procès*, vol. 1, ch. 3, doc. 27, 92; for items named: Arntzenius, ed., *Procès*, vol. 1, 'Acte d'Accusation,' 15.

23. For measures Polari took to hide the jewels discussed in this paragraph: Arntzenius, ed., *Procès*, vol. 2, pp. 377-8.

24. Arntzenius, ed., *Procès*, vol. 2, 351.

25. Ibid.

26. Arntzenius, ed., *Procès*, vol. 2, 380.

27. Louis Antoine Fauvelet de Bourienne, *Memoirs of Napoleon Bonaparte*, ed. R.W. Phipps, vol. 1 (New York: Charles Scribner's Sons, 1892), 30.

28. Arntzenius, ed., *Procès*, vol. 2, pp. 365-7.

29. For Daux's location: Arntzenius, ed., *Procès*, vol. 2, 380. For Cartier connection: Hans Nadelhoffer, *Cartier* (San Francisco: Chronicle Books, 2007), 18. For the Daux episode: Arntzenius, ed., *Procès*, vol. 2, pp. 381-2.

30. Arntzenius, ed., *Procès*, vol. 2, 435; Arntzenius, ed., *Procès*, vol. 1, ch. 4, doc. 41, 179.

31. For cost of travel, ship name, and departure city: Arntzenius, ed., *Procès*, vol. 2, 435; for travel under the name Palarrio: 'The Jewels of the Princess of Orange,' *The Evening Post* (New York), July 30, 1831, Newspapers.com.

32. Aronson, *Coburgs*, prologue, part 4, Kindle.

33. Aronson, *Coburgs*, prologue, part 3, Kindle.

34. H.T. Colenbrander, ed. *Gedenkschriften Van Anton Reinhard Falck* ('s-Gravenhage: Martinus Nijhoff, 1913), 312.

35. Hermans and Hooghiemstra, eds., *Voor de Troon*, pp. 177-8.

36. Stockmar, *Memoirs*, 153.

37. Colenbrander, ed., *Gedenkstukken*, vol. 10, book 3, 480.

38. Aronson, *Coburgs*, prologue, part 4, Kindle.

39. Charles Robert Vasilievitch de Nesselrode, *Lettres Et Papiers Du Chancelier Comte De Nesselrode 1760-1850*, ed. Anatole Nesselrode, vol.7: 1828-1839 (Paris: A. Lahure, 1908), pp. 185-6.

40. 'Dutch Papers,' *Sun* (London), July 28, 1831, BNA.

Chapter 9: Welcome to New York

1. Number of passengers: William Skiddy, 'Diary, 1805-1839,' *Mystic Seaport Museum*, coll. 304, vol. 1, accessed August 12, 2024, https://research.mysticseaport.org/item/l038915_vol-1/#216. Route details: 'Havre Packets,' *The Evening Post* (New York), February 4, 1829, Newspapers.com. Quote: 'The undersigned, passengers…' *The Evening Post* (New York), May 19, 1817, Newspapers.com.

2. Stephen Fox, *Transatlantic: Samuel Cunard, Isambard Brunel, and the Great Atlantic Steamships* (New York: HarperCollins, 2003), pp. 5-10.

3. Arntzenius, ed., *Procès*, vol. 1, ch. 4, doc. 39, 159.

4. Duke Bernhard of Saxe-Weimar-Eisenach, *Travels through North America, During the Years 1825 and 1826*, vol. 2 (Philadelphia: Carey, Lea & Carey, 1828), 195.

5. Charles E. Rosenberg, *The Cholera Years: The United States in 1832, 1849 and 1866* (Chicago: University of Chicago Press, 1962), 13.

6. De Brauw, *Herinneringen*, 26.

7. 'French & Spanish Boarding,' *The Evening Post* (New York), April 8, 1831, Newspapers.com.

8. De Brauw, *Herinneringen*, pp. 26-27.

9. *Index*, vol. 1, doc. 127, 5.

10. Arntzenius, ed., *Procès*, vol. 1, ch. 4, doc. 48, 215.

11. Arntzenius, ed., *Procès*, vol. 2, 383; Hamilton, *Reminiscences*, 223.

12. Arntzenius, ed., *Procès*, vol. 1, ch. 4, doc. 49, 226.

13. 'Foreign Intelligence, Brussels, Sept. 21,' *British Mercury* (London), September 29, 1824, BNA.

14. For Roumage's history: *Causes Criminelles Célèbres Du Dix-Neuvième Siècle*, vol. 3 (Paris: H. Langlois et Cie, 1828), pp. 6–35.

15. For the bond deal gone wrong: *Causes Criminelles*, pp. 16–23. For the legal aftermath and Roumage quote: *Causes Criminelles*, pp. 33–54.

16. *Causes Criminelles*, 81.

17. For the escape story: 'Orleans, July 29,' *Morning Chronicle* (London), August 3, 1825, BNA. For the monogram: Arntzenius, ed., *Procès*, vol. 1, ch. 2, doc. 25, 87.

18. For the arson accusation, see bound issues in: *Le constitutionnel: journal du commerce, politique et littéraire* (France: Boniface, 1829). In particular: 'Interieur, Paris, 26 Octobre,' October 27, 1829; 'Interieur, Paris 25 Novembre | Tribunal Correctionnel de Paris,' November 26, 1829; 'Interieur, Paris 18 Octobre 1829 | - Roumage, condamné pour une escroquerie des plus scandaleuses…,' October 19, 1829. For trial, see: 'The People vs. Roumage,' *The Evening Post* (New York), November 7, 1829, Newspapers.com.

19. Arntzenius, ed., *Procès*, vol. 2, 384.

20. Arntzenius, ed., *Procès*, vol. 1, ch. 4, doc. 51, 238 and Arntzenius, ed., *Procès*, vol. 2, 451.

21. Arntzenius, ed., *Procès*, vol. 2, 384.

22. All information in this paragraph: Arntzenius, ed., *Procès*, vol. 2, 385.

23. Arntzenius, ed., *Procès*, vol. 2, pp. 386–7.

24. Arntzenius, ed., *Procès*, vol. 2, 387.

25. Textbook: Arntzenius, ed., *Procès*, vol. 2, 438. Battery Park: Barry Moreno, *Castle Garden and Battery Park* (Charleston, SC: Arcadia Publishing, 2007), pp. 8, 14–15, 19. Song: De Brauw, *Herinneringen*, 177.

26. Arntzenius, ed., *Procès*, vol. 2, 387.

27. Arntzenius, ed., *Procès*, vol. 1, ch. 4, doc. 48, 213.

Chapter 10: The First Betrayal

1. Arntzenius, ed., *Procès*, vol. 1, ch. 4, doc. 48, 213.

2. Arntzenius, ed., *Procès*, vol. 1, ch. 4, doc. 46, pp. 204–5.

3. Arntzenius, ed., *Procès*, vol. 1, ch. 4, doc. 44, 194; Arntzenius, ed., *Procès*, vol. 1, ch. 4, doc. 51, 239.

4. Arntzenius, ed., *Procès*, vol. 1, ch. 4, doc. 51, 242.

5. 'The Robbery of the Dutch Crown Jewels,' *New York Daily Herald*, December 20, 1850, Newspapers.com.

6. Hamilton, *Reminiscences*, pp. 123, 125.

7. Hamilton, *Reminiscences*, 132.

8. Van Buren, *Autobiography*, 263.

9. Swartwout and Burr history: Andreas Reichstein, *Rise of the Lone Star: The Making of Texas* (College Station, TX: Texas A&M University Press, 1989), 108; R. Kent Newmyer, *The Treason Trial of Aaron Burr: Law, Politics, and the Character Wars of the New Nation* (Cambridge: Cambridge University Press, 2012), 52.

10. Raymond J. Sheehan, *The Original Sins: America's Fight Against Corruption in the Era of Manifest Destiny* (Maitland, FL: Xulon Press, 2016), 62.

11. Treasury's funds: Andrew Jackson, *The Papers of Andrew Jackson*, vol. 7 (1829), ed. Daniel Feller, Thomas Coens, Laura-Eve Moss, and Harold D. Moser (Knoxville, TN: University of Tennessee Press, 2007), 156. Quote about Swartwout: Jackson, *Papers*, vol. 7, pp. 156-7.

12. Jackson, *Papers*, vol. 7, 180.

13. Hamilton, *Reminiscences*, 132.

14. Hamilton, *Reminiscences*, pp. 173-4.

15. Arntzenius, ed., *Procès*, vol. 1, ch. 2, doc. 6, 27.

16. Arntzenius, ed., *Procès*, vol. 1, ch. 4, doc. 51, 244.

17. Arntzenius, ed., *Procès*, vol. 1, ch. 4, doc. 48, pp. 217, 241 and ch. 2, doc. 8, 40. For the currency conversion: 'CPI Inflation Calculator,' *OfficialData.Org*, accessed August 12, 2024, https://www.officialdata.org/us/inflation/1830?amount=20000.

18. 'Biljage tot het A.H.B. No. 108 | Aan de Redactive van het A.H.B.,' *Algemeen Handelsblad (*Amsterdam), September 8, 1831, delpher.nl.

19. 'NY, U.S., Wills and Probate Records, 1659-1999 for Joshua B Seely,' *Ancestry.com*, accessed August 13, 2024. https://www.ancestry.com/search/collections/8800/records/1934103?tid=151195839&pid=252099306530&ssrc=pt.

20. 'U.S., Newspaper Extractions from the Northeast, 1704-1930 for William A Seely,' *Ancestry.com*, accessed August 13, 2024. https://www.ancestry.com/search/collections/50015/records/515130?tid=151195839&pid=252099307314.

21. Seely's experience: 'Communication,' *The Evening Post* (New York), October 29, 1813, Newspapers.com; Daniel Rogers, *The New-York City-Hall Recorder, for the Year 1817*, vol. 2, no. 5 (New York: Clayton and Kingsland, 1817) pp. 61-8. Quote: 'We have great pleasure in stating…,' *Poughkeepsie Journal*, July 6, 1825, Newspapers.com.

22. Quote: *Index*, vol. 1, doc. 127, 64. Salary: *Index*, vol. 1, doc. 127, 7. Currency conversion: 'CPI Inflation Calculator,' *OfficialData.org*, accessed August 12, 2024, https://www.officialdata.org/us/inflation/1830?amount=12000. Appearance: 'U.S., Passport Applications, 1795-1925 for William A Seely,' *Ancestry.com*,

accessed August 13, 2024. https://www.ancestry.com/search/collections/1174/records/60897?tid=151195839&pid=252099307314.

23. Arntzenius, ed., *Procès*, vol. 1, ch. 2, doc. 25, 79.

24. Arntzenius, ed., *Procès*, vol. 1, ch. 2, doc. 25, 78.

25. 'Seizure by the Custom House,' *The Evening Post* (New York), July 29, 1831, Newspapers.com; 'The Jewels of the Princess of Orange,' *The Evening Post* (New York).

26. This paragraph contains Polari's version of the seizure; for detail: Arntzenius, ed., *Procès*, vol. 2, 388ff.

27. Arntzenius, ed., *Procès*, vol. 1, ch. 2, doc. 13, 56; *Index*, vol. 1, doc. 127, 33.

28. 'The Jewels of the Princess of Orange,' *The Evening Post* (New York); *Index*, vol. 1, doc. 127, 32; Arntzenius, ed., *Procès*, vol. 2, 438.

29. Quote: Hamilton, *Reminiscences*, 223. Payout: Jonathan D. Sarna, *Jacksonian Jew: The Two Worlds of Mordecai Noah* (New York: Holmes & Meier Publishers, Inc., 1981), 87.

Chapter 11: Buried Treasure

1. De Brauw, *Herinneringen*, 146.

2. Henry R. Stiles, *A History of the City of Brooklyn*, vol. 2 (Brooklyn, NY: Published by subscription, 1869), 133. For Whitman and the Military Garden: Walt Whitman, *Specimen Days & Collect* (Philadelphia, PA: Rees Welsh & Co., 1882), 16. Also: Walt Whitman, 'An Old Brooklyn Landmark Going,' *The Walt Whitman Archive*, gen. ed. Matt Cohen, Ed Folsom, and Kenneth M. Price, accessed August 13, 2024, https://whitmanarchive.org/item/per.00207.

3. Arntzenius, ed., *Procès*, vol. 2, 390.

4. Ibid.

5. Arntzenius, ed., *Procès*, vol. 1, ch. 2, doc. 6, 28.

6. Police response: Arntzenius, ed., *Procès*, vol. 1, ch. 2, doc. 6, 28; Quote: 'Biljage tot het A.H.B. No. 108,' *Algemeen Handelsblad*.

7. Arntzenius, ed., *Procès*, vol. 1, ch. 2, doc. 6, 28.

8. Arntzenius, ed., *Procès*, vol. 1, ch. 4, doc. 51, 253.

9. Arntzenius, ed., *Procès*, vol. 1, ch. 4, doc. 44, 193.

10. Arntzenius, ed., *Procès*, vol. 1, ch. 4, doc. 51, 253; Arntzenius, ed., *Procès*, vol. 2, 504.

11. Arntzenius, ed., *Procès*, vol. 2, 391.

12. 'Good league': Arntzenius, ed., *Procès*, vol. 2, 391; 'The Stolen Jewels of the Prince of Orange,' *New York Daily Herald*, January 21, 1850, Newspapers.com. 'Inaccessible thicket': *Index*, vol. 1, doc. 127, 8.

13. Arntzenius, ed., *Procès*, vol. 2, 392; Arntzenius, ed., *Procès*, vol. 1, ch. 4, doc. 36, 136 and ch. 4, doc. 44, 195.

14. Arntzenius, ed., *Procès*, vol. 2, 392.

15. De Brauw, *Herinneringen*, 146; Arntzenius, ed., *Procès*, vol. 2, 392.

16. Arntzenius, ed., *Procès*, vol. 1, ch. 2, doc. 6, 29.

17. Arntzenius, ed., *Procès*, vol. 1, ch. 4, doc. 51, 258.

18. Arntzenius, ed., *Procès*, vol. 1, ch. 2, doc. 25, 81.

Chapter 12: The Second Betrayal

1. Arntzenius, ed., *Procès*, vol. 1, ch. 4, doc. 40, pp. 170-1.

2. Arntzenius, ed., *Procès*, vol. 1, ch. 4, doc. 42, 184.

3. Timing: Arntzenius, ed., *Procès*, vol. 1, ch. 4, doc. 42, 184. Rosine: Arntzenius, ed., *Procès*, vol. 1, ch. 4, doc. 40, 174. For value: *Index*, vol. 1, doc. 127, 8.

4. Arntzenius, ed., *Procès*, vol. 1, ch. 4, doc. 33, 118.

5. Arntzenius, ed., *Procès*, vol. 1, ch. 2, doc. 6, 30.

6. Arntzenius, ed., *Procès*, vol. 1, ch. 4, doc. 39, 161.

7. 'The Jewels of the Princess of Orange,' *The Evening Post* (New York).

8. Arntzenius, ed., *Procès*, vol. 1, ch. 2, doc. 10, 47.

9. 'Biljage tot het A.H.B. No. 108,' *Algemeen Handelsblad*.

10. DuFlon offer: *Index*, vol. 1, doc. 127, 8; Arntzenius, ed., *Procès*, vol. 1, ch. 2, doc. 6, 29. Police quote: Arntzenius, ed., *Procès*, vol. 1, ch. 2, doc. 6, 29.

11. Arntzenius, ed., *Procès*, vol. 2, 393.

12. Ibid.

13. Arntzenius, ed., *Procès*, vol. 1, ch. 2, doc. 6, 29; Arntzenius, ed., *Procès*, vol. 2, 393.

14. Polari's strength: Arntzenius, ed., *Procès*, vol. 1, ch. 2, doc. 6, 29. Homan: 'The Stolen Jewels,' *Rhode-Island Republican*, August 9, 1831, Newspapers.com. Seely quote: *Index*, vol. 1, doc. 127, 46.

15. Resistance quote: De Brauw, *Herinneringen*, 147. Lawyer quote: Arntzenius, ed., *Procès*, vol. 2, 392.

16. *Index*, vol. 1, doc. 127, 9.

17. Arntzenius, ed., *Procès*, vol. 1, 'Acte d'Accusation,' 31.

18. Francis Rawle, 'Edward Livingston,' in *The American Secretaries of State and Their Diplomacy*, ed. Samuel Flagg Bemis, vol. 4 (New York: Pageant Book Company, 1958), 213.

19. Charles Havens Hunt, *Life of Edward Livingston* (New York: D. Appleton and Company, 1864), 274.

20. Hunt, *Livingston*, pp. 278-9.

21. 'Biljage tot het A.H.B. No. 108,' *Algemeen Handelsblad*.

22. For the Café de la Victoire story: 'Aan de Redactive van het A.H.B.,' *Algemeen Handelsblad* (Amsterdam), September 8, 1831, delpher.nl; Arntzenius, ed., *Procès*, vol. 1, ch. 2, doc. 14, 57; *Index*, vol. 1, doc. 127, 34. For the Paris story: Arntzenius, ed., *Procès*, vol. 1, ch. 2, doc. 19, 62. For the Brussels story: *Index*, vol. 1, doc. 127, 35.

23. For Seely's memory: *Index*, vol. 1, doc. 127, 11. For Hamilton's: Hamilton, *Reminiscences*, 223.

24. Arntzenius, ed., *Procès*, vol. 1, ch. 2, doc. 25, 82.

25. Arntzenius, ed., *Procès*, vol. 1, ch. 4, doc. 38, 156.

26. Arntzenius, ed., *Procès*, vol. 1, ch. 4, doc. 50, 235.

27. *Index*, vol. 1, doc. 127, 13; Arntzenius, ed., *Procès*, vol. 1, 'Acte d'Accusation,' 12; Arntzenius, ed., *Procès*, vol. 1, ch. 2, doc. 22, 72.

28. Arntzenius, ed., *Procès*, vol. 1, ch. 4, doc. 50, 234.

29. Bellevue history: David Oshinsky, *Bellevue: Three Centuries of Medicine and Mayhem at America's Most Storied Hospital* (New York: Doubleday, 2016), pp. 18, 37. Robert J. Carlisle, ed., *An Account of Bellevue Hospital with a Catalogue of the Medical and Surgical Staff from 1736 to 1894* (New York: The Society of the Alumni of Bellevue Hospital, 1893), 24.

30. 'Prisoners and Patients,' *The Evening Post* (New York), May 24, 1831, Newspapers.com.

31. Arntzenius, ed., *Procès*, vol. 2, 481.

32. Hamilton, *Reminiscences*, 320.

33. Arntzenius, ed., *Procès*, vol. 1, ch. 2, doc. 12, pp. 50-52.

Chapter 13: A Reputation Rehabilitated

1. Van Zanten, *Koning*, chap. 7, "Tien dagen wraak."

2. Charles White, *The Belgic Revolution of 1830*, vol. 1 (London: Whittaker and Co., 1835), 299.

3. 'Portret van Anna Paulowna,' *Koninklijke Verzamelingen.nl*, accessed August 15, 2024, https://www.koninklijkeverzamelingen.nl/collectie/portret-van-anna-paulowna-6177.

4. 'London – Thursday, Oct. 13 | Her Royal Highness the Princess of Orange…' *Saint James's Chronicle* (London), October 13, 1831, BNA.

5. Aronson, *Coburgs*, chap. 1, part 1, Kindle.

6. Campaign details: Paarlberg & Slechte, eds., *Willem II*, 196 (for quote); Van Zanten, *Koning*, chap. 7, 'Tien dagan wraak'; Jackman, ed., *Relations*, 236; Doorn, *Rusland*, 164.

7. Nesselrode, *Lettres*, 213.
8. Wellesley, *Supplementary Despatches,* vol. 10, 168.
9. 'Holland,' *Halifax Express*, September 3, 1831, BNA.
10. Nesselrode, *Lettres*, 219.
11. Jackman, ed., *Relations*, 242.
12. Nesselrode, *Lettres*, 209.
13. Stockmar, *Memoirs*, 145.
14. Negotiations: Stockmar, *Memoirs*, 208; Koch et al., *House of Orange*, 175.
15. Nesselrode, *Lettres*, 235.
16. Colenbrander, ed., *Gedenkstukken*, vol. 10, book 3, 494.

Chapter 14: The Third Betrayal

1. Jackson, *Papers*, vol. 9, pp. 532-3.
2. Request: *Index*, vol. 1, doc. 127, 16; 'Carrara and the Jewels,' *The Evening Post* (New York), September 2, 1831, Newspapers.com. Provisional mandate: Jackson, *Papers*, vol. 9, 533.
3. Arntzenius, ed., *Procès*, vol. 1, ch. 4, doc. 50, 235.
4. Arntzenius, ed., *Procès*, vol. 1, 'Acte d'Accusation,' 13; Arntzenius, ed., *Procès*, vol. 1, ch. 2, doc. 25, 86.
5. Arntzenius, ed., *Procès*, vol. 1, ch. 4, doc. 48, 218.
6. Arntzenius, ed., *Procès*, vol. 1, ch. 4, doc. 33, 120.
7. Arntzenius, ed., *Procès*, vol. 1, ch. 4, doc. 51, 259.
8. Fare information is for the *Monongahela*, sailing under Captain Dixey, in September of 1832. £30 is listed as the equivalent of $133 1/3. 'Line of Packets for Liverpool,' *The Philadelphia Inquirer*, September 24, 1832, Newspapers.com.
9. Arntzenius, ed., *Procès*, vol. 1, ch. 2, doc. 26, 90.
10. Arntzenius, ed., *Procès*, vol. 1, ch. 4, doc. 35, 128.
11. Arntzenius, ed., *Procès*, vol. 1, ch. 4, doc. 35, pp. 128-9.
12. Arntzenius, ed., *Procès*, vol. 1, ch. 4, doc. 48, 218.
13. PA trip details: Arntzenius, ed., *Procès*, vol. 1, ch. 4, doc. 51, 260; Arntzenius, ed., *Procès*, vol. 1, ch. 4, doc. 33, pp. 116-7; Arntzenius, ed., *Procès*, vol. 1, ch. 4, doc. 45, 200; *Index*, vol. 1, doc. 127, 15.
14. Departure time: Arntzenius, ed., *Procès*, vol. 1, ch. 4, doc. 45, 200. Mail coach details: Steven M. Roth, 'Stage Operations and the Mails in New Jersey,' *New Jersey Postal History Society* 41, no. 1 and 2 (February and May 2013): 6ff, accessed August 15, 2024, https://njpostalhistory.org/media/pdf/rothstage.pdf. Handkerchief to face: Arntzenius, ed., *Procès*, vol. 1, ch. 4, doc. 45, 200.

15. Arntzenius, ed., *Procès*, vol. 1, ch. 4, doc. 45, 201.

16. Arntzenius, ed., *Procès*, vol. 1, ch. 4, doc. 36, 140.

17. Arntzenius, ed., *Procès*, vol. 1, ch. 4, doc. 36, 141.

18. Arntzenius, ed., *Procès*, vol. 1, ch. 4, doc. 39, 161.

19. Arntzenius, ed., *Procès*, vol. 1, ch. 4, doc. 34, 125; Arntzenius, ed., *Procès*, vol. 1, ch. 4, doc. 48, 218.

20. Arntzenius, ed., *Procès*, vol. 1, ch. 4, doc. 45, pp. 201-3; Arntzenius, ed., *Procès*, vol. 1, ch. 4, doc. 36, 148.

21. Seely's plan, from here to section end: *Index*, vol. 1, doc. 127, 15.

22. For Huygens's visit to Polari: Arntzenius, ed., *Procès*, vol. 1, 'Acte d'Accusation,' 12; pardon offer: *Index*, vol. 1, doc. 127, 17.

23. Susanne knew his secrets: Arntzenius, ed., *Procès*, vol. 1, ch. 2, doc. 21, 70; reputation quote: 69; scheming quote: 67.

24. Cache worth: *Index*, vol. 1, doc. 127, 18; Bergonzio present: Arntzenius, ed., *Procès*, vol. 2, 475; no jewels: Arntzenius, ed., *Procès*, vol. 1, ch. 2, doc. 23, pp. 74-5.

25. *Index*, vol. 1, doc. 127, pp. 36-40.

26. Huygens surrenders stones: *Index*, vol. 1, doc. 127, pp. 36-40; Jackson's order: Jackson, *Papers*, vol. 9, 533.

27. *Index*, vol. 1, doc. 127, 15.

28. Ibid.

29. See Susanne's fifth interrogation: Arntzenius, ed., *Procès*, vol. 1, ch. 4, doc. 36, pp. 141-8.

30. Arntzenius, ed., *Procès*, vol. 1, 'Acte d'Accusation,' 13; 'Jewels of the Princess of Orange,' *Morning Post* (London), September 26, 1831, BNA.

31. Arntzenius, ed., *Procès*, vol. 1, ch. 4, doc. 38, 155; ch. 3, doc. 27, 93; ch. 3, doc. 30, 99.

32. For Roumage's version of events: Arntzenius, ed., *Procès*, vol. 1, ch. 4, doc. 48, pp. 217-8; taken to London: 'Jewels of the Princess of Orange,' *The Evening Post* (New York), November 10, 1831, Newspapers.com.

33. Willink's analysis of the jewels: Arntzenius, ed., *Procès*, vol. 1, 'Acte d'Accusation,' 16; Arntzenius, ed., *Procès*, vol. 1, ch. 3, doc. 28, pp. 95-97.

34. Colenbrander, ed., *Gedenkstukken*, vol. 9, book 2, 570.

35. George Bradshaw, *Bradshaw's Illustrated Hand-Book for Travellers in Belgium, on the Rhine, and through Portions of Rhenish Prussia* (London: W.J. Adams, 1853), 168.

36. For Roumage's version of events: Arntzenius, ed., *Procès*, vol. 1, ch. 4, doc. 48, pp. 218-220.

37. Arntzenius, ed., *Procès*, vol. 1, ch. 4, doc. 48, 222.

Chapter 15: Law & Disorder

1. Jackson, *Papers*, vol. 9, 677.
2. Henry Dudley Teetor, 'The Burr-Hamilton Duel, and the Duel Ground at Weehawken,' *Magazine of Western History* XII, no. 3 (July 1890): 233.
3. 'The Mercantile Advertiser…' *The Evening Post* (New York), October 4, 1831, Newspapers.com.
4. Swartwout and McLane's relationship: John A. Munroe, *Louis McLane: Federalist and Jacksonian* (New Brunswick, NJ: Rutgers University Press, 1973), pp. 246, 448; Eugene Irving McCormac, 'Louis McLane,' in *The American Secretaries of State and Their Diplomacy*, vol. 4, ed. Samuel Flagg Bemis (New York: Pageant Book Company, 1958), 276.
5. Hamilton, *Reminiscences*, 223.
6. Hamilton, *Reminiscences*, pp. 223-4.
7. Both quotes in this paragraph: Hamilton, *Reminiscences*, 224.
8. Jackson, *Papers*, vol. 9, 678.
9. For Susanne's first interrogation: Arntzenius, ed., *Procès*, vol. 1, ch. 4, doc. 32. For the buried jewels outside Brussels: p. 111.
10. Arntzenius, ed., *Procès*, vol. 1, ch. 4, doc. 35, 130; ch. 4, doc. 38, pp. 155, 160.
11. For the review of recovered jewels: Arntzenius, ed., *Procès*, vol. 1, ch. 3, doc. 31, pp. 100-105; ch. 1, doc. 2, 7; vol. 1, 'Acte d'Accusation,' pp. 16-17.
12. Le Strange, ed., *Correspondence*, vol. 2, pp. 328-330.
13. *Index*, vol. 1, doc. 127, 36.
14. *Index*, vol. 1, doc. 127, 18; 'We learn from the Washington Globe…', *The Evening Post* (New York), January 11, 1832, Newspapers.com.
15. De Brauw, *Herinneringen*, pp. 208-9.
16. 'Escape of Prisoners from Bridewell,' *The Evening Post* (New York), February 20, 1830, Newspapers.com.
17. 'A morning paper mentions that Carara…' *The Evening Post* (New York), January 24, 1832, Newspapers.com; De Brauw, *Herinneringen*, pp. 150-1.
18. De Brauw, *Herinneringen*, 151.
19. Jackson, *Papers*, vol. 10, 26.
20. Jackson, *Papers*, vol. 10, 27.
21. Hamilton, *Reminiscences*, 225.
22. *Index*, vol. 1, doc. 127, 18; Arntzenius, ed., *Procès*, vol. 1, ch. 6, doc. 53, pp. 275-6; Jackson, *Papers*, vol. 10, 27.

23. Hamilton, *Reminiscences*, pp. 223-4.

24. *Index*, vol. 1, doc. 127, pp. 50-52.

Chapter 16: A Hero, a Spy, and a Scoundrel

1. Marius Draaisma, 'De Polari-affair, 1829-1834: Een juwelendiefstal wordt een diplomatiek incident,' Master's thesis (Rijksuniversitat Groningen, n.d.), accessed August 16, 2024, https://be1830.be/onewebmedia/De%20affaire%20 Polari%20%28juwelenroof%20Willem%20van%20Oranje%29.pdf, 29.

2. 'The Jewels of the Princess of Orange,' *Phenix Gazette (Alexandria Gazette)*, March 21, 1832, Newspapers.com.

3. Both quotes from Disbrowe, *Old Days*, 234.

4. Noorduyn, *Brussel in Augustus 1836*, 3.

5. Arntzenius, ed., *Procès*, vol. 1, ch. 5, doc. 52, 262.

6. For Raymond's dig: Arntzenius, ed., *Procès*, vol. 1, ch. 5, doc. 52, pp. 261-3; Arntzenius, ed., *Procès*, vol. 1, 'Acte d'Accusation,' pp. 17-18.

7. For Raymond's trip back: 'The Jewels of the Princess of Orange,' *Phenix Gazette (Alexandria Gazette)*, March 21, 1832, Newspapers.com; 'The Jewels of the Princess of Orange,' *Poughkeepsie Journal*, April 11, 1832, Newspapers.com.

8. 'The Jewels of the Princess of Orange,' *Poughkeepsie Journal*.

9. For second review of recovered jewels: Arntzenius, ed., *Procès*, vol. 1, ch. 1, doc. 2, 10; ch. 5, doc. 52, 264, pp. 264, 266-7; Verhaegen, 'Le Vol,' pp. 334-5. For the list of jewels identified: Arntzenius, ed., *Procès*, vol. 1, ch. 5, doc. 52, pp. 267-8.

10. Arntzenius, ed., *Procès*, vol. 1, 'Acte d'Accusation,' 19; ch. 5, doc. 52, 272.

11. 'The Jewels of the Princess of Orange,' *Poughkeepsie Journal*, April 11, 1832, Newspapers.com.

12. Arntzenius, ed., *Procès*, vol. 1, ch. 4, doc. 50, 235.

13. Jackson, *Papers*, vol. 10, 214.

14. Jackson, *Papers*, vol. 10, pp. 214-5.

15. Arntzenius, ed., *Procès*, vol. 2, pp. 396-7.

16. Arntzenius, ed., *Procès*, vol. 2, 397.

17. Arntzenius, ed., *Procès*, vol. 2, 398.

18. De Brauw, *Herinneringen*, pp. 144-5.

19. 'The following certificate has appeared…' *Morning Courier & New York Enquirer* (New York), April 9, 1832, Newspapers.com.

20. Ibid.

21. De Brauw, *Herinneringen*, pp. 153-5.

22. Arntzenius, ed., *Procès*, vol. 2, pp. 500-01.

23. 'The Hague, April 5,' *Albion and the Star* (London), April 9, 1832, BNA; 'Holland | The Hague, April 13,' *London Evening Standard*, April 17, 1832, BNA.

24. For third review of recovered jewels: Arntzenius, ed., *Procès*, vol. 1, ch. 6, doc. 53, pp. 274-88, 282.

25. *Index*, vol. 1, doc. 127, pp. 47-49.

26. Van Buren, *Autobiography*, pp. 9-10.

Chapter 17: Cholera

1. 'Foreign News | There is no news of any moment…,' *The Evening Post* (New York), November 2, 1830, Newspapers.com; Constantine's death: Jackman, ed., *Relations*, 19.

2. Corine Hendriks and Martijn Storms, 'Leiden Cholera Epidemics Mapped out, Literally,' *UniversiteitLeiden.nl*, September 7, 2020, https://www.universiteitleiden.nl/en/news/2020/09/leiden-cholera-epidemics-mapped-out-literally.

3. Jackman, ed., *Relations*, 247.

4. Hendriks and Storms, 'Leiden Cholera.'

5. 'To David Hosack, M.D. of New York,' *The Evening Post* (New York), October 3, 1831, Newspapers.com.

6. Quote and stats in this paragraph: Geoffrey Bilson, *A Darkened House: Cholera in Nineteenth-Century Canada* (Toronto: University of Toronto Press, 1980), chap. 2, Kindle.

7. 'Quarantine Ground,' *The Evening Post* (New York), April 10, 1832, Newspapers.com.

8. 'Cholera Department,' *Herald of the Times* (Newport, RI), August 2, 1832, Newspapers.com.

9. Charles E. Rosenberg, *The Cholera Years: The United States in 1832, 1849 and 1866* (Chicago: University of Chicago Press, 1962), pp. 17-18.

10. Walter Bowne, 'Proclamation,' *The Evening Post* (New York), June 16, 1832, Newspapers.com.

11. J.E. De Kay, 'Gentlemen – In reply to your request for information,' *The Evening Post* (New York), June 16, 1832, Newspapers.com.

12. Rosenberg, *Cholera Years*, 25.

13. De Brauw, *Herinneringen*, pp. 157-8.

14. Rosenberg, *Cholera Years*, 3.

15. Edward H. Dixon, *Scenes in the Practice of a New York Surgeon* (New York: De Witt & Davenport, 1855), pp. 15-16.

16. Rosenberg, *Cholera Years*, 3.

17. For quotes from this letter in this paragraph: *Index*, vol. 1, doc. 127, pp. 42-43.

18. Arntzenius, ed., *Procès*, vol. 2, 477.

19. 'The Report of the Board of Health...,' *The Evening Post* (New York), July 6, 1832, Newspapers.com.

20. 'The Commissioners of the Alms House...,' *The Evening Post* (New York), July 6, 1832, Newspapers.com.

21. Rosenberg, *Cholera Years*, 32.

22. Rosenberg, *Cholera Years*, 30.

23. 'The Cholera,' *Phenix Gazette (Alexandria Gazette)*, July 10, 1832, Newspapers. com.

24. Hamilton, *Reminiscences*, 246.

25. 'The Cholera,' *The Evening Post* (New York), August 2, 1832, Newspapers.com.

26. Dixon, *New York Surgeon*, pp. 14-15.

27. Arntzenius, ed., *Procès*, vol. 2, pp. 481-2.

28. Death date: 'Mr. George B. Raymond,' *Philadelphia Inquirer*, July 10, 1832, Newspapers.com; *Index*, vol. 1, doc. 127, 20. Nine children: 'New York, U.S., Wills and Probate Records, 1659-1999 for George B Raymond,' *Ancestry.com*, accessed August 19, 2024. https://www.ancestry.com/search/collections/8800/records/2683534?tid=&pid=&queryId=f9d7cb52-04b9-44aa-a757-fb406bb6ecd9.

29. *Index*, vol. 1, doc. 127, 20.

30. Oshinsky, *Bellevue*, pp. 42-43; Carlisle, *An Account*, 35.

31. Jackson, *Papers*, vol. 10, 827; Hamilton, *Reminiscences*, 226.

32. Arntzenius, ed., *Procès*, vol. 2, 480.

33. Jackson, *Papers*, vol. 10, 827.

34. Joan Haslip, *The Crown of Mexico* (New York: Avon Books, 1973), 75.

Chapter 18: Extradition

1. *Index*, vol. 1, doc. 127, 21.

2. Sarna, *Jacksonian Jew*, 87.

3. For Livingston's participation: De Brauw, *Herinneringen*, 188. For the escorts: Arntzenius, ed., *Procès*, vol. 1, ch. 2, doc. 26, pp. 89-90.

4. De Brauw, *Herinneringen*, 189.

5. De Brauw, *Herinneringen*, 188.

6. *Index*, vol. 1, doc. 127, 21.

7. De Brauw, *Herinneringen*, 194. Seely remembered 10 men, not 14, in: *Index*, vol. 1, doc. 127, 46.

8. For Polari's quote and de Brauw's summary, see his *Herinneringen*, pp. 191-4.

9. *Index*, vol. 1, doc. 127, 20.

10. De Brauw, *Herinneringen*, 192.

11. De Brauw, *Herinneringen*, 215; following Polari quote ("irons"), 196.

12. De Brauw, *Herinneringen*, 201.

13. This quote and the following: De Brauw, *Herinneringen*, 216.

14. This quote and the following: De Brauw, *Herinneringen*, 203.

15. De Brauw, *Herinneringen*, 214.

16. 'Carrara,' *The Long-Island Star* [reprinting from the *Commercial Advertiser*], September 5, 1832, Newspapers.com.

17. 'Carrara, or Constant Polari,' *American and Commercial Daily Advertiser* (Baltimore, MD) [reprinting from the *New York Journal*], August 28, 1832, Newspapers.com.

18. Draaisma, *Polari-affair*, 49.

19. 'Polari, alias Carara,' *Morning Courier and New-York Enquirer*, September 1, 1832, FultonHistory.com.

20. 'Polari, alias Carrara,' *Phenix Gazette (Alexandria Gazette)*, November 22, 1832, Newspapers.com.

21. This quote and the following: Arntzenius, ed., *Procès*, vol. 2, pp. 352-3.

22. All Polari's quotes in this paragraph come from his second letter from prison: Arntzenius, ed., *Procès*, vol. 2, pp. 402-405.

23. Arntzenius, ed., *Procès*, vol. 2, 408.

Chapter 19: The Brink of War

1. Jackman, ed., *Relations*, 249.

2. Le Strange, ed., *Correspondence*, vol. 2, pp. 413, 419.

3. Charles Stuart Wortley, *Journal of an Excursion to Antwerp during the Siege of the Citadel in December, 1832* (London: John Murray, 1833), 42.

4. K. Baedeker, *Belgium and Holland Including the Grand-Duchy of Luxembourg* (London: Dulau and Co., 1897), 127.

5. Koch, *Willem I*, chap. 8, 'Koning van een halve staat.'

6. 'Private Correspondence,' *Morning Herald* (London), October 5, 1832, BNA.

7. Arntzenius, ed., *Procès*, vol. 2, 416.

8. Arntzenius, ed., *Procès*, vol. 2, 423.

9. Arntzenius, ed., *Procès*, vol. 2, 460.

10. Arntzenius, ed., *Procès*, vol. 2, 448.

11. Arntzenius, ed., *Procès*, vol. 2, 502.

12. Arntzenius, ed., *Procès*, vol. 2, 503.

13. Jackson, *Papers*, vol. 10, 831.

14. *Index*, vol. 1, doc. 127, 50.

15. Arntzenius, ed., *Procès*, vol. 2, 473.

16. Wortley, *Excursion*, 165.

17. 'Copy of the Answer of General Chasse to the Summons of Marshal Gerard,' *Weekly Times* (London), December 8, 1832, BNA.

18. Wortley, *Excursion*, pp. 13-14.

19. Noorduyn, *Brussel in Augustus 1836*, 59.

20. Wortley, *Excursion*, pp. 190-91.

21. Arntzenius, ed., *Procès*, vol. 2, 507.

22. Arntzenius, ed., *Procès*, vol. 2, 528.

23. 'Nederlanden | 's Gravenhage, den 2 April,' *Utrechtsche courant*, April 5, 1833, delpher.nl.

24. *Index*, vol. 1, doc. 127, pp. 43-44.

25. 'M. Roger B. Huygens…,' *The Evening Post* (New York), July 3, 1833, Newspapers.com.

26. *Index*, vol. 1, doc. 127, pp. 47-9.

27. *Index*, vol. 1, doc. 127, 49.

28. *Index*, vol. 1, doc. 127, pp. 44-47.

29. Hamilton, *Reminiscences*, 226.

30. For Seely's passport: 'U.S., Passport Applications, 1795-1925 for William A Seely,' *Ancestry*. For booking: 'Passengers,' *The Evening Post* (New York), November 12, 1833, Newspapers.com.

31. S.A. Howland, *Steamboat Disasters and Railroad Accidents in the United States* (Worcester: Warren Lazell, 1840), 157.

32. *Index*, vol. 1, doc. 127, pp. 49-50.

Chapter 20: A Dubious Confession

1. See the full confession in: Arntzenius, ed., *Procès*, vol. 2, pp. 533-44.

2. Arntzenius, ed., *Procès*, vol. 2, 536.

3. Arntzenius, ed., *Procès*, vol. 2, 542.

4. Arntzenius, ed., *Procès*, vol. 2, 553.

5. Arntzenius, ed., *Procès*, vol. 2, 555.

6. Arntzenius, ed., *Procès*, vol. 2, 558.

7. Arntzenius, ed., *Procès*, vol. 2, 563.

8. Arntzenius, ed., *Procès*, vol. 2, 568.

9. 'Vessels Entered for Loading,' *Liverpool Albion*, December 16, 1833, BNA.

10. Scott Norsworthy, '1833 Banquet, Albany St Nicholas Society,' *Melvilliana* (blog), December 20, 2018, accessed August 20, 2024, https://melvilliana. blogspot.com/2018/12/1833-banquet-albany-st-nicholas-society.html.

11. *Index*, vol. 1, doc. 127, 50.

12. *Index*, vol. 1, doc. 127, pp. 50–52.

13. Arntzenius, ed., *Procès*, vol. 1, 'Acte d'Accusation,' 32.

14. Arntzenius, ed., *Procès*, vol. 2, 574.

15. Arntzenius, ed., *Procès*, vol. 2, 575.

16. Ibid.

17. Arntzenius, ed., *Procès*, vol. 2, 594.

Chapter 21: The Trial

1. '(Private Correspondence) Court of Assizes for the Southern Division of the Province of Holland,' *English Chronicle and Whitehall Evening Post* (London), March 11, 1834, BNA.

2. Arntzenius, ed., *Procès*, vol. 2, 578.

3. 'Particuliere Correspondentie,' *Algemeen Handelsblad* (Amsterdam), March 10, 1834, delpher.nl.

4. Arntzenius, ed., *Procès*, vol. 2, 578.

5. *Verslag Der Teregtzitting van Het Hof van Assises, Provincie Holland (Zuider-Kwartier), Gehouden Den 7den Maart 1834, in Zake van Constant Polari, Beschuldigd van Diefstal in Het Paleis van HH. KK. HH. Den Prins En de Prinses van Oranje Te Brussel* ('s Gravenhage: De Gebroeders van Cleef, 1834), pp. 48–50.

6. *Verslag*, 51.

7. *Verslag*, 53.

8. *Verslag*, pp. 53–54.

9. *Verslag*, pp. 60–61; 'Particuliere Correspondentie,' *Algemeen Handelsblad*; 'Court of Assizes,' *English Chronicle and Whitehall Evening Post*.

10. Arntzenius, ed., *Procès*, vol. 1, 'Acte d'Accusation,' 28.

11. 'Court of Assizes,' *English Chronicle and Whitehall Evening Post*.

12. Arntzenius, ed., *Procès*, vol. 2, pp. 580–1.

13. Arntzenius, ed., *Procès*, vol. 2, 589.

14. Arntzenius, ed., *Procès*, vol. 2, 595.

15. 'Court of Assizes,' *English Chronicle and Whitehall Evening Post*.

16. *Verslag*, 86.

17. *Verslag*, 94.

18. Arntzenius, ed., *Procès*, vol. 2, 608.

19. 'Court of Assizes,' *English Chronicle and Whitehall Evening Post.*

20. *Verslag*, 98.

21. Arntzenius, ed., *Procès*, vol. 2, 615.

22. Arntzenius, ed., *Procès*, vol. 2, 620.

23. '…in Brussels': Arntzenius, ed., *Procès*, vol. 2, 623. '…conviction': Arntzenius, ed., *Procès*, vol. 2, 624; *Verslag*, 113.

24. Arntzenius, ed., *Procès*, vol. 2, 625.

25. Ibid.

26. Arntzenius, ed., *Procès*, vol. 2, 626.

27. Ibid.

28. 'Polari and the Princess of Orange's Jewels,' *London Courier and Evening Gazette*, March 21, 1834, BNA.

29. 'Private Correspondence,' *Evening Mail* (London), March 21, 1834, BNA.

30. ' 's Gravenhage, den 3den April,' *Overijsselsche courant* (Zwolle, Netherlands), April 8, 1834, delpher.nl.

31. For the public 'execution': 'The Hague, April 2 – Polari having failed,' *Albion and the Star* (London), April 8, 1834, BNA.

32. Arntzenius, ed., *Procès*, vol. 2, 628.

33. *Index*, vol. 1, doc. 127, pp. 52-53.

34. *Index*, vol. 1, doc. 127, pp. 53-54.

35. Draaisma, 'Polari-affair,' 53.

36. Draaisma, 'Polari-affair,' 55.

37. 'Meeting of the French and Italian Adopted Citizens,' *The Evening Post* (New York), November 3, 1834, Newspapers.com.

38. "Foreign Ministers," *Niles National Register* (St. Louis, MO), May 9, 1835, Newspapers.com.

39. John Van Buren, 'John Van Buren to MVB, c. June 1834,' *The Papers of Martin Van Buren*, accessed February 13, 2024, https://vanburenpapers.org/document-mvb05211.

40. *Index*, vol. 1, doc. 127, 55.

41. 'New York, U.S., Arriving Passenger and Crew Lists (including Castle Garden and Ellis Island), 1820-1957 for William A Suly,' *Ancestry.com*, accessed September 5, 2024. https://www.ancestry.com/search/collections/7488/records/1022382865?tid=151195839&pid=252099307314.

42. *Index*, vol. 1, doc. 127, 56.

43. For Seely's calculations: *Index*, vol. 1, doc. 127, 24. For currency conversion: Alan Eliasen, 'Historical Currency Conversions,' *Futureboy.us*, accessed August 21, 2024, https://futureboy.us/fsp/dollar.fsp?quantity=42000¤cy= dollars&fromYear=1835.

Chapter 22: A Walking Stick in America

1. G.J. Hooykaas, ed., *De Briefwisseling van J.R. Thorbecke: Vol. 1 (1830–1833)* ('s Gravenhage: Martinus Nijhoff, 1975), 422.
2. Meeter, *Holland*, 302.
3. Koch, *Willem I*, chap. 8, 'Koning van een halve staat.'
4. Van Zanten, *Koning*, chap. 7, 'Een afgedwongen abdicatie?'
5. Koch, *Willem I*, chap. 9, 'Het laatste optreden.'
6. Paarlberg and Slechte, eds., *Willem II*, 201.
7. Arntzenius, ed., *Procès*, vol. 1, ch. 1, doc. 2, 10.
8. Paarlberg and Slechte, eds., *Willem II*, 201.
9. Doorn, *Rusland*, 231.
10. For Polari's request to write a memoir: Draaisma, 'Polari-affair,' 53. For mention in the press: 'Binnenland | Men schrift uit Woerden…,' *Algemeen Handelsblad* (Amsterdam), April 15, 1837, delpher.nl.
11. 'Utrecht den 22 Februarij,' *Groninger courant*, February 25, 1842, delpher.nl.
12. 'Death on February 21, 1842 in Woerden (Netherlands),' *Open Archive*. Accessed August 21, 2024. https://www.openarchieven.nl/rel:ee499357-2e94-8f13-d9f7-730fd4573e56/en.
13. 'Utrecht den 22 Februarij,' *Groninger courant*; 'Utrecht den 22, Februarij,' *Utrechtsche provinciale en stads-courant: algemeen advertentieblad*, February 23, 1842, delpher.nl.
14. Meeter, *Holland*, pp. 16–17.
15. 'Crown Diamonds,' *Utica Daily Observer*, March 30, 1877, NYSHistoricNewspapers.org.
16. *Report of the Committee of Investigation, Chosen by Ballot by the House of Representatives January 17 and 19, 1839, on the Subject of the Defalcations of Samuel Swartwout and Others* (Washington, DC: Thomas Allen, 1839), 8.
17. *Report of the Committee*, 29.
18. Sheehan, *Original Sins*, 70.
19. 'Death of Samuel Swartwout,' *New-York Daily Tribune*, November 24, 1856, Newspapers.com.
20. Hamilton, *Reminiscences*, 320.

21. Hamilton, *Reminiscences*, 346.

22. *Index*, vol. 1, doc. 127, 24.

23. *Index*, vol. 1, doc. 127, pp. 60-61.

24. *Index*, vol. 1, doc. 127, 61.

25. *Index*, vol. 1, doc. 127, pp. 25-28.

26. 'Thirty-First Congress,' *The Evening Post* (New York), January 11, 1850, Newspapers.com.

27. 'The Jew and the Jewels,' *New York Daily Herald*, March 18, 1850.

28. Sarna, *Jacksonian Jew*, pp. 211-12.

29. Sarna, *Jacksonian Jew*, 208.

30. 'The Robbery of the Dutch Crown Jewels – The Conduct of the Dutch Government,' *New York Daily Herald*, December 20, 1850, Newspapers.com.

31. 'New York, U.S., Wills and Probate Records, 1659-1999 for Wm A Seely.' Ancestry.com. Accessed August 22, 2024. https://www.ancestry.com/search/collections/8800/records/5212862?tid=&pid=&queryId=7e9389c4-11c0-4926-8d5d-b8ddeb15fbc4e.

32. *Documents of the Board of Aldermen of the City of New York*, part 1, vol. 33 (New York: E. Jones & Co., 1867), docs. 8, 5.

33. Tomsinski, 'De Romanovs,' 58.

34. Ibid.

35. Ibid.

36. Ibid.

37. Paarlberg and Slechte, eds., *Willem II*, 188.

38. Martijn Akkerman, 'Anna Paulowna en Haar Juwelen,' in Sander Paarlberg and Henk Slechte, eds., *Willem II: De Koning en De Kunst* (Dordrecht: W Books, 2014), 42.

39. Simone Lamain, "De Russische echtgenote van Willem II: Anna Paulowna," *Blauw Bloed* (blog), March 7, 2024, accessed August 4, 2024, https://blauwbloed.eo.nl/royaltynieuws/vier-koninginnen-2-koningin-anna-paulowna.

40. Robert von Mohl, *Lebens-Erinnerungen von Robert von Mohl 1799-1875*, vol. 2 (Stuttgart: Deutsche Verlags-Anstalt, 1902), 302.

41. Lady Walburga Paget, *Scenes and Memories* (New York: Charles Scribner's Sons, 1912), 42.

Bibliography

All sources cited are included in the notes. This bibliography includes only the most helpful books and resources on the topic.

Almedingen, E.M. *So Dark a Stream: A Study of the Emperor Paul I of Russia 1754–1801*. London: Hutchinson, 1959.

Arntzenius, Pieter Nicolaas, ed. *Procès de Constant Polari, Condamné Le 8 Mars 1834, Par La Cour d'assises de La Hollande, (Partie Méridionale), Pour Cause de Vol Des Diamans et Joyaux de S.A.I. et R. Madame La Princesse d'Orange*. 2 vols. La Haye: Chez Th. Lejeune, 1835.

Aronson, Theo. *The Coburgs of Belgium*. London: Lume Books, 2020. Kindle.

Aspinall, A., ed. *Letters of the Princess Charlotte 1811–1817*. London: Home and Van Thal, 1949.

Bemis, Samuel Flagg, ed. *The American Secretaries of State and Their Diplomacy, Vol. IV*. New York: Pageant Book Company, 1958.

Bosscha, Johannes. *Het Leven van Willem Den Tweede Koning Der Nederlanden En Groothertog van Luxemburg*. Amsterdam: C.M. Van Gogh, 1865.

Brands, H. W. *Andrew Jackson: His Life and Times*. New York: Anchor Books, 2006.

Brauw, J. de. *Herinneringen Eener Reize Naar Nieuwyork Gedaan in de Jaren 1831 En 1832*. Leiden, The Netherlands: C.C. van der Hoek, 1833.

Brownlow, Emma Sophia, Countess of. *Slight Reminiscences of a Septuagenarian from 1802 to 1815*. London: John Murray, 1867.

Burrows, Edwin G., and Mike Wallace. *Gotham: A History of New York City to 1898*. New York, NY: Oxford University Press, 2000.

Causes Criminelles Célèbres Du Dix-Neuvième Siècle. Vol. 3. Paris: H. Langlois et Cie, 1828.

Clifford, Lady de. *A Short Journal of a Tour, Made Through Part of France, Switzerland, and the Banks of the Rhine, to Spa, Antwerp, Ghent, &c*. Richmond, Surrey: F.H. Wall, n.d.

Colenbrander, H.T., ed. *Gedenkstukkender Algemeene Geschiedenis van Nederland van 1795 Tot 1840*. 10 vols. Den Haag: Martinus Nijhoff, 1905–1913.

Corti, Egon Caesar. *Leopold I of Belgium: Secret Pages of European History.* Translated by Joseph McCabe. London: T. Fisher Unwin Ltd., 1923.

Disbrowe, Charlotte. *Old Days in Diplomacy: Recollections of a Closed Century.* London: Jarrold & Sons, 1903.

Doorn, Jacqueline. *Rusland en Orange.* Zaltbommel: Europese Bibliotheek, 1974.

Draaisma, Marius. 'De Polari-affair, 1829-1834: Een juwelendiefstal wordt een diplomatiek incident.' Master's thesis, Rijksuniversitat Groningen, n.d.

Hamilton, James A. *Reminiscences of James A. Hamilton; or, Men and Events at Home and Abroad during Three Quarters of a Century.* New York: Charles Scribner & Co., 1869.

Hansen, Maria. 'Twaalf kranten zijn even warm als een deken: het leven van jonkheer Roger Bangeman huygens, Graaf van Löwendal.' *Virtus* 9, no. 1-2 (2002): 49–55.

Hermans, Dorine, and Daniela Hooghiemstra, eds. *'Voor de Troon Wordt Men Niet Ongestraft Geboren': Ooggetuigen van de Koningen van Nederland, 1813-1890.* Amsterdam: Bakker, 2008.

Hunt, Charles Havens. *Life of Edward Livingston.* New York: D. Appleton and Company, 1864.

Index of Miscellaneous Documents Printed by Order of the Senate of the United States during the First Session of the Thirty-First Congress, 1849-'50. 2 vols. Washington, DC: Wm. M. Belt, 1850.

Jackman, S. W., ed. *Romanov Relations: The Private Correspondence of Tsars Alexander I, Nicholas I and the Grand Dukes Constantine and Michael with Their Sister Queen Anna Pavlovna, 1817-1855.* London: Macmillan, 1969.

Jackman, Sydney W., ed. *Chère Annette: Letters from Russia 1820-1828; the Correspondence of the Empress Maria Feodorovna of Russia to Her Daughter the Grand Duchess Anna Pavlovna the Princess of Orange.* Stroud, Gloucestershire, UK: Alan Sutton Publishing Inc., 1994.

Jackson, Andrew. *The Papers of Andrew Jackson.* Edited by Daniel Feller, Thomas Coens, Laura-Eve Moss, and Harold D. Moser. Volumes 7 (1829), 9 (1831), and 10 (1832). Knoxville: University of Tennessee Press, 2007.

Jena, Detlef. *Katharina Pawlowna Großfürstin von Russland - Königin von Württemberg.* Regensburg: Verlag Friedrich Pustet, 2003.

Klauss, Jochen and Stifting Weimarer Klassik und Kunstsammlungen, eds. *'Ihre Kaiserliche Hoheit' Maria Pawlowna Zarentochter am Weimaraner Hof.* Weimar: Stiftung Weimarer Klassik und Kunstsammlungen, 2004.

Knight, Cornelia. *Autobiography of Miss Cornelia Knight, Lady Companion to the Princess Charlotte of Wales.* London: W.H. Allen and Co., 1861.

Koch, Jeroen. *Koning Willem I: 1772 - 1843*. Amsterdam: Uitgeverij Boom, 2013. Kobo.

Koch, Jeroen, Dik van der Meulen, and Jeroen van Zanten. *The House of Orange in Revolution and War: A European History, 1772-1890*. Translated by Andy Brown. London: Reaktion Books, 2022.

Le Strange, Guy, ed. *Correspondence of Princess Lieven and Earl Grey*. Translated by Guy Le Strange. 3 vols. London: Richard Bentley and Son, 1890.

Marszalek, John F. *The Petticoat Affair: Manners, Mutiny, and Sex in Andrew Jackson's White House*. Baton Rouge: Louisiana State University Press, 1997.

Martin, Marie. *Maria Féodorovna En Son Temps, 1759-1828: Contribution à l'histoire de La Russie et de l'Europe*. Paris: L'Harmattan, 2003.

McGrew, Roderick E. *Paul I of Russia 1754-1801*. Oxford: Clarendon Press, 1992.

Meacham, Jon. *American Lion: Andrew Jackson in the White House*. New York: Random House, 2008.

Meeter, E. *Holland: Its Institutions; Its Press, Kings, and Prisons*. London: J.F. Hope, 1857.

Meulen, Dik van der. *Koning Willem III: 1817-1890*. Amsterdam: Uitgeverij Boom, 2013. Kobo.

Mikhailowitch, Grand Duke Nicholas, ed. *L'Impératrice Élisabeth, Épouse d'Alexandre Ier*. 3 vols. St. Petersburg: Manufacture des Papiers de l'État, 1908.

Munroe, John A. *Louis McLane: Federalist and Jacksonian*. New Brunswick, NJ: Rutgers University Press, 1973.

Nesselrode, Charles Robert Vasilievitch de. *Lettres Et Papiers Du Chancelier Comte De Nesselrode 1760-1850*. Edited by Anatole Nesselrode. Vol. 6: 1819-1827. Paris: A. Lahure, 1908.

Noorduyn, Jacobus. *Herinneringen van een uitstapje naar Brussel in Augustus 1836*. Gorinchem, Netherlands: Jacobus Noorduyn, 1836.

Oshinsky, David. *Bellevue: Three Centuries of Medicine and Mayhem at America's Most Storied Hospital*. New York: Doubleday, 2016.

Paarlberg, Sander, and Henk Slechte, eds. *Willem II: De Koning en De Kunst*. Dordrecht: W Books, 2014.

Paget, Lady Walburga. *Scenes and Memories*. New York: Charles Scribner's Sons, 1912.

Report of the Committee of Investigation, Chosen by Ballot by the House of Representatives January 17 and 19, 1839, on the Subject of the Defalcations of Samuel Swartwout and Others. N.P.: Thomas Allen, 1839.

Rosenberg, Charles E. *The Cholera Years: The United States in 1832, 1849 and 1866.* Chicago: University of Chicago Press, 1962.

Sarna, Jonathan D. *Jacksonian Jew: The Two Worlds of Mordecai Noah.* New York: Holmes & Meier Publishers, Inc., 1981.

Saxe-Weimar-Eisenach, Bernhard, Duke of. *Travels through North America, During the Years 1825 and 1826.* 2 vols. Philadelphia: Carey, Lea & Carey, 1828.

Sheehan, Raymond J. *The Original Sins: America's Fight Against Corruption in the Era of Manifest Destiny.* Maitland, FL: Xulon Press, 2016.

Shelley, Frances. *The Diary of Frances Lady Shelley 1787-1817.* Edited by Richard Edgcumbe. New York: Charles Scribner's Sons, 1912.

Smith, Margaret Bayard. *The First Forty Years of Washington Society.* Edited by Gaillard Hunt. New York: Charles Scribner's Sons, 1906.

Stockmar, Baron E. von. *Memoirs of Baron Stockmar.* Edited by F. Max Müller. London: Longmans, Green and Co., 1872.

Van Buren, Martin. *The Autobiography of Martin Van Buren.* 2 vols. Edited by John C. Fitzpatrick. Annual Report of the American Historical Association for the Year 1918. Washington, DC: Government Printing Office, 1920.

Verhaegen, P. 'Le Vol Des Bijoux de La Princesse d'Orange a Bruxelles En 1829.' *Annales de La Société d'Archeologie de Bruxelles* 15 (1901): 330–36.

Verslag Der Teregtzitting van Het Hof van Assises, Provincie Holland (Zuider-Kwartier), Gehouden Den 7den Maart 1834, in Zake van Constant Polari, Beschuldigd van Diefstal in Het Paleis van HH. KK. HH. Den Prins En de Prinses van Oranje Te Brussel. 'S Gravenhage: De Gebroeders van Cleef, 1834.

White, Charles. *The Belgic Revolution of 1830.* 2 vols. London: Whittaker and Co., 1835.

Wolf, Simon. *Mordecai Manuel Noah: A Biographical Sketch.* Philadelphia: The Levytype Company Publishers, 1897.

Zanten, Jeroen van. *Koning Willem II - 1792-1849.* Amsterdam: Boom Uitgevers, 2014. Kobo.

Index

Adams, John Quincy, 22, 38, 41

Adams, Louisa, 41

Agoult, Comte Hector-Philippe d', 27

Alexander I, Emperor of Russia, 1, 4,
11–12, 15, 18, 33, 38, 94

Alexander II, Emperor of Russia, 172

Alexandrina Victoria, Princess of Kent,
see Victoria, Queen of Great
Britain

Algiers, 57, 68, 93, 151

Allen, Francis P., 105, 107

Alorna, Pedro de Almeida Portugal,
3rd Marquis d', 26

amethysts, *see* jewels, amethysts

Amour Sacré de la Patrie (aria from
La Muette de Portici), 30, 72

Amsterdam, 109, 127–28

Anduaga, Don Joaquin de, 34

Anna Pavlovna, Princess of Orange and
Grand Duchess of Russia
and Belgian revolution, 33, 65, 96, 98
and jewels, 2, 63, 94, 167, 172–3
as queen, 167
as widow, 172
birth, 11
character, 1–2
childhood and education, 12
children, 16, 19, 172–73

death, 172

dowry, 3, 15

identifies missing items, 6–7

identifies recovered jewels, 115,
122–23, 126

marriage, 15, 22

married life, 16–19, 26–28, 36, 99

new palace and mother's death, 19

notified of theft, 6

on night of theft, 1, 4

portraits of, 2, 96

marriage proposal from Napoleon, 12

reaction to cholera outbreak, 128

theft aftermath, 29, 34, 115, 123, 142

theft's effect on health, 8–9

Triopathy, 11, 28

warned of Willem's behavior, 28

will and jewel dispersal, 172–73

Antwerp, 4, 34, 70, 99, 142, 145–46

Auber, Daniel, 30

Bagot, Sir Charles, 30

Bangeman Huygens, Chevalier
Christiaan, *see* Hugyens, Chevalier
Christiaan Bangeman

Barbier, Théodore-Emmanuel, 4–5

Belgian revolution, 125
battle for Brussels, 32

Belgium declares independence, 35

blamed for case difficulties, 144

Dutch response in 1831, 65

hostility between Belgium and
Netherlands, 65, 98, 120, 142

incitement of August 25, 30–31

London Conference begins, 35

origin, 17, 30

Prince Willem joins rebels, 34

Prince Willem's negotiations, 32

provisional government declared, 33

siege of Antwerp, 142, 145

spread of rebellion, 31

Ten Days' Campaign, 96–98

throne offered to Leopold, 63–65

Twenty-Four Articles, 98

Willem I's response, 31–32

Belgium, 14, 17, 31, 33–35, 47, 64–65,
96, 98–99, 112, 120–22, 133, 142,
157, 161, 166

Bellevue (New York prison complex),
94–96, 102, 106, 108–109, 116–17,
124–26, 130–33, 135–36, 139

Bennett, James Gordon, 171

Bergonzio, Eugene, 68, 71, 73, 84–85,
87, 102, 106, 164

Bernhard, Prince of Saxe-Weimar-
Eisenach, 23

Berrien, John, 40, 43–44

Berthier, Louis-Alexandre, 26

Blanche, Susanne

agrees to dig up Brussels cache, 101

agrees to separate from Polari, 72

arrest in Liverpool, 108

arrives in New York, 66

arrives in The Hague, 110

arrives in Liverpool, 108

begins to suspect Roumage, 102–104,
108

birth of Rosine, 49

confides in Roumage, 71–72, 74,
86, 88

corset sewn with diamonds, 60, 62,
66, 69

digs up jewels with Roumage, 88

directs Raymond to buried jewels,
121

first meets Roumage, 68

helps Polari hide jewels in US, 82,
84–85, 87–88

helps Polari smuggle jewels overseas,
62–63, 67

interrogations in The Hague, 114,
143

joins Polari in Brussels, 60

last visit to Polari, 102

learns about US laws, 71, 73

leaves New York, 102

Polari comments on theft to her, 60

Polari's violence toward, 60, 68, 71,
73–74, 82, 102, 125

relationship with Polari, 49, 55–56,
59, 68, 70, 72, 74, 102, 131, 138,
140

relationship with Roumage, 87, 93

released by Dutch authorities, 163

sees stolen jewels, 61

surrenders jewels, 109

visits Polari in prison, 93

with Anna's jewels, 59, 74, 157

Bonaparte, Napoleon, *see* Napoleon
    Bonaparte (Emperor of the
    French)
Boutersem, battle of, 97
Box, Henri, 166
Branch, John, 40, 43–44
Brussels1–2, 4, 6–10, 13–14, 16–19, 25,
    27–28, 30–34, 46, 49–53, 55–57,
    59–60, 62, 65, 73–74, 77, 88–89,
    93, 96, 98, 101, 104, 108–109,
    114, 121, 132, 141, 144, 146, 155,
    160–61, 168
Buchanan, James, 170
Burr, Aaron, 39, 75, 76, 92, 112

Cabinet of Andrew Jackson, 39–44,
    113–14
Calhoun, John C., 41
cameos, *see* jewels, cameos
Carara, Charles Dominique (alias of
    Constant Polari), 49, 67, 77, 84,
    89, 143, 146, 161
carnelian, *see* jewels, carnelian
Casimir, Prince of Orange, 19
Catherine the Great (Empress
    Catherine II), 1, 11, 16, 122
Catinelli, Colonel Carlo, 48
Cavanillas, Nicolas, 3–4, 7–8, 35
Charlotte, Princess of Wales, 13, 15, 17,
    35, 63, 133
Chassé, General Baron David Hendrik,
    145
Chernysheva, Natalia Petrovna, 1, 4,
    6–7, 115, 122, 155, 157
cholera, 37, 126, 128–33, 144, 148

Clancarty, Lord (Richard Trench,
    2nd Earl of Clancarty), 17
Clay, Henry, 22, 38, 170
Clifford, Lady de (Mary Elizabeth
    Bourke Southwell), 27
Collet, Joseph, 67, 74, 84, 86, 88, 95,
    117–18, 125–26
Columbia (packet ship), 39
Congress of Vienna, 14
Constant Rebecque, Baron Jean Victor
    de, 13, 31–32
Constantine Pavlovich, Grand Duke of
    Russia, 19, 128

Davis, Jefferson, 171
Davizac, Auguste, 127
De Bas, Jan, 153, 155, 157, 159–63
De Brauw, Jacob, 67, 72, 125–26, 130,
    134–38, 140
De Knyff de Gontrœul, Chevalier
    Pierre Michel-Charles, 4–8, 31,
    143, 155–56
De Potter, Louis, 33
Deguerre, Joseph, 71, 164
Demidov, Count Nikolai Nikitich, 26
Desaye, Victoire, 50, 140, 160
Devan, Thomas, 132
diamantaire, 3–5, 19, 150–51, 153, 156,
    159, 173
diamonds, *see* jewels, diamonds
Dixey, Charles, 102
Dixon, Edward H., 130, 132
Donker Curtius, D., 164–65
Drabbe, Arend-Jacob-Adrien, 142–44,
    146

Du Flon
    family, 86–87, 89–90
    Jean François Louis 'Poppy', 82, 86
    Military Garden, 74, 82, 84–85, 87,
        93, 107
Dutalis, Joseph-German, 7, 63, 89

Earl of Liverpool (packet ship), 9
Eaton Affair, 38–45
Eaton, John Henry, 38, 40, 42, 44
Eaton, Margaret O'Neal Timberlake,
        38, 41–44, 76
Edgcumbe, Lady Emma Sophia, 14
Eighteen Articles (treaty), 65
emeralds, *see* jewels, emeralds

Falck, Anton Reinhard, 64, 109
Ferdinand VII, King of Spain, 27
François Depaw (packet ship), 165
François I (packet ship), 63, 66, 68–69,
        103
Frederik, Prince of Orange, 6, 31–33,
        97, 121
Fury (packet ship), 9

Gagern, Friedrich von, 25
Gazette (schooner), 135, 137, 139
George IV, King of Great Britain, 13
Gérard, Count Étienne Maurice, 97,
        142, 145
golden breakfast service, 8, 151, 153
Gregoire, Xavier, 140
Grey, Charles (2nd Earl Grey), 64
Guryev, Count Nicholas Dmitrievich,
        25–28

Hamilton, Alexander, 39, 76, 92, 112
Hamilton, James Alexander, 39–41, 44,
        48, 75–77, 81, 93, 95, 107, 113–14,
        118–19, 132, 148, 169–70
Hasselt, battle of, 97
Hatzfeldt, Prince Franz Ludwig von, 17
Hays, Benjamin J., 83, 134, 136–37, 139
Hays, Jacob, 80, 134
Hendrik, Prince of Orange, 173
Hercules (steamship), 125, 135–37
Hopson, James, 80, 83, 91, 95
Huygens, Chevalier Christiaan
        Bangeman
    advises Seely on payment, 147,
        149, 152
    and Eaton Affair, 42–45
    appointed Dutch envoy to
        America, 22
    diplomatic duties, 23, 44, 116, 119,
        144
    early career, 22
    first meeting with Roumage, 77
    friendship with Van Buren, 23, 40,
        91, 127
    Hamilton visits him in Denmark, 169
    hires Seely, 79
    home robbed, 23
    last meeting with Seely, 119
    offers Polari a pardon, 91, 106, 116
    ordered to hand over jewels from
        Roumage, 107
    recovers Anna's confiscated jewels
        from Customs, 119
    requests extradition of Polari and
        jewels, 92

returns to the Netherlands, 126
role in investigating jewel theft, 9, 78,
     80, 83–84, 86, 89–91
role in prosecuting Polari, 94–95,
     100–101, 104, 106, 112–13, 118,
     127
second marriage, 22
views jewels seized by Customs, 89
Huygens, Constantia Wilhelmina
     Vrijthoff van den Santheuvel, 22,
     42–44, 95, 113, 119, 125
Huygens, Roger
  carries out extradition, 135–37
  chooses *nolle prosequi*, 118
  combats bad publicity after
     extradition, 139
  diplomatic duties, 116, 144,
     147, 152
  disobeys order to return to
     Netherlands, 148
  fails to meet Seely, 148, 152,
     163–64
  hires De Brauw as spy, 125
  illness after extradition, 144
  in Russia, 169–70
  plans extradition, 134–35
  recalled to the Netherlands, 147
  refuses to sign pardon, 124
  role in prosecuting Polari, 106, 118,
     120, 126, 130, 132–34
  sued by servant, 164
  trains under father, 22

Ingham, Samuel, 40, 43–44
Irving, Washington, 21

Jackson, Andrew, 37–45, 75–77, 100,
     107, 112–14, 116, 118–19, 124,
     131, 133, 144, 147, 164, 169
Jackson, Rachel, 38–39, 41
jewel theft
  Brooklyn cache seized in Liverpool,
     109
  Brussels cache recovered, 121
  Customs seizure given to Huygens,
     119
  discovery, 3
  initial Dutch court charges (The
     Hague), 146
  initial investigation (Brussels), 4–8
  investigation re-opened after Polari's
     confession, 151
  missing items, 6–7
  new indictment after confession, 153
  Polari's discovery story, 50–53
  recovered jewels displayed at trial,
     155
  reward, 9, 53, 78, 80, 89, 94, 119,
     123, 127, 147, 171
  US Customs seizure, 80–81
  Willink inventories Brooklyn
     cache, 109
jewels
  amethysts, 2, 60–61, 81, 89, 122, 127
  cameos, 6, 52, 58, 60, 89, 114, 121–22
  carnelian, 6, 127
  diamonds, 1–2, 4, 6, 19, 22, 35, 51–
     52, 55–62, 66, 68, 71, 73–74, 77,
     80–81, 85, 87–89, 94–95, 103–106,
     109, 114–15, 122, 127, 151–53,
     164, 167, 172

emeralds, 6, 22, 52, 61, 81, 89, 94–95,
        104, 123, 127
gemstone floral bouquet, 6, 123
opals, 6, 51–52, 122
pearls, 2, 5–6, 19, 61, 80–82, 85,
        88–89, 94–95, 104, 109, 115, 127,
        152, 159, 173
peridots, 127
rubies, 6, 52, 61, 123
sapphires, 6, 10, 22, 61–63, 66, 68,
        77, 81, 85, 94–95, 104, 106, 123,
        127, 167, 173
snake bracelet, 6, 59, 61
topaz, 1, 6, 22, 61, 68, 81, 127
turquoise, 2, 6, 61, 95, 115, 122,
        127, 167

Kent, Duchess of, 35, 64
Kneuterdijk Palace, 114–15, 122,
        127–28
Krudener, Baron Paul de, 38, 42, 44
Kruseman, Cornelis, 96

La Belle Alliance (tavern), 50, 60
Larpent, F. Seymour, 13
Leopold I, King of the Belgians
        (formerly Prince of Saxe-Coburg-
        Saalfeld), 15, 35, 63–65, 96–98,
        116, 133
Lieven, Prince Christopher
        Andreyevich, 35
Liverpool, 101–102, 104–105, 108–110,
        114–15, 123, 145, 152, 173
Livingston, Edward, 92, 100, 107,
        113–14, 118, 131–32

Livingston, Edward P., 134–35
London, 13–14, 17, 33–35, 39, 44,
        63–65, 96, 99, 104, 108–109, 119,
        152, 161, 169
London Conference, 35, 44, 64
Louis Philippe, King of the French, 64,
        97, 133, 142
Louise, Princess of Orange, 15
Louise, Queen of the Belgians (née
        Princess Louise of Orléans), 133
Löwendal, Elise de Danneskiold, 22
Lyon, 48–49, 52, 55–59, 62–63, 74, 126,
        143–44, 146

Machado, Don Justo José de26–29, 34,
        52, 98, 166
Maria Feodorovna, Dowager Empress
        of Russia, 1, 2, 11–12, 15–16, 19,
        49, 127
Marie Louise, Archduchess of
        Austria, 48
Martini, Adrien, 147–48
Matuszewicz, Count Andrezj Josef, 64
Máxima, Queen of the Netherlands, 173
Maxwell, William H., 70, 93
McLane, Louis, 39, 41, 113–14, 118
McLean, John, 40, 44
Meeter, Eilert, 168
Mendizábal, Juan Álvarez, 26–27
Metternich, Prince Klemens von, 98
Michael Pavlovich, Grand Duke of
        Russia, 11
Mier, Count Felix von, 28
Military Garden, see Du Flon, Military
        Garden

Monongahela (packet ship), 102–103,
105, 107
Morris, Thomas, 80–81
Moussaye, Marquis Louis-Toussaint de
la, 28, 32

Napoleon (packet ship), 145, 148, 152
Napoleon Bonaparte (Emperor of
the French), 12–15, 26, 47–48,
62, 125
Nesselrode, Count Karl Vasilyevich, 19
Nesselrode, Countess Maria
Dmitrievna, 65, 97–98
New England (steamboat), 148
New York City, 21, 23, 39, 41, 45, 63,
66–67, 70, 75–76, 78–79, 82, 94,
101, 118–19, 123, 125, 128–33,
135, 148, 152–53, 161, 164, 168–
69, 172
Nicholas I, Emperor of Russia, 7, 11,
19, 25, 27–29, 33–36, 60, 64, 89,
92, 116, 122, 128, 169, 172
Noah, Mordecai M. (M.M.), 113, 134,
139, 171

opals, *see* jewels, opals
Orléans, duc d', *see* Louis Philippe,
King of the French
Orléans, Princesse Louise d', *see* Louise,
Queen of the Belgians

packet ships, 9, 63, 66, 101, 103, 105,
107–109, 119, 123, 148, 152, 165
see also, Columbia, Earl of
Liverpool, François Depaw,
François I, Fury, Monongahela,
Napoleon, Sylvanus Jenkins
Paget, Lady (Walpurga Hohenthal), 173
Palace of the Prince of Orange, Brussels
(now Palace of the Academies),
3–5, 8–9, 19, 27, 32, 36, 50, 60, 98,
143, 151, 156, 158–59
Parfait, Étienne, 2–3, 7
Paris, 14–15, 26, 60–63, 69, 93–94, 96
Paul I, Emperor of Russia, 11, 42, 122,
173
Paul Petrovich, Grand Duke of Russia,
see Paul I, Emperor of Russia
pearls, *see* jewels, pearls
Pereira, Achilles de, 25–29, 46, 166
peridots, *see* jewels, peridots
Philadelphia, 22, 23, 68, 101–103, 105,
107, 128, 147
Philipse, Anthoni Willem, 9, 115,
122–123, 140, 150–51
Polari, Constant
abducted from Bellevue, 136
alibi in letter written from prison,
140
and blind man, 53
arrest in New York, 90–91
arrives in New York, 66
behavior in boarding house, 68
blames Roumage and Susanne, 131
British military service, 48
buries jewels in Saint-Josse-ten-
Noode, 60
commissions hollow cane, 55
commissions hollow umbrella
shaft, 59

confession (in The Hague), 150–51

confirms jewels are Anna's, 63

discovers jewels in the woods, 50–52

discusses theft with Susanne, 60

during Customs raid, 80–81

first meets Roumage, 68

flees from authorities, 82–84, 86–87, 89–90

French military service, 47

hides remaining jewels in Brooklyn woods, 84–85

illness and death, 168

imprisonment, 163, 167

in Bellevue, 94–95, 117

in Brussels after Lyon bankruptcy, 49–50

in Lyon, 49

interrogated after arrest (NY), 92

interrogations in Dutch custody, 140, 143, 150–53

learns about US Customs laws, 71

learns of jewel theft, 49

learns Susanne betrayed him, 106

on ship bound for America, 66

partnership with Roudez, 56–58

prepares to smuggle jewels overseas, 61–62

punishment after conviction, 163

reburies jewels in spring 1830, 52

refuses Dutch pardon, 91, 106, 116, 124

relationship with Susanne, 49, 55, 59, 68, 71–72, 102, 106

requests visit from Susanne, 93

returns to Brussels, 59

reveals Brooklyn burial site, 106

rumors about, 168–69

sells diamonds in Frankfurt, 55

sells diamonds in New York, 71

settles in Lyon, 48

Swiss birth and youth, 47

tells Susanne he has Anna's jewels, 61

trial, 155–61

trial verdict, 160–61

violent fight with Susanne, 73

with cholera, 132

wonders if jewels are real, 52–53

Polari, Rosine, 49, 56, 60–63, 66–67, 69, 72–75, 82, 84, 87–88, 93, 101–102, 123, 131, 134–35, 136, 138, 140–41, 163, 168

Poroshin, Semyon Andreevich, 11

Price, William M., 70, 93

Raymond, George B., 93, 102, 104–105, 108–109, 120–24, 130, 132–33, 144

Red Marble Room, 5, 158

Riker, Richard, 112

Robert, Jean (alias of Jean Roumage), 70, 102, 105, 108, 164

Roudez, 56–58, 62, 93, 126, 140, 144, 146, 151

Roumage, Constant, 69, 105

Roumage, Frédéric, 69, 101, 103, 105, 164

Roumage, Jean

arrest in Liverpool, 108

arrives in New York, 70

arrives in The Hague, 110

arrives in Liverpool, 108

blames Raymond, 123
boards *Monongahela*, 103
bond purchase, 69–70
conviction in France, 70
decides to inform on Polari, 75
digs up jewels with Susanne, 88
disappears from record, 164
early life and career, 69
evicted from the Netherlands, 127
gives stones to Huygens, 94
informs on Polari, 75, 77, 85, 89
leaves New York, 102
meets Polari and Susanne, 68
on *Monongahela*, 103–104
plans to retrieve Brussels cache,
    100–102
questioned by authorities, 109
questions Seely on Susanne's
    behalf, 79
relationship with Susanne, 71–2, 74,
    86–87, 93–94
sees Polari with diamonds, 68
shelters Polari, 84
tracks Polari and Susanne to Pearl
    Street, 69
Roumage, Victor, 69, 164
Rowley, Sir Josias, 48
rubies, *see* jewels, rubies

Saint-Josse-ten-Noode, 8, 60, 121, 157
Salviati, Peter Heinrich August von, 25
sapphires, *see* jewels, sapphires
Schieffelin, Jonathan, 68, 73
Scholten van oud Haarlem, Christiaan
    Jacobus, 151, 153

Schultz, Karl Ivanovich, 3–4, 6, 8, 115,
    155–56
Seely, Hannah (née Fountain) 78,
    148–149, 152, 164, 165
Seely, William Austin
    advises Roger against extradition, 134
    and cholera, 133
    approached by Dutch minister, 78
    arrests Polari, 90
    arrives in Europe, 152
    attempts to get paid, 119, 146–48,
        152, 163–65, 170
    attends Polari's extradition, 135–36
    death, 171
    early career, 78
    first attempt to arrest Polari, 83
    hires George Raymond, 93
    history with Roumage, 70, 72
    income, 79
    last meeting with Huygens, 119
    personal history, 78
    petitions Congress for payment, 170
    petitions Gov. Throop to extradite
        Polari, 100
    questions Roumage's brothers, 105
    returns to New York from The
        Hague, 165
    role in capturing Polari, 80, 83–84, 89
    role in prosecuting Polari, 95,
        106–107, 119, 126, 130, 132
    second attempt to arrest Polari, 85
    takes Polari case, 79
    tracks Susanne and Roumage,
        104–105
Skiddy, William T., 66, 69

Smith, Margaret Bayard, 43

Soestdijk Palace, 172

Sophie, Princess of Orange (later
    Grand Duchess of Saxe-Weimar-
    Eisenach), 172–74

St. Petersburg, 2–3, 15, 19, 26, 38, 128,
    155, 169

stolen items
    bracelets, 6, 61, 95, 115, 122, 127
    brooches, 6, 115, 127
    buckles, 6, 61, 95, 114, 127
    comb, 115
    diamond and turquoise arrow, 122
    earrings, 61, 122, 127
    gemstones, *see* jewels
    gold box, 95
    golden fans, 51, 59–60, 123
    jeweled cross, 51
    jeweled fleurs-de-lis, 115
    jeweled watch seals, 61
    necklaces, 61, 115, 122
    portraits of Russian imperial family,
      6, 60, 114
    shawl, 2, 4, 8–9, 150, 156, 160
    tiaras, 2, 6, 36, 115, 122
    turquoise and gold cross, 6, 167

Swartwout, Samuel, 67, 74–77, 80–82,
    89, 91, 106–107, 112–13, 118, 123,
    134, 139, 169

Sybourg, Elisabeth-Louise de, 12, 16

Sylvanus Jenkins (packet ship), 105, 107

Talleyrand-Périgord, Charles Maurice
    de, 99

Taney, Roger B., 100, 118

Taylor, George W., 102, 125, 134–37,
    139

Tervuren, 1, 3, 6, 8

The Hague, 9, 12, 16, 19, 32, 34–35, 79,
    96–97, 109–110, 116, 120–23, 126,
    130, 140, 142, 145–46, 148, 152,
    155, 160–63, 165, 167, 170, 172

Thorp, George B., 126

Throop, Enos T., 100, 112, 119, 134

Ticino, Switzerland, 47, 161

topaz, *see* jewels, topaz

Triopathy, 11, 19, 28, 33

turquoise, *see* jewels, turquoise

Twenty-Four Articles (treaty), 35, 98,
    116, 166

United Kingdom of the Netherlands,
    14, 17, 33, 35, 49, 142, 145

US Customs, 9, 40, 67, 71, 75–77,
    80–81, 83, 91, 100, 105–107,
    112–14, 123, 127, 131–32, 134,
    139, 147, 158–59, 171

Van Buren, John, 23, 40

Van Buren, Martin, 9, 23, 40–44,
    75–76, 91, 112, 127, 132,
    164, 169

Van der Burgh, H., 155–156, 158, 160

Van der Hulst, Jean Baptiste, 2, 36, 115,
    167

Van Halen, Don Juan, 33–34

Van Hemert, J.W. Junius, 155, 157, 159

Van Maanen, Cornelis Felix, 6–9, 19,
    25, 31, 110, 114–115, 120–23, 127,
    142, 150, 152, 163–64

Van Wagenen, Isabella (later Sojourner
    Truth), 21
Victoria, Queen of Great Britain, 35, 64

Waddell, William Coventry, 119
Washington, DC, 22–23, 37–44, 116,
    124, 147, 170
Waterloo, battle of, 14, 17, 23, 26, 29,
    32, 34–35, 46, 48, 50, 96–97, 142,
    145, 171
Wellesley, Arthur (Viscount, later
    Duke of Wellington), 13–14, 17,
    37, 40, 97
Wellington, Duke of, *see* Wellesley,
    Arthur
Westenberg, David, 153, 155
Wilhelmina, Queen of the Netherlands,
    16, 122, 166
Willem Frederik, Prince of Orange, *see*
    Willem I, King of the Netherlands
Willem I, King of the Netherlands
    abdication and death, 167
    acknowledges Belgium, 166
    and Belgian revolution, 33, 65, 97,
        99, 145
    as king, 16, 18, 21, 30, 97
    attempt to crush Belgian revolt, 31–32
    conflict with son, 16–18, 34, 64
    exile, 13
    hopes son will marry Princess
        Charlotte of Wales, 13
    isolation after wife's death, 166
    learns of theft, 6
    meets Van Buren, 127
    praises Livingston's work, 92

    recalls Huygens, 144
    refuses to acknowledge Belgium, 98,
        116, 142
    refuses Seely's request for
        arbitration, 165
    returns from exile, 14
    role in prosecuting Polari, 134, 163
    second marriage, 166–67
Willem V, Stadtholder of the
    Netherlands, 12, 22
Willem, Prince of Orange (later King
    Willem II of the Netherlands)
    and Belgian revolution, 32–34, 64–65
    and blackmail, 18
    and French conspirators, 18
    arrives home after theft, 7
    as fiancé of Charlotte of Wales, 13
    as king, 167
    birth, 12
    blackmailed, 166
    childhood, 12
    conflict with father, 16–17, 166–67
    death, 172
    did not want guards in palace, 29
    during Ten Days' Campaign, 96–97
    headquarters at Tilburg, 99
    in British army, 13
    in Brussels to quell revolt, 31–32
    in London during Great Powers'
        conference, 35, 64
    injured at Waterloo, 14
    lectured by Grand Duke
        Constantine, 19
    marriage, 15, 22
    married life, 1, 17, 19, 36

no longer suspected of theft, 98
prefers Belgium to the Netherlands,
    16, 18
relationship with Pereira, 26–29
reputation at nadir, 34
sexuality, 18, 166, 168
suspected of theft, 25, 29, 61
thanks George Raymond, 123
travels to Paris after Waterloo, 14–15
unwilling to help Seely get paid, 165
Willem, Prince of Orange (later King
    Willem III of the Netherlands),
    16, 172

Willink, Daniel, 105, 108–109, 115,
    145, 173
Willink, Willem, 110, 115
Woerden (Dutch prison), 163,
    167–68
Wortley, Charles Stuart, 145

York (packet ship), 123

Zimmerman, John C., 77–78, 80, 83,
    89, 91–92, 125, 127, 130
Zuylen van Nijevelt, Jacob van,
    110, 163